SynergiCity

WITHDRAWN

REINVENTING THE POSTINDUSTRIAL CITY

SynergiCity

EDITED BY PAUL HARDIN KAPP AND PAUL J. ARMSTRONG

FOREWORD BY RICHARD FLORIDA

University of Illinois Press | Urbana, Chicago, and Springfield

© 2012 by the Board of Trustees
of the University of Illinois
All rights reserved
Manufactured in the United States of America
C   5   4   3   2   1
∞ This book is printed on acid-free paper.

Library of Congress Cataloging-in-Publication Data
SynergiCity : reinventing the postindustrial city /
edited by Paul Hardin Kapp and Paul J. Armstrong;
foreword by Richard Florida.
    pages   cm

Includes bibliographical references and index.
ISBN 978-0-252-03681-1 (hardback)
1. City planning — United States.
2. Cities and towns — United States.
3. Deindustrialization — Social aspects — United States.
I. Kapp, Paul Hardin, author, editor of compilation.
II. Armstrong, Paul J., author, editor of compilation.
HT167.S89 2012
307.1'2160973 — dc23   2012024408

Contents

The Death and Life of Great Industrial Cities

RICHARD FLORIDA

I PARAPHRASE THE GREAT JANE JACOBS FOR A reason. Left for dead, abandoned by globalizing and deindustrializing corporations, and mortally wounded by some of the most destructive urban renewal strategies of modern history, great industrial cities across America and the world are now in the throes of a great, bottom-up push for revitalization and renewed life.

This transformation is nothing short of astounding, really.

Great industrial cities in the United States and around the world had been declining for the better part of half a century, well before they took the brunt of the great economic crisis of 2008. As globalization led manufacturing offshore in search of lower wages and China became the world's new factory, automation, robotization, and other new technologies — what economists antiseptically dub "skill-biased technical change" — wrought devastating changes in blue-collar manufacturing communities. While some larger cities in the so-called Rustbelt — notably Chicago and Toronto — have been able to navigate these trends and remake their economies around knowledge, creativity, and service, many smaller cities have been more hard-pressed. The timing of their decline has been uneven. Pittsburgh was hard hit earlier on in the 1970s and 1980s, while Detroit reached its tipping point more recently.

From Rustbelt to revitalization belt, let's not fall into the trap of geographic or locational fatalism. Toronto and Chicago and now Pittsburgh and others chronicled in these pages aren't the only older, colder cities that have been able to turn themselves around. College towns throughout the region stand as exemplars of knowledge-based innovation and creative economies. Ann Arbor, Michigan, in the shadow of Detroit, has a resilient, knowledge-based economy that looks more like Boulder's or Austin's. The same with Madison, Wisconsin, and many other college towns and cities throughout the region — a tribute to the enduring importance of core knowledge-based institutions, like research universities and teaching hospitals.

As for me personally, I have a soft spot — I adore older industrial cities. Hailing from Newark, New Jersey, I still have vivid memories of the eyeglass factory where my father worked. I've lived in Pittsburgh and now Toronto. I love the industrial heritage of these places, their historic neighborhoods and bridges, their great architecture, the old buildings that, to paraphrase Jane Jacobs, are the sources of so many new ideas.

Economic growth today is powered no longer principally by raw materials, great waterways and railroad lines, or giant factories but by the places that have the richest clusterings of people who come together in dense ecosystems, generating ideas and products faster than they can elsewhere. Our great industrial cities stand at the forefront of this transformation. These cities have the density and the infrastructure, the history and authenticity, the walkable neighborhoods and quality, affordable housing, the great universities and medical centers, the leading cultural complexes and cutting-edge music and cultural scenes that are the fuel of the creative economy.

And together as a unit, they also have the tremendous size and scale needed to renew and prosper in our increasingly spiky world. Many of the cities discussed in this book are part of the great megaregion dubbed Chi Pitts by the great economic geographer Jean Gottman a half century ago. With 46 million people and $1.6 trillion in economic output, this cluster of great cities is the world's third largest; its population and its economy dwarf those of many countries. In my book *The Great Reset*, I argue that the region needs to be knit even closer together with better transit, especially high-speed rail, which can create a more integrated labor market and talent pool, increasing the velocity of people, goods, and ideas.

The ongoing economic crisis has impelled many people to look for deeper meaning and purpose in life — and for better places to live, with good, family-supporting jobs and affordable housing, where they can realize a new American Dream of doing purposeful and meaningful work in a real, authentic community that embraces and energizes them and their loved ones, that lets them be part of building something bigger than themselves. That's the new Dream that great industrial cities can provide and that they are embracing.

As the case studies in Paul Hardin Kapp and Paul J. Armstrong's *SynergiCity: Reinventing the Postindustrial City* prove, there is much reason for optimism. Some of our Rustbelt cities have been developing intriguing strategies of renewal, deeply informed by ideas about the creative class and based around sustainability, heritage, and ecological urbanism. The key to their ongoing turnaround, as I have noted elsewhere and as this book extensively documents, lies in letting go of all the old discredited top-down strategies and embracing organic, community-based efforts. As Don Carter's chapter on my old hometown Pittsburgh documents, it's not the megaprojects — the heavily subsidized convention centers and downtown sports stadiums — that ultimately make the difference but the "bottom-up energy" coming from community groups, architects and designers, entrepreneurs and techies, and city-builders and place-makers of all stripes and from all corners of the community. Carter knows of what he writes. He's a practitioner as well as a thinker, who's not afraid to wade into the mulch of real urbanism and get his hands dirty. I was proud to be his comrade-in-arms during my formative time in Pittsburgh, working alongside him to help set in motion some of these efforts and push others to the fore of the regional conversation

and strategy, even as entrenched squelchers tried to derail them. These efforts cannot be minimized: the persistence of forward-looking, collaborative, and inclusive regional practitioners and thoughtleaders, even in the face of highly placed opposition and backlash, has played and continues to play a key role in revitalization strategies across great industrial regions.

Instead of handing over neighborhoods or even whole sections of cities outright to city hall or private developers, this book shows that the solution to many cities' plights lies within them. Empowering residents to take control of and build on community assets, engaging them in community-based organizations that can spearhead revitalization and build real quality of place, yields real results. It takes time — 20 to 30 years is not uncommon — and it doesn't happen by itself. Politicians, planning professionals, academics, architects and landscape designers, real estate developers, local institutions and businesses, and citizens' groups must learn not just to cooperate with each other but to actively collaborate, to create synergies, as it were. But to the extent that they adopt a holistic approach to planning and build on a city's intrinsic strengths, they can accomplish miracles.

Introduction

PAUL HARDIN KAPP AND PAUL J. ARMSTRONG

As a designer you are capable of developing a concept which melds buildings together, creates synergy, and is exciting. If you worry about the details at the beginning [of the design process], you just get fragments. [If] you let the plan flow out of you . . . it [becomes] a reality.

Edmund Bacon, 1991–92 Plym Distinguished Professor of Architecture,
University of Illinois, Urbana-Champaign

EDMUND BACON, THE FORMER URBAN PLANNER for the city of Philadelphia, once described urban synergy as a process that successfully synthesizes disparate and often competing economic, social, and political forces in which the result is greater than the sum of the constituent parts (Warfield 1995). SynergiCity, therefore, is more than merely a master plan proposal: It is a visionary concept for the wholesale redevelopment of the postindustrial city. It is an evolution of a process we initiated, first as a graduate architecture design studio and, later, as a research project that proposed to transform the postindustrial city from a forgotten footnote in history into a lively, dynamic urban center. Our research then became a dialogue — among a group of urban design experts throughout the nation — that analyzed the postindustrial city and its sustainable redevelopment in terms of urban design and planning, architecture, and sustainability. This book is the end result.

During the spring 2009 and 2010 academic terms, two teams of graduate architecture students under our supervision at the School of Architecture at the University of Illinois, Urbana-Champaign, de-veloped master plan proposals for the Warehouse District of the city of Peoria, Illinois. We selected Peoria because of its industrial history, strategic location on the Illinois River, and the scale and potential for redevelopment of its existing warehouse district. As urban designers and preservation architects, we saw opportunities for ecological development of the entire district, ranging from development of infrastructure and transportation to adaptive use of existing buildings with new architecture and urban spaces. In developing the master plan proposals, we determined two primary goals for the warehouse district redevelopment: environmental stewardship and economic development. As a "steward" of the Illinois River, Peoria has an obligation to protect and sustain the natural environment and its most precious resources: clean air, fresh water, and its people. Consequently, developing sustainable design proposals that synthesize ecology and economic development with social needs is imperative.

Soon after we began our first design studio, events in Illinois and throughout the nation compelled us to consider broader implications of redesigning the existing warehouse district. In January 2009, the Great Recession began to take hold in Peoria and throughout the Midwest. Caterpillar, Peoria's largest employer and a Fortune 50 company, announced that it would lay off 20,000 workers, sending a tremor throughout the Illinois economy. In our architectural studio, we began to consider broader economic challenges facing Peoria. Could Peoria reinvent itself? And, on a broader scale, how could the design professions — architecture, planning, urban design, historic preservation, and landscape architecture — play a significant role in meeting challenges facing other postindustrial cities in the Midwest and elsewhere?

Economic and industrial decline is very real in Illinois and its surrounding states. Addressing the Commerce Committee of the Illinois General Assembly in February 2011, Dr. Geoffrey J. D. Hewings, professor of economics and director of the Regional Economics Application Laboratory at the University of Illinois, presented a sobering summary of the state of the Illinois economy. Illinois was losing both jobs and population; it had lost 320,000 jobs in the 2008–2009 recession. In fact,

Illinois had never recovered from the last recession of 2000-2001 and had been in an "employment recession" for the past 10 years. This had resulted in a loss of 455,000 jobs in Illinois since the state's last peak job period in November 2000. Hewings asserted that in the past decade Illinois had lost over $6 billion in tax revenue; furthermore, thousands of talented and skilled workers had migrated out of state to seek work and opportunities. If not addressed, the loss of human capital through out-migration, he warned, could have dire consequences, such as a continuing loss of at least $1 billion in annual revenue and a continued decline of the state's average per capita income. In closing, Hewings told the legislators that the two primary goals for growing the Illinois economy should be to stem the outflow of talented young people and to find ways to generate more wealth for all Illinois citizens (Hewings 2011).

As architecture design instructors with useful ideas, we felt it necessary to engage in the conversation for economic renewal in the Midwest. Although it would be inaccurate to declare that the industrialized economy in the Midwest no longer exists, it is safe to say that it is undergoing a profound change: the economy of production is evolving from goods to ideas and invention. In order for the midwestern states to return to their former economic prominence, the innovation economy will need every opportunity to flourish. Part of the solution is to design, build, and transform urban environments for this new economy. As professionals specializing in the built environment, we felt it necessary to explore how new urban districts can fulfill the needs of the new economy. Part of the answer lies in the industrial districts of the past. Currently, the postindustrial areas of midwestern

cities are either underutilized or not utilized at all. While globalization is partly to blame, the challenge of brownfield remediation and a pervasive attitude that these districts are antiquated and inconsequential have hampered development efforts. This has led these districts to be declared "postindustrial" — places belonging to a once industrial age in American history and repositories of forgotten artifacts that include factories, warehouses, freight ports, railroads, streets, and alleys. However, when we studied these urban areas in greater detail, we found that these districts still have great value and potential. These postindustrial districts are composed of millions of square feet of durable buildings, miles of extensive streets and infrastructure, and often miles of shorelines and waterways in the Midwest. They have the capability of providing venues for both economic production and lively places to live and work. They can be urban and natural, efficient and innovative. Addressing the redesign and redevelopment of these postindustrial landscapes is one way that states such as Illinois can reverse out-migration of talent and resources and redevelop both wealth and industry in cities such as Peoria.

Postindustrial development is not only practical, it is fiscally, environmentally, and socially responsible. Why abandon blocks of warehouses and infrastructure to develop rural land into suburban sprawl? With shrinking operational budgets, midwestern cities are no longer able to build and maintain new infrastructure. However, to its advantage, the Midwest is blessed with vast natural resources, most notably potable water, which should not only be conserved and carefully managed from an environmental point of view but also in social and economic terms. Socially, redevelop-

ing the postindustrial district in ways that nurture creative contributions from all citizens can have the potential to reverse embedded cultural and educational inequalities, while at the same time providing environments for better economic production. In considering these factors, postindustrial redevelopment can be a convergence and a synergy of the innovation economy with the natural and humanmade resources of the existing built environment.

In exploring ways to reinvent the postindustrial city, we found the ideas of noted urban theorist Richard Florida compelling and worth considering — specifically, the idea of "creative capital," the emergence of the "megaregion," and finally, the concept of "Urban Metabolism." As faculty members at the University of Illinois, we have witnessed firsthand how creative invention is routinely produced at our campus. Then we have watched the creators take their ideas elsewhere, either to the West Coast or the East Coast. We challenged the studio by asking: "Why is an idea created in Champaign, Illinois, then produced in Silicon Valley, California?" This led us to consider ways late-nineteenth-century and early-twentieth-century warehouse and industrial districts can become the "idea" factories of the twenty-first century. We also explored Florida's idea of megaregions, which he defines as systems of multiple cities and their suburbs, where two-thirds of the global economic output is produced and nearly nine in 10 new patented innovations are developed (Florida 2010). The Boston–New York–Washington Corridor, the "Char-Lanta" (Charlotte, North Carolina–Atlanta, Georgia) Corridor, and the Portland-Seattle-Vancouver Corridor are all examples Florida uses in describing the megaregion. It can be argued today that the Midwest is already a megaregion, with active trade occurring between its states.[1] How should this economic and innovative productivity be harnessed? How can architecture and urban design contribute to a city's effort of building a flourishing, innovative economy and, subsequently, a megaregion?

Part of the answer lies in the idea Florida labels "Urban Metabolism": a city's ability to convert sources of energy, both physical (food, oil, etc.) and intellectual (creative capital, invention), into wealth. This is caused by the "talent-clustering" of creative people who, through everyday interactions, create and develop new ideas that result in greater wealth for the city and the region. So how does one bring about a talent-cluster? By providing environmentally sustainable areas of urban density that allow people to work and live affordably, to enjoy healthy and active lifestyles, and to engage in culture and heritage. This is the urban design solution for creating a new innovation-based economy in postindustrial cities. This is SynergiCity.

Structure of the Book

This book is written for urban planners and designers, architects, landscape architects, political and public officials, developers, entrepreneurs, social scientists, community activists, and anyone who is interested in the redevelopment of postindustrial cities. This book does not discuss dollars or monetary investment in postindustrial redevelopment in detail; rather, it discusses values and ethics in design and development strategies. Thirteen thematic chapters are organized into three parts and a conclusion that synthesizes the book's key points. These chapters introduce the reader to the

strategies that create successful and sustainable postindustrial cities. The contributors are leading academic, professional, and political experts from throughout the United States who bring specialized knowledge and experience from diverse fields, including urban planning, architecture, landscape architecture, behavioral science, real estate and development, and policy-making. Case studies illustrate the key points and strategies of cities that have reinvented themselves into vibrant, livable communities. As such, this is the only book that addresses the postindustrial city in a comprehensive manner and specifically evaluates the future of midsize cities, which have been, historically, the most vulnerable to the stresses created by environmental, economic, and social turmoil.

Part I explores the facets of redesigning postindustrial districts for new and sustainable uses. In chapter 1, Donald K. Carter establishes the theme of conservation for the book. He evaluates the impact of postindustrial development on cities such as Pittsburgh as they transform themselves from heavy industry and manufacturing centers to knowledge-based, livable, pedestrian-oriented urban communities. Cities can grow "smarter" by adapting sustainable planning principles through stewardship of the natural environment. He suggests that regions of the United States should be reclassified as "water-belt" or "drought-belt" rather than "rust belt" and "sun belt" — an idea supporting the concepts of sustainable development that resonate throughout the book. Fresh, potable water is one of the most vital resources in the Midwest and is worth protecting at virtually any cost. Chapter 2 examines the role of postindustrial design and its application to the Warehouse District of the city of Peoria. In chapter 3, Paul Hardin Kapp states that

historic preservation is the first and most critical step in redeveloping the postindustrial city and illustrates the pivotal roles of preservation and adaptive reuse in defining sustainable cities and communities. In chapter 4, Paul Armstrong explores ways urban design can increase Urban Metabolism in the postindustrial city. This chapter addresses the motives, aspirations, and outcomes involved in developing former industrial areas sustainably by balancing environmental, economic, and social redevelopment. In chapter 5, Lynne Dearborn explains why urban districts should be redeveloped not only to produce wealth but also to become environments that educate. In chapter 6, John Norquist makes a compelling argument that today's manufacturing processes, which are quieter and safer than in the past, can be allowed and encouraged in urban neighborhoods.

Part II focuses on environmental stewardship in postindustrial cities. In chapter 7, Mark Gillem examines ways brownfield remediation has led to exciting and profitable postindustrial redevelopment in cities throughout the United States, for example Baltimore, Portland (Oregon), and San Francisco. Protecting and managing the watershed and developing urban landscapes for recreation and other uses are examined in chapters 8 and 9. In chapter 10, Norman Garrick proposes a different way of managing vehicular movement in the postindustrial district by proposing maximum parking lot spaces rather than the currently accepted minimum. Each of these contributors shows how sustainable, responsive urbanism can further an innovation economy and create new forms of place making through the integration of ecology and urbanism.

Part III, focuses on ways to implement the ideas and principles of SynergiCity within the existing postindustrial city. Examples and case studies demonstrate how postindustrial redevelopment can be both exciting and rewarding. In chapter 11, Bob Greenstreet, dean of the School of Architecture and Urban Planning at the University of Wisconsin, Milwaukee, cites how the university and the city of Milwaukee have formed a successful ongoing town-gown partnership as a catalyst for urban design and development that has revitalized the city culturally and economically. In chapter 12, Ray Lees, partner at PSA-Dewberry Architects, and Craig Hullinger, ex officio director of the Peoria Development Office, offer an inside perspective on the planning and design process in Peoria as a case study. They illustrate how Peoria is integrating new architecture with existing buildings for living, working, and gathering socially. In chapter 13, Emil Malizia examines the prospects for merging civic vision with economic realities at the project and strategic levels. He analyzes the financial strategies, risks, and rewards of postindustrial redevelopment. Paul Hardin Kapp synthesizes all of the contributors' thoughts and ideas in the conclusion.

The problem of reinventing the postindustrial district is not unique to Peoria. Many industrial cities throughout the United States face similar issues, particularly midsize cities in the Midwest such as Milwaukee; St. Paul and Minneapolis; St. Louis, Missouri; and Rockford, Illinois, to name a few. After we researched and analyzed these cities as case studies, it became apparent to us that sustained revitalization and growth takes an average of 20 to 30 years of planning and development. It also requires intensive collaborations among cities, institutions, planning and design professionals, developers, politicians, and many others. Our research revealed that the proposed model of SynergiCity

has worked successfully in many cities throughout the nation. Examples of successful postindustrial redevelopment are featured throughout the book, including Milwaukee's Third Ward and Lowertown in St. Paul, Minnesota; both developments began in the early 1980s and are now catalysts for redevelopment of adjacent districts. Midtown Alley in St. Louis is a commercial redevelopment of existing buildings and public spaces that connects the University of St. Louis with the downtown and civic center. Renaissance Development, a local developer, has transformed the demolished property of a failed public housing project into a prospering urban business district. These developments are only a few of the numerous postindustrial developments featured in SynergiCity.

In the final analysis, this book shows that postindustrial cities can be affordable, sustainable, and livable places to foster new economies and sustained growth. However, reinventing the postindustrial city is a challenge that requires a true synergy of diverse design professions and ideas if it is to be successful. Developers and cities will be successful in these ventures only if they work together and take a holistic approach to planning and building that incorporates urban planning and design, landscape design, architecture, historic preservation, and adaptive use of existing buildings. This is already happening in cities throughout the Midwest. The sustainable redevelopment of both brownfields and natural green spaces has produced exceptional results from Minneapolis to St. Louis.

Entrepreneurship is ingrained in the culture in the Midwest, where there is an abundance of natural resources, including an ample supply of fresh water and an affordable cost of living. And its housing and commercial real estate are more affordable

than those in other regions of the country. It has Tier 1 universities and colleges that are recognized throughout the world as leaders in research and education. Why, then, wouldn't new and innovative businesses with state-of-the art products and technology find the Midwest an attractive place to grow and prosper? Cities such as Peoria already provide the basic infrastructure of transportation, buildings, parks, institutions, and recreational amenities for creative capital ventures to prosper in the Midwest. Therefore, they have the potential to become livable, vibrant, and sustainable urban communities where enterprise is welcomed, urban growth and environmental stewardship is sustained, and the next Fortune 50 Company emerges.

◆ ◆ ◆

We are grateful to each of our partners and contributors. Without them the design proposals and this book would not have been possible. We are especially indebted to Ray Lees, principal of PSA-Dewberry, who arranged for numerous meetings and public reviews. We acknowledge Mayor Jim Ardis of the City of Peoria and Craig Hullinger, ex officio director of the Office of Economic Development, the City of Peoria Planning Department, and Dr. Amir Al-Khafaji of the Peoria Sustainability Commission for their support and guidance. Special thanks to Pat Sullivan of J & P Development in Peoria, who participated in reviews and provided tours of buildings. Weiming Lu, urban planner and former president of the St. Paul Lowertown Development Corporation, offered invaluable insights into the planning and development of postindustrial cities. We also wish to acknowledge the support of our contributors, who persevered in delivering quality manuscripts. We acknowledge the many design and planning professionals who have laid the intellectual foundation for this book. Special thanks to Richard Florida, who graciously agreed to write the foreword and who defined the "Creative Class," and to Donald K. Carter, Emil Malizia, and John Norquist for believing in "the cause." Don Carter also thanks Richard Florida, William H. Hudnut III, David Lewis, Rick Stafford, and Joel Tarr, who read and commented on early drafts of his chapter, and Elise Gatti, who assisted in its research and editing. Finally, we are especially grateful for the sustained efforts of our students, who contributed their time, effort, and talents to the design concepts and master plans featured in this book.

We also wish to express our gratitude for the financial and moral support from the University of Illinois Research Board; Robert Graves, dean of the College of Fine and Applied Arts at the University of Illinois, Urbana-Champaign, for providing financial support through a College Creative Research Grant; and David Chasco, director of the School of Architecture at the University of Illinois, Urbana-Champaign, for his support of the SynergiCity project.

Note

1. Incidentally, if the Midwest were a sovereign country, it would have the seventh largest economy in the world (Hewings 2011).

References

Florida, Richard. 2010. *The Great Reset: How New Ways of Living and Working Drive Post-crash Prosperity.* New York: HarperCollins.

Hewings, Geoffrey J. D. 2011. "State of the Illinois Economy, 2011: 'Connecting the Dots.'" Presentation to State Legislators, February 8, Springfield, Illinois.

Warfield, James. 1995. "Creating Urban Synergy: The Philadelphia Project." In *Architectural Design of Tall Buildings, Tall Building Council on Tall Buildings and Urban Habitat,* edited by Mir M. Ali and Paul J. Armstrong, 168. New York: McGraw Hill.

PART I

Designing
SynergiCity

CHAPTER ONE

Hope for the Future of the Postindustrial City

DONALD K. CARTER

Well I went back to Ohio | But my city was gone | There was no train station | There was no downtown

"My City Was Gone" (1982)—The Pretenders (music and lyrics by Chrissie Hynde)

THE TERM "POSTINDUSTRIAL" WAS FIRST POPU-larized by Daniel Bell in his 1973 book *The Coming of Post-industrial Society*, in which he forecast that mature national economies were moving and would continue to move from being manufacturing based to service based. The United States indeed went in that direction and prospered overall. What Bell did not predict were the severe regional disparities that would result between the so-called Rust Belt cities of the Northeast and Midwest and the Sun Belt cities of the South and Southwest. Over the next 40 years, Rust Belt cities were characterized by depopulation, disinvestment, and decline while Sun Belt cities were characterized by population explosion, economic growth, and sprawl. Graph 1.1 illustrates the magnitude of this geographic shift, comparing population change in two representative cities, Pittsburgh (Rust Belt) and Phoenix (Sun Belt), and their respective Metropolitan Statistical Areas (MSAs) between 1950 and 2009. The symp-toms of decline in the Rust Belt are well known, the causes have been identified, and the diagnosis has been consistently grim for cities like Detroit and Youngstown, Ohio.

This chapter will present a more optimistic future for the postindustrial cities of the Rust Belt. The transformation of the "Steel City" of Pittsburgh into a technology and financial center will be featured as a case study. Although "Shrinking Cities"—a term some consider pejorative—have indeed bled jobs and people for decades in the Northeast and Midwest, the cities themselves remain national treasures not to be tossed aside like the silver ghost towns of Nevada. Shrinking cites with well-planned postindustrial redevelopments, such as SynergiCity, have the best attributes of "Smart Growth," including walkable neighborhoods, affordable housing, historic downtowns and main streets, strong universities and hospitals, cultural amenities, parks, unused infrastructure capacity, development density sufficient to support public transit, and abundant water.

By contrast, the burgeoning cities of the Sun Belt are low-density, auto-dependent, and surviving on ever-diminishing supplies of borrowed water. Sun Belt economies have been driven not by diverse economies but by the business of growth itself, such as home building and construction, which the Great Recession of 2008-2009 revealed as illusory and unsustainable (Florida 2010). A new termi-nology now seems appropriate. Rust Belt becomes "Water Belt." Sun Belt becomes "Drought Belt."

We cannot undo the post-1950 global economic patterns that led to these regional inequities, but we can provide strategies for the rebirth of our in-dustrial heartland in the postindustrial economy, especially if redevelopment is tackled on a regional basis, not just in the central cities. The regional cit-ies of the Water Belt may now, half a century later, have regained a competitive advantage. They have

GRAPH 1.1. Populations of Pittsburgh (Rust Belt) v. Phoenix (Sun Belt) in 1950 and 2009. (Courtesy of Donald Carter)

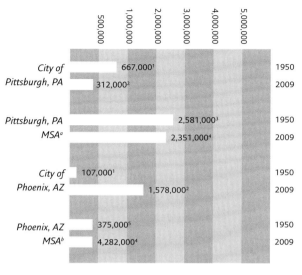

City of Pittsburgh, PA	667,000[1]	1950
	312,000[2]	2009
Pittsburgh, PA MSA[a]	2,581,000[3]	1950
	2,351,000[4]	2009
City of Phoenix, AZ	107,000[1]	1950
	1,578,000[2]	2009
Phoenix, AZ MSA[b]	375,000[5]	1950
	4,282,000[4]	2009

[a] The Pittsburgh, PA, MSA consists of Alleghny, Armstrong, Beaver, Bulter, Fayette, Washington, and Westmoreland counties (U.S. Census Bureau 2008).

[b] The Phoenix-Mesa-Scottsdale, AZ, MSA consists of Maricopa and Pinal counties (U.S. Census Bureau 2008).

[1] U.S. Census Bureau 1950   [4] U.S. Census Bureau 2009a
[2] U.S. Census Bureau 2009b   [5] U.S. Census Bureau 1995a
[3] U.S. Census Bureau 1995d

GRAPH 1.2. Population Change in Buffalo, Detroit, and Pittsburgh, 1950-2009. (Courtesy of Donald Carter)

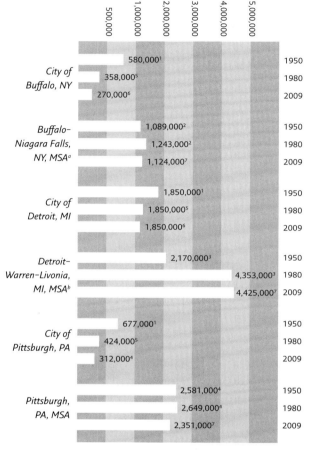

City of Buffalo, NY	580,000[1]	1950
	358,000[5]	1980
	270,000[6]	2009
Buffalo–Niagara Falls, NY, MSA[a]	1,089,000[2]	1950
	1,243,000[2]	1980
	1,124,000[7]	2009
City of Detroit, MI	1,850,000[1]	1950
	1,850,000[5]	1980
	1,850,000[6]	2009
Detroit–Warren-Livonia, MI, MSA[b]	2,170,000[3]	1950
	4,353,000[3]	1980
	4,425,000[7]	2009
City of Pittsburgh, PA	677,000[1]	1950
	424,000[5]	1980
	312,000[4]	2009
Pittsburgh, PA, MSA	2,581,000[4]	1950
	2,649,000[4]	1980
	2,351,000[7]	2009

[a] The Buffalo-Niagra Fall, NY, MSA consists of Erie and Niagra counties (U.S. Census Bureau 2008).

[b] The Detroit-Warren-Livonia, MI, MSA consists of Lapeer, Livingston, Macomb, Oakland, St. Clair, and Wayne counties (U.S. Census Bureau 2008).

[1] U.S. Census Bureau 1950   [5] U.S. Census Bureau 1980
[2] U.S. Census Bureau 1995c   [6] U.S. Census Bureau 2009b
[3] U.S. Census Bureau 1995b   [7] U.S. Census Bureau 2009a
[4] U.S. Census Bureau 1995d

space to grow internally on vacant and underutilized land. They have adaptable buildings and walkable neighborhoods. They have roads and utilities in place. They have strong institutional resources. They are places of authenticity and heritage. They have the persistence, strength, and resiliency of the people who did not leave. They have water.

There is every reason to believe that many of these American heartland cities can, with proper planning and investment, repopulate and prosper as some of the expanding U.S. population (300 million people in 2010 to 400 million in 2050) migrates to sustainable and livable cities with high quality of life, affordability, amenities, and economic opportunity. This can be the future of American postindustrial cities and can be a replicable model for postindustrial cities internationally.

Pathology of Postindustrial Cities

Well we're living here in Allentown
And they're closing all the factories down
Out in Bethlehem they're killing time
Filling out forms, standing in line
"Allentown" (1982) (music and lyrics by Billy Joel)

There is an established pathology for American postindustrial cities. The *symptoms* are well known and follow a well-documented pattern: loss of industrial jobs; subsequent loss of support and multiplier jobs; out-migration and population loss; lack of private investment; tax base decline; neglect and disinvestment in infrastructure and public services; abandoned factories; brownfields; vacant houses; vacant land; declining real estate values; loss of family equity; increased poverty; and finally, loss of hope and psychological depression.

The United States is not alone in experiencing postindustrial decline. In 1988, the International Remaking Cities Conference was held in Pittsburgh with over 350 delegates from industrial regions such as the Ruhr Valley in Germany, the Midlands in England, and the Monongahela Valley in Pittsburgh. Urban designers, market economists, architects, and citizens shared ideas for the reinvigoration of postindustrial cities that informed subsequent redevelopment policy in the Pittsburgh region (Davis 1989).

Graph 1.2 tracks population for three representative postindustrial U.S. cities and their respective MSAs from 1950 to 2008: Buffalo, Pittsburgh, and Detroit. Note that the central cities suffered large declines in population compared to their regions, which experienced moderate growth or decline. This reflects the 65-year pattern of suburbanization of America that accompanied the emptying out of the urban core, a national trend termed by Rolf Pendall (2003) as "sprawl without growth."

The *causes* of the decline of postindustrial cities in the Northeast and Midwest are likewise well known: loss of basic industries to low-cost, nonunion producers in the Sun Belt, Far East, and Mexico; an entrepreneurial vacuum creating no new industries to replace the lost jobs; the lure of suburbia; racial conflict; white flight; middle-class flight; concentration of poverty and crime in the urban core; investment in highways over public transit; steady decline of funding for essential services such as schools, parks, and public works; and the overall deterioration of the built environment, including streets, bridges, and buildings. Why stay?

The standard *prognosis* for postindustrial cit-

ies has been bleak. At worst, these cities are dead and will not come back. At best, they will become Shrinking Cities populated by an increasingly aged and poor population. They will have to do less with less. Like Camden, New Jersey, they will become "wards of the State" (Gillette 2005: 39). Whole parts of cities will be abandoned. Indeed, some of this is happening already in Detroit, Buffalo, and Flint, Michigan, where "managed decline" is the new strategy (Oswalt 2006a; Pallagst et al. 2009) and once-vibrant neighborhoods are being transformed into urban farms, recreational amenities, green infrastructure zones, and natural areas. Such downsizing strategies have been successfully adopted in depopulated cities in the former East Germany in an attempt to match cities' footprints to their new populations (Müller 2010). This still may be the fate of some cities. But there is an alternative scenario, best exemplified by the remaking of Pittsburgh, the quintessential industrial city and personification of the Rust Belt.

What Happened in Pittsburgh

Now Main Street's whitewashed windows and
    vacant stores
Seems like there ain't nobody wants to come down
    here no more
They're closing down the textile mill across the
    railroad tracks
Foreman says these jobs are going boys and they
    ain't coming back to
Your hometown, your hometown, your hometown,
    your hometown
"My Hometown" (Music and lyrics by Bruce
    Springsteen, 1984)

The song lyrics quoted about the breakdown of the Midwest's great industrial cities by Chrissie Hynde, Billy Joel, and Bruce Springsteen are from the 1980s. That is not a coincidence; it was indeed a dire time. Pittsburgh and many of its sister cities across the Northeast and Midwest lost their industrial bases in the space of a few years and went into precipitous, seemingly irreversible decline. That has not been the outcome for Pittsburgh. There are lessons to be learned in recounting how Pittsburgh was transformed in one generation from "Steel City" to "Knowledge City" (Carnegie Mellon University 2002) and how it became "a center for technology and green jobs, health care and education" (Obama 2010). The remaking of Pittsburgh did not happen by chance or luck. It was the result of a realistic assessment of assets and problems, imaginative long-range economic regional planning, a shared vision, a tradition of successful public-private partnerships, involvement of concerned private organizations, authentic citizen participation, strategic investments, organized feedback and evaluation,

FIGURE 1.1. Downtown Pittsburgh (daytime), c. 1940. Street lights were turned on during the day. Businessmen put on clean shirts in the afternoon. (Photographer unknown. Image courtesy of Smoke Control Lantern Slide Collection, Archives Services Center, University of Pittsburgh)

and patience to stay the course. First, a brief history of industrial Pittsburgh is in order to understand the city's underlying "DNA." Its current vibrancy is built on the legacy of three successive eras: Industrial Powerhouse (1865-1945); Renaissance (1945-1985); and Regrouping and Transformation (1985-present).

INDUSTRIAL POWERHOUSE (1865-1945)

The unprecedented industrial growth of Pittsburgh between the Civil War and World War I was the foundation for all that followed. That expansive era was made possible by nearby natural resources, particularly coal, oil, and gas; good transportation connections via rivers, canals, and railroads; an abundance of immigrant workers; and the genius and resourcefulness of a remarkable group of entrepreneurs: Andrew Carnegie, Henry Clay Frick, H. J. Heinz, Andrew Mellon, and George Westinghouse, to name the most famous.

Pittsburgh was truly a boomtown, albeit a polluted one, indelibly characterized by James Parton in 1868 as "Hell with the lid taken off" (Cronin 2008). In the 1870s, Pittsburgh was called the "'Forge of the Universe,' turning out half the glass, half the iron, and much of the oil produced in the United States" (Toker 2009). Between World War I and World War II, Pittsburgh maintained its place as one of the largest industrial centers in the world, despite suffering an economic downturn during the Great Depression of the 1930s. The armaments needed for World War II brought the city back to full employment as new factories were built overnight and pollution poured from the smokestacks and into the rivers. Streetlights were on at midday. Pollution meant prosperity (fig. 1.1).

RENAISSANCE (1945-1985)

In 1943, as World War II raged, Pittsburgh civic and business leaders, led by Democrat mayor David L. Lawrence and Republican business magnate Richard K. Mellon, son of the famed banker Andrew Mellon, determined that cleaning up the image of the city was critically important. This era has been dubbed "Renaissance I"; it included a smoke control ordinance, locks and dams on the rivers to prevent flooding, four major urban redevelopment projects (Gateway Center, Lower Hill, North Side, and East Liberty), and an urban highway system. Corporate headquarters were built for U.S. Steel, Alcoa, Mellon Bank, and Westinghouse. A new key player on the private side, the Allegheny Conference on Community Development, was formed in 1945 and was comprised of the CEOs of Pittsburgh's corporations, banks, private foundations, and universities.

"Renaissance II" is associated with Mayor Richard Caliguiri (1977-1988). During his time in office, a $2 billion downtown development boom occurred with six new office towers and a convention center hotel (fig. 1.2). The construction of a light rail subway system downtown and an exclusive busway to the eastern part of the city further strengthened the employment function of the urban core. Caliguiri also developed strategies for neighborhood revitalization, including housing rehabilitation and new infill development. Midway through his term of office, the steel industry in the Pittsburgh region collapsed, and 133,000 manufacturing jobs were lost in the span of eight years (Bureau of Economic Analysis 2010).

REGROUPING AND TRANSFORMATION (1985-2010)

Not only did the Pittsburgh region lose basic manufacturing jobs, but in 1985, Gulf Oil, a Fortune 500 company founded and headquartered in Pittsburgh, ceased to exist as it merged with Chevron, moving all operations to Houston and San Francisco. Rockwell International and Koppers likewise disappeared in mergers and acquisitions. Westinghouse faced financial problems that led to its eventual breakup into separate companies and subsequent loss of jobs in Pittsburgh. Things looked bleak. Families left the region for points south and west in quest of jobs. "Rust Belt" started to sound about right.

Improbably, in the midst of these losses, Rand McNally's *Places Rated Almanac* crowned Pittsburgh the nation's "Most Livable City" in 1985, displacing Atlanta, to its disbelief and dismay, and producing derisive snickers coast to coast. That surprising designation offers an important key to the continued resilience of Pittsburgh: quality of life. The city received medium and high marks for climate and terrain, housing, health care, transportation, education, the arts, recreation, and economic outlook. In essence, the Most Livable City designation was and is a measure of quality of life, and Pittsburgh was exceptional. Pittsburgh was named Most Livable City by the *Places Rated Almanac* again in 2007. In 2009, the British magazine *Economist* rated Pittsburgh the Most Livable U.S. City and twenty-ninth in the world. A year later, *Forbes* named metropolitan Pittsburgh the Most Livable City in the country and the Best Place to Buy a Home (Kalson 2010). Other recent accolades for the Pittsburgh region include "Number 1 Commercial Real Estate Market" in 2009, from Moody's Investors Service, and "Second Best Place to Raise Kids," from *Business Week* (2008).

Nevertheless, it was clear in 1985 that an economy based on heavy manufacturing was over. The often-quoted dictum from the richest American

FIGURE 1.2. View of Downtown Pittsburgh, "The Golden Triangle," 2008. The Allegheny and Monongahela Rivers meet to form the Ohio River. Over 300,000 persons work downtown. (Courtesy of Bobak Ha'Eri)

ever, Andrew Carnegie—"Put all your eggs in one basket, and then watch that basket"—does not apply if the eggs *and* the basket have disappeared. In the 1980s, Pittsburgh still had the key indicators of quality of life, but if well-paying jobs continued to disappear, so would quality of life.

Something had to be done, and it was. Between 1985 and 1995, the regional economic agenda for the next 25 years was set. This process involved leaders in the public and private sectors, in much the same way Renaissances I and II had. But something else also began to happen—an unprecedented bubbling up of quality-of-life initiatives from individuals, volunteer groups, and nongovernmental organizations, many of them in turn funded by the corporations and foundations. There was receptivity to new things and willingness to take risks. This bottom-up energy was especially exhibited by young adults in their twenties and thirties who began populating older neighborhoods, renovating houses, creating art, and starting new businesses. Two important civic groups, the Pittsburgh Urban Magnet Program (PUMP) and GroundZero Action Network, were created by and for young adults. Word of mouth fed a trickle and then a steady flow of young expatriate Pittsburghers who were coming back home ("boomerangs") and young newcomers eager to take advantage of the low cost of living, available jobs, and a vibrant cultural scene.

Charting the changes from the mid-1980s, when all seemed lost, makes a remarkable story. The first important transformative effort after the collapse of Big Steel was the formation in 1985 of Strategy 21, a consortium of the city of Pittsburgh, the county of Allegheny, the University of Pittsburgh, and Carnegie Mellon University that developed a strategy "to transform the economy of the Pittsburgh/ Allegheny region as it enters the 21st century" (Strategy 21 1985: 1). Strong emphasis was placed on creating a diversified economy to take "maximum advantage of emerging economic trends toward advanced technology and international marketing and communications systems" (Strategy 21 1985: 1). The Allegheny Conference on Community Development and local foundations were silent partners and major funders of the effort. Strategy 21 projects included the Software Engineering Institute (1986), the Pittsburgh Super Computing Center (1986), a new international airport terminal (1992), and major infrastructure improvements and brownfield reclamation projects throughout the region.

In the 25 years since 1985, manufacturing jobs have decreased by 40%, but total employment in the Pittsburgh region has grown by 13%, with growth in the health care, education, research, technology, finance, and arts sectors (Bureau of Economic Analysis 2010). New research institutes were created, including the Pittsburgh Transplantation Institute, National Robotics Center, and Gates Center for Computer Science. Scores of new nongovernmental organizations emerged, including Leadership Pittsburgh, the Green Building Alliance, Pittsburgh Downtown Partnership, Sustainable Pittsburgh, Riverlife, and Bike Pittsburgh.

New cultural organizations joined the four established world-class institutions (the Pittsburgh Symphony, Pittsburgh Opera, Pittsburgh Ballet, and Carnegie Museum), including the Pittsburgh Cultural Trust (with four downtown theaters), the Andy Warhol Museum, the Senator John Heinz History Center, and the August Wilson Center for African American Culture. In addition, art galleries, live music venues, performance groups, and neighborhood arts initiatives emerged, accompanied by new coffee shops and restaurants. Four large public buildings were built downtown: the David L. Lawrence Convention Center, PNC Park (baseball), Heinz Field (football), and the Consol Energy Center (hockey).

The most recent transformative project is the Pittsburgh Promise. Based on the highly successful 2005 Kalamazoo Promise, Pittsburgh Promise provides college scholarships for graduates of the Pittsburgh public schools or one of its charter high schools who have maintained a grade point average of 2.5 and a 90% attendance record from the ninth grade. The Pittsburgh Promise was jump-started in 2009 with a $100 million grant and pledge from the University of Pittsburgh Medical Center (UPMC), with substantial additional funding and matching contributions anticipated from businesses, foundations, and individuals over the next nine years to reach the goal of $250 million.

Several demographic trends are promising. In the last 25 years, regional population loss has slowed each decade, to the point that the population has now stabilized at about 2.4 million, with a slight increase projected for 2010 (Rotstein 2010). The region's net domestic out-migration in 2007 was lower than that of 16 of the top 40 regions, including Boston, Chicago, San Diego, and Silicon Valley (Miller 2008). The median age of employed Pittsburghers has started to drop, as younger people are drawn to the quality of life and a steady economy (Bowling 2008). Even senior citizens are finding Pittsburgh an attractive relocation destination. A study by the University of Pittsburgh and the Rand Corporation found that one-third of the elderly who moved to Pittsburgh between 1995 and 2000 migrated from Florida (Zlatos 2006).

Thorny issues nevertheless remain for the Pittsburgh region, including a surplus of vacant land and buildings; declining neighborhoods; racial and socioeconomic inequities; aging infrastructure, such as combined sewer overflows and bridge maintenance; stressed municipal finances; fragmented government; and an underfunded public transit system. These problems are shared with most of the deindustrialized cities in the Northeast and Midwest as they struggle to make a comeback. Philadelphia, Youngstown, Pennsylvania, Cleveland, and Detroit are exploring innovative approaches to the vacant land problem, including urban agriculture, return of nature to the city, and densifying certain neighborhoods along with dedensifying others. Many postindustrial cities are striving to capitalize on the strengths of their universities and medical centers. Yet Pittsburgh, of all those cities in the Northeast and Midwest, stands out today as exemplary in its transformation given the circumstances it faced in 1985. What lessons from Pittsburgh can be replicated in other postindustrial cities?

Lessons from Pittsburgh

Pittsburgh's path of recovery over the last 25 years, although difficult, is an example of how to build on current assets and respect past strengths while boldly embracing the future. The Pittsburgh story suggests that hope for the future of postindustrial cities will depend on the hard work and creativity of today's citizens, institutions, businesses, and governments working together with a shared vision. Below are 10 lessons for postindustrial cities from the remaking of Pittsburgh.

POPULATION GROWTH IS NOT NECESSARILY THE ANSWER

For so-called shrinking cities, the typical lament has been "If only we had more people. . . ." That is the wrong metric. Most of the deindustrialized regions of the Northeast and Midwest, although not growing, are in fact viable even at their reduced size. Many, like Pittsburgh, have stabilized in population at a size that can provide the services and amenities of world-class regions. For example, the population of the Pittsburgh region (2.4 million) is equal to or greater than 75% of the major metropolitan regions of Europe. This includes Copenhagen (2.4 million), Zurich (2.5), Vienna (2.2), Stockholm (2.2), Turin (2.2), and Dublin (1.6), to name just a few (OECD 2006). It is not likely that any of these regions will grow substantially in the next 20 years, but they will remain vibrant and viable. The same can be said about Pittsburgh.

Population size is not the issue, nor is population growth. Paul Gottlieb, in his 2002 paper for the Brookings Institution *Growth without Growth: An Alternative Economic Development Goal for Metropolitan Areas*, makes the argument that per capita growth in income is more important than population growth. He groups U.S. cities into four categories: Wealth Builders; Population Magnets; High-Growth Traditional; and Low-Growth Traditional. He argues that Wealth Builder cities tend to be in the "Frost Belt" and have high-tech economies. According to his analysis, the top three Wealth Builder cities are St. Louis, Pittsburgh, and Boston. Population Magnets like San Diego or Orlando tend to be in the Sun Belt and have economies based on tourism and low-paying, low-tech jobs. Gottlieb concludes: "We do not normally think

of metropolitan areas like Milwaukee, St. Louis, or Pittsburgh as economic success stories, but by this particular welfare measure they are" (Gottlieb 2002: 25).

HAVE A LONG-TERM REGIONAL VISION

The unit of economic competitiveness is no longer the central city but the metropolitan region (Calthorpe and Fulton 2001). Despite the fragmentation of local government, the Pittsburgh region has been able to forge a unified economic vision.

Following Strategy 21 in 1985, a second regional visioning effort was initiated in 1993, with the publication of a white paper by Robert Mehrabian, president of Carnegie Mellon University. Commissioned by the Allegheny Conference, the study compared the Pittsburgh region's economic indicators to those of the 24 largest regions in the country. The comparison was sobering. From 1970 to 1990, the Pittsburgh region had the largest decline in manufacturing jobs, the slowest growth in service jobs, and the greatest loss of population. On the other hand, the report identified inherent strengths on which to base an economic recovery: a strong downtown; a concentration of university and corporate research; a dedicated and trained workforce; a growing core of high-value, high-tech manufacturing and specialty companies; and an extraordinary range of high-quality recreational and cultural amenities. The report proposed a nine-month public engagement process to develop a consensus vision for the region. That process involved over 5,000 people and resulted in a report, *The Greater Pittsburgh Region: Working Together to Compete Globally*, published the following year (Mehrabian and O'Brien 1994). The Working Together Consortium, comprised of representatives from government, business, labor, education, community and religious organizations, and counties throughout the region, was subsequently formed to implement the plan.

The Strategic Investment Fund was established in 1996 by private corporations and foundations to complement and support public sector investments in economic development. Originally endowed with $40 million, it received a second round of capitalization of $30 million in 2002. The Fund provides gap-financing loans of $500,000–$4,000,000 for two categories of development: regional core investments, and industrial site reuse and technology development.

One of the most important actions of the Working Together Consortium affecting quality of life was the enactment of State Law 77, which enabled the adoption of a 1% added sales tax in Allegheny County in 1994. The 1% tax increment was split three ways: 0.25% to municipalities for tax relief; 0.25% to Allegheny County for tax relief; and 0.5% to the newly created Regional Asset District. The portion of the tax designated for the Regional Asset District provides operating support to the Pittsburgh Zoo, National Aviary, Phipps Conservatory, Carnegie Museums, Carnegie Libraries, County Parks, Convention Center, stadiums, and many smaller cultural organizations. From 1994 to 2010, the Regional Asset District has provided $1.1 billion to these regional assets.

A further regional initiative, "Power of 32," began in 2010 with the goal of creating a regional vision for the 32 counties surrounding Pittsburgh. With the tag line "32 Counties, 4 States, 1 Vision," Power of 32 will gather 4.2 million people from southwestern Pennsylvania, eastern Ohio, northern West Virginia, and western Maryland in a large-scale visioning project modeled after "Envision Utah" and "Louisiana Speaks."

MAKE LOCAL GOVERNMENT MORE EFFICIENT

The implementation of the Regional Asset District sales tax in 1995, in effect a regional tax-sharing mechanism, was an important first step in restructuring local government, a major goal of the Working Together Consortium. It was followed in 1998 by a ballot initiative changing the governance of Allegheny County from three elected county commissioners, with its foundation in an outmoded rural model, to an elected county executive and 15 councilors. In 2005, Allegheny County voters approved the conversion of previously elected offices, such as the clerk of courts and coroner, to merit-based appointments by the county executive and county council. The city of Pittsburgh and Allegheny County began discussions regarding city-county consolidation based on successful consolidations in Indianapolis/Marion County and Louisville/Jefferson County. However, other than a city-county summit in 2004 and a 2008 public agreement between the current mayor and county executive to work toward consolidation, there has been little progress in merging departments. As they have in the past, when progress has stalled on important regional issues, the local foundation community in July 2010 stepped in to create and fund the Allegheny Forum. The Forum consists of 300 invited residents representing the county's demographic and partisan makeup who have been tasked with simplifying the "gnarled, centuries-old issue of divided governance." Their first assignment will be to look at the sustainability of maintaining 109 separate police forces across Allegheny County.

FOSTER PUBLIC-PRIVATE PARTNERSHIPS

The remaking of Pittsburgh could not have taken place in the last 65 years without the extraordinary public-private partnerships described previously. Government, corporations, and philanthropic foundations worked together on issue after issue, whether environmental cleanup, transit, or public schools. It may be difficult for other cities to replicate the large behind-the-scenes investments by Pittsburgh's private foundations that bear the names of the industrialists and financiers of the Industrial Powerhouse years (Mellon, Heinz, McCune, Benedum, Hillman, Hunt, and Buhl, among others). This may be one area where Pittsburgh has a decided advantage. Nevertheless, philanthropic and corporate resources are available in every community. The important lesson is to engage local foundations and corporations, whoever they are, in the remaking effort. For example, an adventuresome, farsighted Chattanooga foundation, the Lyndhurst Foundation, spearheaded the acclaimed revitalization of the Chattanooga downtown and riverfront.

DIVERSIFY THE ECONOMY

The city of Pittsburgh's decisions in the 1980s and 1990s to diversify the economy into high-tech industries and research have paid large dividends. Today, the Pittsburgh region has a smaller share of employment in manufacturing than the national average, but its share of employment in the education and health services industry is 1.5 times larger than the average in the United States (Miller and Rudick 2007). All those lost manufacturing jobs (and more) were replaced over three decades by jobs in research, medicine, finance, and services and in new fields such as robotics, information technology, and green industries. This was a deliberate strategy backed by studies and strategic investments by government, corporations, universities, and foundations, working together with one shared vision. An indicator of this strategy is that the Pittsburgh region's unemployment rate has been lower than or equal to the national rate since early 2007 (Rotstein 2010).

STRENGTHEN THE CORE

Despite its economic woes beginning in the mid-1980s, the city of Pittsburgh, the heart of the region, had significant assets: a strong downtown; distinct historic and walkable neighborhoods; two major research universities; a world-renowned medical center; a well-used public transit system; unrivaled cultural amenities for a city of its size; and a critical mass of large philanthropic foundations with a commitment to investing in the region.

Beginning with Renaissance I after World War II and continuing today, a major goal of community leaders has been to strengthen the central city of Pittsburgh and its downtown. Some mistakes were made along the way, as in other cities, most notably ill-conceived urban renewal projects that displaced low-income residents and businesses, and highway projects that severed neighborhoods from the rest of the city. But the overall result has been good, as the downtown remains the economic hub of the region, with employers providing 140,000

jobs, including corporations, banks, law firms, government offices, professional offices, hotels, two department stores, hundreds of retail stores and restaurants, and five performing arts theaters. The major public facilities built in the last 10 years (two stadiums, the arena, and the convention center) are located downtown and were central accomplishments of the Regional Destination Strategy of the Working Together Consortium. Downtown housing is increasing, aided by government programs and philanthropic efforts, and a continuous network of green spaces has been created along the rivers in the urban core. Parallel investments in housing, amenities, economic development, and brownfield redevelopment have been made in Pittsburgh's neighborhoods by the city under Mayor Tom Murphy (1994-2006), the Strategic Investment Fund, and other civic initiatives.

COMMIT TO SUSTAINABLE DEVELOPMENT

Pittsburgh pioneered the environmental cleanup of industrial pollution in the late 1940s, as described in the Renaissance section. Pittsburgh became known for leading-edge engineering and construction companies involved in brownfield remediation, air and water quality technologies, and best practices in stormwater management. In the 1990s as part of the Working Together Consortium, two new Smart Growth organizations were created: the Green Building Alliance, which predated the U.S. Green Building Council, and Sustainable Pittsburgh. Pittsburgh was ahead of the curve on "green building," becoming a national leader in Leadership in Energy and Environmental Design (LEED) certified buildings, including the first LEED certified conven-

tion center, botanical conservatory, and multipurpose arena. City and county governments have sustainability coordinators. Pittsburgh corporations, universities, hospitals, and real estate developers have embraced sustainability principles in their construction programs. The Strategic Investment Fund gives special consideration in its loans to projects that include brownfield redevelopment and green technology. Sustainable development has thus become an environmental ethic and brand for Pittsburgh as well as an economic driver.

CAPITALIZE ON FRESH WATER

Fresh water resources are expected to be a key determinant worldwide of the health of all metropolitan regions in the next 50 years. Water is a finite resource—a closed system that cycles over and over from evaporation to precipitation. Only 2.5% of the world's supply is fresh water, and two-thirds of that is frozen in Earth's polar ice caps. The remaining 97.5% is ocean salt water unusable for human consumption, industry, or agriculture without treatment (Lange 2010).

Climate change and unsustainable development practices are creating water shortages through the world, including the United States. A 2010 study by the Natural Resources Defense Council found that one-third of all counties in the lower 48 states—more than 1,100 counties—will be subject to higher risks of water shortages by midcentury. The regions in the nation with naturally abundant and rechargeable fresh water supplies, such as Pittsburgh and the other postindustrial regions of the upper Midwest, with the Great Lakes, major rivers, and large ever-renewing underground aquifers, have a decided advantage over regions in the

FIGURE 1.3. Kayakers on the Allegheny River, 2008. The three rivers in Pittsburgh are lined with 25 miles of bicycle and pedestrian trails where railroad lines and factories once prevented public access. (Photo by John Altdorfer. Courtesy of John Altdorfer)

South and Southwest. Rapidly growing regions like Atlanta and Phoenix have exceeded their natural water supplies. Water must be borrowed from other states at great expense and usually after intense disputes over riparian rights. At the same time, their underground aquifers are being pumped out faster than they are being recharged, also at great expense. Continued growth in these regions may become untenable as the fresh water supply inexorably diminishes, while the postindustrial cities of the Midwest remain water rich.

Las Vegas is the first region in the nation to reach a dangerous tipping point in water resources, as Lake Mead continues to shrink and the Owens Valley aquifer is being pumped dry (Sonoran Institute

2010). By contrast, Pittsburgh and the Midwest will continue to have abundant water for agriculture, industry, drinking, and new development, while regions in the Drought Belt may have reached their peaks and may become the Shrinking Cities of the twenty-first century. "Water is going to be more important than oil in the next 20 years," says Dipak Jain, dean of the Kellogg School of Management at Northwestern University in Evanston, Illinois (quoted in Lippert and Efstathiou 2009).

INVEST IN EDUCATION

An educated workforce is essential to economic success, whether in remaking a city or building a new

one. Pittsburgh has committed to increasing the effectiveness of its workforce over the last 25 years, and with good results. A recent report published by the University of Pittsburgh's University Center for Social and Urban Research, comparing the educational attainment of workers aged 24 to 34 in the top 40 metropolitan areas of the nation, found that 48.1% of Pittsburghers in this cohort have obtained at least a bachelor's degree. This puts Pittsburgh in fifth place after Boston, San Francisco, Washington, D.C., and Austin (Briem 2010). The deindustrialized cities of the Northeast and Midwest saw their inner-city school systems decline in enrollment, test scores, and graduation rates while the surrounding suburban school districts flourished. Central city scholarship programs like the Kalamazoo Promise counter that trend. Since the inception of the Kalamazoo Promise in 2005, enrollment in the public school system has increased 17.6%, ending 20 years of steady decline (Miller-Adams 2009). Middle-class families are moving to the city to take advantage of the scholarship program. More college preparatory courses are being offered in high school as a result. Finally, because the Kalamazoo Promise scholarships can only be used at public colleges and universities in Michigan, there is more likelihood of retaining those young people in the region when they graduate, an outcome the Pittsburgh Promise hopes to achieve.

INVEST IN QUALITY OF LIFE

Pittsburgh deserved its many citations as Most Livable City. It has also been consistently in the top 10 U.S. cities for other measures such as cultural tourism and being artist friendly. Top rankings appear every year for such quality-of-life issues as suitability to raising a family, housing afford-ability, bicycle friendliness, and accessibility of the outdoors. From the creation of the Regional Asset District in 1985 to the construction of 25 miles of riverfront bikeways in the 1990s and 2000s, Pittsburgh has invested heavily in amenities, including major cultural and sports facilities. Richard Florida wrote his seminal 2002 book *The Rise of the Creative Class* while in Pittsburgh on the faculty of Carnegie Mellon University. Funding for his initial research into amenities for young adults came from the Heinz Endowments and the Richard King Mellon Foundation, two of Pittsburgh's largest foundations. Florida's conclusions about the potent combination of talent, technology, tolerance, and territory validated for community leaders in Pittsburgh the importance of investing in quality of life.

There is optimism today in the Pittsburgh region, an upbeat spirit, much of it related to quality of life. Part of that is pride in having survived the collapse of the 1980s, in being named Most Livable City four times, and, of course, in winning two Super Bowls and three Stanley Cups in those years. But it is more tangible than that. People can see for themselves 25 miles of bike trails that did not exist along the rivers 10 years ago. They can see rowers and kayakers on the rivers (fig. 1.3). They can see new stadiums, new housing in once declining neighborhoods, restoration of historic buildings on main streets, an expanding arts community, neighborhood festivals, an influx of young people, and most important, new businesses and jobs.

References

Bell, Daniel. 1973. *The Coming of Post-industrial Society: A Venture in Social Forecasting.* New York: Basic Books.

Bowling, Brian. 2008, September 23. "City Shifts to Younger Work Force, Census Says." *Pittsburgh Tribune-Review.* www.pittsburghlive.com/x /pittsburghtrib/news/cityregion/s_589592.htm.

Briem, Christopher. 2010, March. "Education Attainment in the Pittsburgh Regional Workforce." *Pittsburgh Economic Quarterly.* www.ucsur.pitt.edu /files/peq/peq_2010-03.pdf.

Brookings Institution. 2007. *Committing to Prosperity: Moving Forward on the Agenda to Renew Pennsylvania.* Washington, DC: Brookings Institution.

Bureau of Economic Analysis. 2010. Regional Economic Accounts. CA25—Total Employment by Industry, 1985-2008. www.bea.gov/regional/reis /default.cfm?selTable=CA25.

Calthorpe, Peter, and William Fulton. 2001. *The Regional City.* Washington, DC: Island Press.

Carnegie Mellon University. 2002, summer. "President Bush Visits Oakland, Greets University Presidents." *Carnegie Mellon Magazine.* www.cmu.edu /magazine/02summer/newsbriefs.html#bush.

Cronin, Mike. 2008, September 7. "Reactions Mixed on Comparison of City to Hell." *Pittsburgh Tribune-Review.* www.pittsburghlive.com/x/pittsburghtrib /news/specialreports/250-anniversary/s_586956 .html.

Davis, Barbara, ed. 1989. *Remaking Cities: Proceedings of the 1988 International Conference in Pittsburgh.* Pittsburgh: University of Pittsburgh Press.

Florida, Richard. 2002. *The Rise of the Creative Class: And How It's Transforming Work, Leisure,*

Community and Everyday Life. New York: Basic Books.

———. 2010. *The Great Reset: How New Ways of Living and Working Drive Post-crash Prosperity.* New York: HarperCollins.

Gillette, Howard, Jr. 2005. *Camden after the Fall: Decline and Renewal in a Post-industrial City.* Philadelphia: University of Pennsylvania Press.

Gleeson, Robert E. 2004. *Toward a Shared Economic Vision for Pittsburgh and Southwestern Pennsylvania: A White Paper Update.* Prepared for the Center for Economic Development, H. John Heinz III School of Public Policy and Management, Carnegie Mellon University.

Gottlieb, Paul D. 2002. *Growth without Growth: An Alternative Economic Development Goal for Metropolitan Areas.* Washington, DC: Brookings Institution.

Grimm, Fred. 2009, January 17. "A City Goes from Misery to Marvelous." *Miami Herald.*

Grogan, Paul, and Tony Proscio. 2000. *Comeback Cities: A Blueprint for Urban Neighborhood Revival.* Boulder, CO: Westview Press.

Hudnut, William H., III. 1998. *Cities on the Rebound: A Vision for Urban America.* Washington, D.C.: Urban Land Institute.

Hynde, Chrissie. 1990. "My City Was Gone." In *Learning to Crawl.* CD performed by The Pretenders. Sire Records 0759923980-2. Reissued 1990.

Jensen, Brian K., and James W. Turner. 2000. "Act 77: Revenue Sharing in Allegheny County." *Government Finance Review* 12: 17-21.

Joel, Billy. 1982. "Allentown." In *The Nylon Curtain,* performed by Billy Joel. Columbia Records QC 38200. Vinyl recording.

Kalson, Sally. 2010, May 4. "Pittsburgh Named Most

Livable City Again." *Pittsburgh Post-Gazette*, Local sec.

Kromer, John. 2010. *Fixing Broken Cities: The Implementation of Urban Development Strategies*. New York: Routledge.

Lange, Karen E. 2010, April. "Get the Salt Out." *National Geographic*.

Lippert, John, and Jim Efstathiou, Jr. 2009, May 3. "Thirsty Las Vegas Is a Case Study of the Next Global Crisis." *Seattle Times*, Business/Technology sec. http://seattletimes.nwsource.com/html /businesstechnology/2009164039_lasvegaswater03 .html.

Lorant, Stefan. 1999. *Pittsburgh: The Story of an American City*. 5th ed. Pittsburgh: Esselmont Books.

Lubove, Roy. 1969. *Twentieth-Century Pittsburgh*. Vol. 1. *Government, Business, and Environmental Change.* Pittsburgh: University of Pittsburgh Press.

———. 1996. *Twentieth-Century Pittsburgh.* Vol. 2. *The Post-steel Era.* Pittsburgh: University of Pittsburgh Press.

Mehrabian, Robert, and Thomas H. O'Brien. 1994. *The Greater Pittsburgh Region: Working Together to Compete Globally.* A Report for the Regional Economic Revitalization Initiative by Carnegie Mellon University and the Allegheny Conference on Community Development.

Miller, Christian, and Brian Rudick. 2007. *The Pittsburgh Metropolitan Statistical Area.* Federal Reserve Bank of Cleveland. www.clevelandfed.org /research/trends/2007/0407/01regact_032607 .cfm.

Miller, Harold D. 2008, April 13. "Regional Insights: What Can Keep People from Leaving Pittsburgh?" *Pittsburgh Post-Gazette*, Business sec. www .post-gazette.com/pg/08104/872629-28.stm#.

Miller-Adams, Michelle. 2009. *The Kalamazoo Promise: Building Assets for Community Change.* W. E. Upjohn Institute.

Müller, Rainer. 2010, April 9. "Eastern German Project Provides Hope for Shrinking Cities." *Der Spiegel.* www.spiegel.de/international/germany/0,1518 ,688152,00.html.

Muro, Mark, Bruce Katz, Sarah Rahman, and David Warren. 2008. *MetroPolicy: Shaping a New Federal Partnership for a Metropolitan Nation.* Washington, DC: Brookings Institution.

Nasaw, David. 2006. *Andrew Carnegie.* New York: Penguin Press.

National Resources Defense Council. 2010. *Climate Change, Water, and Risk: Current Water Demands Are Not Sustainable.* www.nrdc.org /globalWarming/watersustainability/files /WaterRisk.pdf.

Obama, Barack H. 2010, June 2. Remarks by the President on the Economy, Carnegie Mellon University. www.whitehouse.gov/the-press-office /remarks-president-economy-carnegie-mellon -university.

OECD. 2006. *Competitive Cities in the Global Economy.* Paris: OECD.

O'Neill, Brian. 2009. *The Paris of Appalachia: Pittsburgh in the Twenty-First Century.* Pittsburgh: Carnegie Mellon University Press.

Oswalt, Philipp, ed. 2006a. *Shrinking Cities.* Vol. 1. *International Research.* Ostfildern: Hatje Cantz.

———, ed. 2006b. *Shrinking Cities.* Vol. 2. *Interventions.* Ostfildern: Hatje Cantz.

Pallagst, Karina, Jasmin Aber, Ivonne Audirac, Emmanuele Cunningham-Sabot, Sylvie Fol, Christina Martinez-Fernandez, Sergio Moraes, Helen Mulligan, Jose Vargas-Hernandez, Thorsten Wiechmann, and Tong Wu. 2009. *The Future of Shrinking Cities: Problems, Patterns and Strategies of Urban Transformation in a Global Context.* Berkeley: Center for Global Metropolitan Studies, Institute of Urban and Regional Development, and Shrinking Cities International Research Network.

Pendall, Rolf. 2003. *Sprawl without Growth: The Upstate Paradox.* Washington, DC: Brookings Institution.

"The Pittsburgh Promise." www.pittsburghpromise .org/.

Power of 32. www.powerof32.org/.

Rotstein, Gary. 2010, June 21. "Pittsburgh's Population Expected to Grow in a Few Years: Region's Exodus Finally Slowing." *Pittsburgh Post-Gazette*, Local sec. www.post-gazette.com/pg/10172/1067091-455.stm.

Sonoran Institute. 2010. *Growth and Sustainability in the Las Vegas Valley*. www.sonoraninstitute.org/ component/docman/doc_download/878-las-vegas -report-09.html.

Springsteen, Bruce. 1982. "My Hometown." In *Born in the U.S.A.* CD. Columbia Records CK 38653.

Stewman, Shelby, and Joel A. Tarr. 1982. "Four Decades of Public-Private Partnerships in Pittsburgh." In *Public-Private Partnership in American Cities: Seven Case Studies*, ed. R. Scott Fosler and Renee A. Berger, 59-127. Lexington, MA: Lexington Books.

Strategy 21: Pittsburgh/Allegheny Economic Development Strategy to Begin the 21st Century. 1985. A proposal to the Commonwealth of Pennsylvania by the City of Pittsburgh, Allegheny County, University of Pittsburgh and Carnegie Mellon University.

Toker, Franklin. 2009. *Pittsburgh: A New Portrait.* Pittsburgh: University of Pittsburgh Press.

U.S. Census Bureau. 1950. Table 18. Population of the 100 Largest Urban Places: 1950. www.census. gov/population/www/documentation/twps0027 /tab18.txt.

———. 1980. Table 21. Population of the 100 Largest Urban Places: 1980. www.census.gov/population/www/documentation/twps0027/tab21.txt.

———. 1995a. Arizona Population of Counties by Decennial Census: 1900 to 1990. www.census.gov/population/cencounts/az190090.txt.

———. 1995b. Michigan Population of Counties by Decennial Census: 1900 to 1990. www.census.gov/population/cencounts/mi190090.txt.

———. 1995c. New York Population of Counties by decennial Census: 1900 to 1990. www.census.gov/population/cencounts/ny190090.txt.

———. 1995d. Pennsylvania Population of Counties by Decennial Census: 1900 to 1990. www.census.gov/population/cencounts/pa190090.txt.

———. 2008. Metropolitan and Micropolitan Statistical Areas and Components, November 2008, with Codes. www.census.gov/population/www/metroareas/lists/2008/List1.txt.

———. 2009a. Table 1. Annual Estimates of the Population of Metropolitan and Micropolitan Statistical Areas: April 1, 2000 to July 1, 2009. www.census.gov/popest/data/metro/totals/2009/index.html

———. 2009b. Table 1. Annual Estimates of the Resident Population for Incorporated Places over 100,000, Ranked by July 1, 2009 Population: April 1, 2000 to July 1, 2009. http://www.census.gov/popest/data/cities/totals/2009/index.html.

———. 2010. About Metropolitan and Micropolitan Statistical Areas. www.census.gov/population/www/metroareas/aboutmetro.html.

Zlatos, Bill. 2006, June 19. Elderly Returning from Sun Belt. *Pittsburgh Tribune-Review*, News sec. www.pittsburghlive.com/x/pittsburghtrib/s_458636.html.

FIGURE 2.1. Rendering of proposed redevelopment of existing warehouses and new multiuse buildings along Adams Street in SynergiCity: Warehouse District, Peoria. (Illustration by Ryan Marshall. Courtesy of School of Architecture, University of Illinois, Urbana-Champaign)

CHAPTER TWO

Why SynergiCity?

PAUL J. ARMSTRONG

FOR THE PAST 15 YEARS, MANUFACTURING CITIES throughout the United States have experienced a significant decline. Manufacturing's share of employment in the United States has been falling for at least 50 years (Bernard et al. 2002). According to the Bureau of Labor Statistics' Establishment Survey, the share of manufacturing employment in 1950 was about 35% and in 2004 was about 13% (Fisher and Rupert 2005). The 2008–2009 recession, which accelerated with the financial collapse on September 15, 2008, has exacerbated this decline, forcing mass closings of manufacturing facilities and layoffs. Leading economists agree that the effects of this recession will be long-lasting and it will challenge the country to restructure the economy. Moreover, the recession emphasized the fact that the majority of the manufacturing base of the American economy is leaving the United States in order to capitalize on cheap labor in developing countries.

The consequences of globalization are far-reaching and deep. The global economy will now compel all facets of the American economy to focus on what it has in the past done very well—innovation. In order for America to transform from an industry-based to an innovation-based economy,

whole-scale changes will need to be made in every aspect of society. Changes will include the design of our cities as well. Larger American cities such as Detroit, New Orleans, St. Louis, Milwaukee, and Pittsburgh have all experienced extreme economic calamities, significant population fluctuations, and drastic reduction in income and corporate tax receipts. As these cities continue to reassess their standing in a postindustrial age, their urban form will need to be assessed as well. Can these cities retain their current geographical size? Is the current urban form of these cities appropriate for the new economy? These are the fundamental questions facing American cities today.

Former American manufacturing cities — particularly those located in the U.S. Rust Belt — are grappling with a large unemployed workforce, declining populations, a large inventory of unoccupied buildings, and a decaying infrastructure. Starting from this crisis, can we transform our industrial cities into centers of creativity and innovation? Finally, can we use the current economic crisis to correct the environmental mistakes of the past in our cities?

Paul Armstrong and Paul Kapp investigated these issues in two graduate architectural design studios

at the School of Architecture, University of Illinois, Urbana-Champaign, during the spring of 2009 and 2010. SynergiCity is a proposal addressed to this challenge in the postindustrial city. It promotes density in urban areas that have an established record of being viable both economically and environmentally, and it proposes to restore floodplain areas of cities that have been developed for other functions back into sustainable uses (fig. 2.1).

Peoria, Illinois

These issues are found not only in larger industrial cities; midsize cities such as Peoria, Illinois, have encountered the same challenges. Peoria is the quintessential midwestern postindustrial city. Because of its proximity to river transportation and access to corn for grain alcohol, Peoria was one of the largest manufacturers of distilled spirits and beer in the United States (Couri 1991). Peoria is also the headquarters of Caterpillar Inc., the world's largest manufacturer of earth-moving machinery (Funding Universe 2004). Caterpillar's own manufacturing history offers a synopsis of the rise, decline, and redirection of manufacturing in the

United States since World War II. In the postwar period, Caterpillar experienced enormous growth until 1983, when it announced its first annual loss in earnings in half a century. Sales slumped to a recent historic low of $5.4 billion, and the company was forced to lay off workers domestically and closed a plant in Newcastle-on-Tyne, England. Caterpillar's worst year came in 2002, when profits amounted to $798 million, which translated into a profit margin of just 4%. Under new leadership since 2003, the company has been targeting emerging markets, particularly China, India, and Russia, for future growth, with a goal of $30 billion in revenues by 2006. However, with the recession of 2008–2009, Caterpillar has been forced to lay off 20,000 employees and close plants once again.

Peoria, which derives its name from a local Native American tribe, was selected by Armstrong and Kapp for the design studio project because of its central location, its relative size, and its significance as a historic "river town." It is the largest city on the Illinois River and the county seat of Peoria County. As of the 2000 census, the city's population was 112,936. The Greater Peoria Metro area, including suburbs and surrounding areas, has a population of 370,000 (NACo 2008).

While Peoria has many strengths, it "has suffered from the absence of a strong common vision, registered in the mixed messages offered by its streets and buildings, and by the evident difficulty in establishing a clear and distinctive character for the new development along the riverfront" (Duany and Plater-Zyberk 2003: 1.1). Cities must reinvent themselves periodically if they are to survive. Relying on manufacturing alone to provide employment, foster economic sustainability and growth, and create the essential foundation for living, education, culture, entertainment, and leisure places cities at risk.

Between 1970 and 2000, Peoria has witnessed an 11.3% decline in population. While this figure is certainly not alarming, it is indicative of a downward trend similar to other industrial cities in the Midwest. As of the 2000 census, the racial makeup of the city was 69.29% white and 24.79% African American, with a median income per household of $36,397 (USCB 2008).

Karina Pallagst, program director of the Center for Global Metropolitan Studies, links urban shrinkage with the "complex . . . forces of globalization" (2008: p. 7). She suggests that this phenomenon should be recognized by cities in "downsizing" urban areas and services.

The *Heart of Peoria*, a study conducted in 2003 by Andres Duany and Elizabeth Plater-Zyberk of DPZ Planners and Architects, recognized the economic and social opportunities in redevelopment of the Warehouse District and riverfront by "bringing new life to the downtown and taking advantage of Peoria's legacy of historic architecture." They also saw its promise as "a potential model for the future redevelopment — particularly as an example of the possibility for fruitful collaboration between public and private interests" (Duany and Plater-Zyberk 2003: IV.9).

Consolidation and Revitalization

"Shrinking cities" has only recently cropped up in the United States as a new term in urban planning and development (Grossman 2007). A shrinking city is "a densely populated urban area with a minimum population of 10,000 residents that has faced population losses in large parts for more than two years and is undergoing economic transformations with some symptoms of a structural crisis" (Wiechman 2007: n.p.).

Some critics believe that shrinkage of U.S. cities can be part of standard postindustrial transformations, which are due to the decline of manufacturing industries, or it can be triggered by "post-industrial transformations of a second generation," which are connected to the high-tech industry (Pallagst 2008: 10). While many planners in the United States have been focusing on revitalizing the distressed inner cities, such as St. Louis and Pittsburgh, less attention has been paid to the fact that there are large-scale areas that are shrinking, particularly in the Northeast/Midwest "Rust Belt."

Shrinkage is proportional to a decrease in urban metabolism, that is, the economic and social vitality of a city. Urban metabolism, defined by Abel Wolman (1965), is a model to facilitate the description and analysis of the flows of the materials and energy within cities. It offers benefits to the studies of the sustainability of cities by providing a unified or holistic viewpoint to encompass all of the activities of a city in a single model.

The city of Rockford, Illinois, is an example where a vision of sustained development was not realized. Its postindustrial central business district was decimated when industries closed. Today vacant warehouses along the Rock River remain as ruins — testaments to better days — and await demolition. Critical intervention, which should have happened 20 years ago, is no longer possible. Meanwhile, businesses have relocated to the State Street "strip," which connects the city to I-39.

While many municipalities in the United States

view shrinkage as pejorative, consolidation can actually present the opportunity in postindustrial cities to maximize Urban Metabolism—a phenomenon, according to noted theorist Richard Florida (2002), that occurs in cities when they are able to grow in GDP, innovation, and patent activity. As they do this, their physical growth happens faster. This typically leads to rising congestion, housing, and business costs. As a city sprawls, the urban metabolism it generates can actually become a negative force that eventually strangles its own vitality. However, Florida argues, "if geographical boundaries are respected, urban metabolism can enhance the vitality of the city both culturally and economically" (2005: 172).

According to the distinguished urban planner Weiming Lu, "It [is] not enough to design good buildings; architects should seek a proper relationship of man to nature and the universe" (Lee 2008: 2). Some urbanists argue that consolidation and targeted development of cities actually can be good environmental stewardship and promote sustainable development (Grossman 2007; Pallagst 2008). However, urban shrinkage can often lead to unplanned landscapes, or *terrains vagues*, that is, vast zones of conspicuous neglect where residual nature is mixed with industry, waste, and infrastructure (Girot 2005: 19). As industries leave and populations drop, nature begins to reassert itself. Resurgent nature may take the form of urban wilderness, forest, meadow, or succession areas. Green space is usually an amenity in cities, but these ambiguous, unmanaged landscapes contribute to anxiety, reduced property values, and a lack of confidence in a neighborhood's future. Containing and reconfiguring emergent nature can be a challenge for shrinking cities, which often lack resources to construct, maintain, and plan for new public landscapes.

SynergiCity does not represent merely a "revitalization" or adaptive reuse of Peoria's existing historic Warehouse District. In the context of this project, SynergiCity is a holistic approach to the sustainable redevelopment of the postindustrial city combining preservation and adaptive reuse of existing buildings with the development of new buildings and services, communications, and transportation infrastructures. While a few of the warehouses in the district could be adaptively reused, many were structurally unsound. Consequently, it was necessary to develop a comprehensive master plan that included sustainable redevelopment of the entire district (plate 2). At the heart of this plan was stewardship of vital natural resources, such as the Illinois River and artesian springs located along the hillsides, as well as promoting sustainable development that balances the social needs of the district with economic growth and ecology.

Vacant land is the most visible byproduct of urban shrinkage. When redevelopment of vacant land is not feasible in the near term or for the foreseeable future, holding strategies and temporary uses can promote stability and uphold adjacent property values. In these cases, landscape beautification offers an established approach. Sustainable development of unused land, some environmentalists argue, may be achieved simply by allowing for natural succession of indigenous plant species to take over. When vacancy is widespread, unused land can improve a city's environmental functions. Vacant land in strategic locations within a watershed can provide storm-water management, create wildlife habitat, and establish concentrated areas of vegetation to improve air quality and reduce urban heat-island effects. Large-scale depopulation allows for the removal of buildings and pavement from floodplains. Low-lying, open land can retain storm water before it reaches rivers, streams, or sewer systems (Pallagst et al. 2009; Spirn 2005).

As part of their research and analysis, the students turned to the *Heart of Peoria* study, which was commissioned from DPZ Planners and Architects by the Heart of Peoria Development Corporation and the city of Peoria. This firm uses urban planning, design, and architecture principles and methods that they pioneered during the planning of Seaside, Florida, during the 1980s and that have been applied in many subsequent projects. Furthermore, the Urban and Architectural Codes that DPZ developed have been adopted by the Congress of New Urbanism as guidelines for the revitalization of existing cities and the development of new and existing suburban communities. DPZ's "chief innovation has less to do with [a city's] buildings and more to do with the space between buildings and the buildings' response to the space" (Easterling 1991: 48). The Urban Code sets up interdependency between road width, landscaping, lot size, and housing type. Regulation of the spatial modeling of the street is perhaps its most important function. It determines when to use a boulevard as well as setback and height requirements to maintain a proportional streetscape. The Architectural Code determines the aesthetics or "style" for buildings. It addresses front porches, window types and dimensions, roof pitches, cladding, and other design features.

Whereas globalization is part of the cause of shrinking cities, its impact is unclear, since economic change does not affect all cities and countries in the same way. On the contrary, shrinkage can show very different characteristics depending on national, regional, and local contexts (Cunningham-Sabot and Fol 2007; Pallagst 2008). Moreover, there is no clear definition of shrinking cities, but rather a range of various interpretations of the phenomenon. There can be a wide spectrum of possibilities for urban decline, ranging from a natural growth-opposing process to decline with negative implications (Brandstetter et al. 2005). For instance, not all cities may want to grow. The city of Portland, Oregon, has adopted a "no growth" policy to limit urban sprawl. Some postindustrial cities — notably Detroit, Michigan, and East St. Louis, Illinois — seem to be in a state of continual decline, with little real prospect for growth in the foreseeable future. However, for most cities urban shrinkage is a cyclical process, embedded in a broader context of growing and shrinking.

One dilemma of dealing with urban shrinkage from a planning perspective is that urban development is strongly interlinked with growth, leading to the perception of shrinkage as a threat or a taboo (Brandstetter et al. 2005). Maintaining a strategy of economic growth with the aim of regaining population growth used to be cities' most common reaction to urban shrinkage, not very often leading to success. In challenging the predominance of growth as the normative doctrine in planning, some researchers wonder whether shrinkage is a problem to be solved or an opportunity not to be missed. Others advocate a new sensitivity in planning that relies on honesty when it comes to coping with future challenges of shrinking cities (Fuhrich and Kaltenbrunner 2005; Martinez-Fernandez and Wu 2007).

Pallagst (2008) presents three challenges that planners and designers must address regarding the problem of urban consolidation. The foremost challenge is to acknowledge that *some cities should become smaller geographically*, not larger. In the United States, where economic and population growth is assumed, shrinkage is anathema to many planners and municipalities. While consolidation initially will result in loss of revenue due to a smaller tax base, many urban theorists believe that in the long term it will produce a net income gain by creating greater efficiencies of resources and people concentrated within a smaller, more compact geographic area. Many U.S. cities, especially those in the "Rust Belt," are faced with the problem of revitalizing their urban infrastructures, including aging transportation networks, waste and water treatment systems, and energy delivery systems. A more compact city would allow for strategic investment directed to a more concentric, densely populated city center, as opposed to less efficient distribution over a vast, decentralized, underserved area.

The second challenge is that *municipal governments must develop a realistic inventory of their physical, economic, intellectual, and cultural resources* at both the urban and regional scales. They must critically evaluate what they have and what they are lacking in each area and develop a strategic plan to address shortfalls. Revitalization of the urban core may be a part of the plan, but it alone cannot be the solution. A balanced, multifocused approach will yield greater dividends in the future than a haphazard or one-dimensional approach.

Finally, *a comprehensive, strategic plan must address economic, social, and environmental sustainability.* This may mean promoting new forms of manufacturing, "green" technologies, and economic initiatives. Enterprise zones and tax increment financing (TIF) districts are just two tradi-

tional methods of promoting economic growth in decaying inner cities. Public-private partnerships among cities, businesses, and academic institutions also should be created to identify and develop new areas of economic growth and to educate and retrain skilled workers for new enterprise markets, especially in areas of green and biomedical technology. In addition, any strategic plan must also include a marketing effort to promote the vision of the district and provisions for a development bank for leveraging financing (Lee 2008).

Creative Capital

The students recognized early in the planning process that they would be designing for a unique demographic group. Richard Florida's definition of "class" emphasizes the way people organize themselves into social groupings and common identities based principally on their economic function (Florida 2002: 67). The "Creative Class include people in science and engineering, architecture and design, education, arts, music, and entertainment, whose economic function is to create new ideas, new technology, and/or new creative content" (2002: 8). Around this creative core, he adds creative professionals in business and finance, law, health care, and related fields who engage in complex problem solving. Generally, they are knowledge intensive, interdisciplinary, technologically savvy, and unhampered by conventions that tend to compartmentalize knowledge and resources.

Florida observes that the Creative Class has already transformed many cities by creating new businesses and enterprises that revitalize cities from within. He describes the "Creative Class" as 40 million workers — 30% of the U.S. workforce — and breaks the class into two broad occupational sections, derived from Standard Occupational Classification codes data sets (BLS 2010): (1) the Super-Creative Core, and (2) Creative Professionals (Florida 2002).

The Super-Creative Core are employed in about 12% of all U.S. jobs. This group is deemed to contain a wide range of occupations (e.g., science, engineering, education, computer programming, research), with arts, design, and media workers making a small subset. Those belonging to this group are considered to "fully engage in the creative process." The Super-Creative Core are considered to be innovative, creating commercial products and consumer goods. Their primary job function is to be creative and innovative. "Along with problem solving, their work may entail problem finding." Creative Professionals are the classic "knowledge-based workers" and include those working in health care, business and finance, the legal sector, and education. They "draw on complex bodies of knowledge to solve specific problems" using higher degrees of education to do so (Florida 2002: 69-70). The Creative Class, therefore, includes educated people who are also broadly classified as middle and upper middle class, but also, according to Florida, would be regarded socially as bohemians because of their unconventional lifestyles.

Instead of "Creative Class," we prefer to use the term "Creative Capital," which is more inclusive and encompasses a broad spectrum of people, enterprises, institutions, innovative technologies, and the arts that will drive economic development and urban sustainability in the future. While Florida's arguments are not universally accepted, we believe that they provide a basis for develop-ing a demographic profile of the type of educated individuals most likely to bring a unique vision and set of skills to bear on the problems postindustrial cities face today. Furthermore, we see no reason that high-tech companies that employ educated and skilled people cannot flourish in the Midwest as they have elsewhere. Midwestern cities generally have enjoyed fewer radical fluctuations in the costs of housing, education, and job creation than cities on the West and East coasts. They have a skilled workforce that can be retrained and a substantial infrastructure of buildings, services, and cultural amenities. While there has been a trend for industries to relocate outside the Midwest in recent decades, we believe that this trend can be reversed with the development of new technologies fostered by public-private partnerships combined with economic incentives. John Norquist (2010), CEO of the Congress of New Urbanism and the former mayor of Milwaukee, agrees. He points out that manufacturing is still strong in the Midwest but has changed with the market and economy.

Creating a City-within-a-City

The students identified five major concepts to guide the design process:

Amble: Creative cities promote pedestrian walking, which contributes to a healthy lifestyle and to the social interaction that is necessary for innovation.

Density: Creative cities need the critical mass for not only work but play.

Sustainability: The people who live in creative cities demand that their cities be sensitive to the environment and use resources wisely.

Epicenters: Major areas or urban nodes are needed in which human activity occurs routinely. These may occur at transportation, commercial, or cultural centers where people congregate.

Synergy: Creative cities thrive on the cooperative action of creative enterprise.

"Sustainable development is development that meets the needs of the present without compromising the ability of future generations to meet their own needs" (WCED 1987). Its "three pillars" are the reconciliation of environmental, social, and economic demands. A socially sustainable community is one that provides equal access to resources for present and future generations. These include the economic resources necessary for education, health and well-being, and prosperity as well as maintaining the quality of the natural environment and the wise use and conservation of its resources. The goal of synergy, beyond its purely economic aspects, is also to develop a more socially diverse and environmentally sustainable community by promoting new technology and innovative problem-solving strategies.

Creating pedestrian-friendly cities in which goods and services are located in proximity to mixed-use residential neighborhoods is a fundamental goal of New Urbanism. This requires walkable, pedestrian-friendly communities that are compact. The street, the square, and the quarter are its major urban components and are serviced by strategically placed public transit nodes located within five- and ten-minute walking radii of major services. New Urbanist planners and architects, such as DPZ, favor a dense, more compact city with contiguous neighborhoods that contain a diverse mix of residential, retail, commercial, and civic functions. Public squares and green spaces are vital for recreation and social interaction, as well as for maintaining sustainable ecological biomes. In Peoria, DPZ took a comprehensive approach to master planning districts within the entire city. These included the Downtown, the Riverfront, the Sears Block Redevelopment, the Warehouse District, and several neighborhoods. The students realized that the Warehouse District was by far the most challenging and compelling area for development, especially with the planned redevelopment of the former Sears Block for the proposed Lakeview Art Museum (Duany and Plater-Zyberk 2003).

TRANSECT PLANNING

In order to address urban design in a sustainable manner, the students applied DPZ's concept of transect planning: sites are considered as an ecological biome in section, each containing a mix of functions, populations, and services, from urban to suburban in character, which are planned in such a way as to promote ecological diversity (plate 3). Accordingly, the Warehouse District was divided into four multiblock transects running downhill from northwest to southeast toward the Illinois River. Each transect was given a unique character that blended functions into livable neighborhoods based on SmartCode planning principles (see below). Students collaborated to develop an overall master plan and then formed smaller teams to develop architectural strategies for each transect. Their decisions were predicated on three major goals: (1) to develop a sustainable community (i.e., a community that strives to balance social equity with economic development and ecology); (2) to promote economic and social diversity by fostering new technology, in manufacturing, media, the arts, energy and ecology, and biomedicine, among others, developed by an emerging creative class; and (3) to create a balanced mix of residential, commercial, civic, and cultural activities at appropriate scales. The result was a plan for a "city-within-a-city" that they named SynergiCity.

SMARTCODE PLANNING

The students also applied concepts related to SmartCode planning, a unified land development ordinance template for planning and urban design. It folds zoning, subdivision regulations, urban design, and basic architectural standards into one compact document. Because the SmartCode enables an urban municipality to develop a shared vision of how it can plan physically for its future social and economic growth by coding specific outcomes that are desired in particular places, it is meant to be locally calibrated by professional planners, architects, and attorneys.

One of the basic principles in the SmartCode is that towns and cities should be structured as a series of walkable neighborhoods. Pedestrian-friendly design requires a mix of land uses (residential, office, and retail), public spaces with a sense of enclosure to create "outdoor rooms," and pedestrian-oriented transportation design. The SmartCode meshes with the diverse and individualistic lifestyles that the Creative Class enjoys, which involve collaboration, participation, and experiential activities that engage complex problem-solving techniques and strategies. This "Street Level Culture," according to Florida, comprises a "teeming blend of cafes, sidewalk musicians, and small galleries and bistros, where it is hard to draw the line between participant and observer, or between creativity and its creators" (2002: 184; plate 1).

The zones within the SmartCode are designed to create complete human habitats (i.e., transects) ranging from the very rural to the very urban. Whereas conventional zoning categories are based on different land uses, SmartCode zoning categories are based on their rural-urban character. All categories within the SmartCode allow some mix of uses. SmartCode zoning categories ensure that a community offers a full diversity of building types, thoroughfare types, and civic space types and that each has appropriate characteristics for its location.

WAREHOUSE DISTRICT

The Warehouse District extends about 1.5 miles from Liberty Street and the Central Business District (CBD) at the north end to Persimmon Street and the Archer Daniels Midland plant at its south end (plate 2). In April 2009, the Peoria City Council voted on a resolution to continue planning for the proposed Lakeview Art Museum, which will be located in the CBD adjacent to the Warehouse District. This dynamic complex will further enhance the cultural and economic bond between the CBD and the Warehouse District. It also promises to become a major attraction not only for the citizens of Peoria but for the region and the entire state of Illinois.

The students proposed four new transects: (1) Arts and Culture Infill, (2) Civic Center, (3) Commercial/Retail, and (4) Mixed Office-Residential (MOR). The Civic Center will contain mixed-use buildings, a public plaza, and retail and commercial spaces (plate 6). At its head will be

FIGURE 2.2. Rendering of proposed development along Adams Street in the Civic Center transect of SynergiCity: Warehouse District, Peoria. The glass and steel SynergiCenter is a focal point for the community as an "ideas incubator" for aspiring entrepreneurs. (Illustration by Cody Bornsheuer and Michael Logunetz. Courtesy of School of Architecture, University of Illinois, Urbana-Champaign)

SynergiCenter, a high-tech glass pavilion, which will provide exhibition space and act as a circulation hub, and a high-rise tower. SynergiCenter will be linked to a lower-level retail mall that is tucked beneath the plaza (fig. 2.2).

TWO MASTER PLANS

During each semester, a different master plan was developed that shared common major planning strategies and themes. While each master plan

bears some affinity to the DZB proposal, it also deviates from it in several significant ways. In the spring 2009 master plan, for example, the most critical (and prescient) decision was to reroute and concentrate all modes of transportation, including the railroad, autos, bicycles, and pedestrians, along the Illinois River. Periodic flooding requires the maintenance of a large tract of undeveloped land between the river and the Warehouse District. The study *Heart of Peoria* proposed locating buildings within this floodplain in "a second phase of devel-

opment extending down to the riverfront," which "includes an extension of the central square down to an open riverfront green, maintained as public realm." New loft buildings would be added on the east side of the street running along this green, and "would have the benefit of both proximity to the amenities of the district and a spectacular view of the river" (Duany and Plater-Zyberk 2003: IV.3).

However, the students discovered during their analysis of the Warehouse District that a 100-year flood of the Illinois River could cause it to rise and inundate large portions of the district, which can be devastating to businesses and cause physical damage to property. They also studied the district in section and found that the river is located in a valley between two bluffs, with East Peoria on one side of the river and Peoria Heights on the other. The Warehouse District actually slopes from west to east toward the river, which creates a difference in elevation of about 40 feet from Adams Street at the highest contour level in the district to Water Street at the lowest.

Early in the planning process, the students decided to redevelop Washington Street as a landscaped east-west boulevard through the entire district. They also proposed a trolley system to link key nodes in the district to a central transportation hub located in the CBD. Visitors to the district arriving by car will park in strategically located parking structures and be able to go anywhere in the district by trolley. Safe "ambling" and bicycling will also be encouraged throughout the district by providing pedestrian-friendly streets, well-defined crosswalks, and bicycle paths.

Throughout each semester there was much discussion of a proposed business-research collaborative, an effort that has engaged the interest of Bradley University, the medical school and hospitals, the nearby agricultural research center, and local industry. The proposed collaborative has also been recognized as potentially an important component of Peoria's economic development in the twenty-first century. In St. Paul, Minnesota, for example, the Lowertown Development Corporation was formed to develop a similar partnership in order "to transform [the Lowertown district] so that people would come back into the city" (Lee 2008). The corporation focused on three types of activi-

ties: first, as a *design center* to create a new vision for the area; second, as a *marketing office* to make people believe in its vision and the market potential for the area and be willing to invest; and third, as a *development bank* to fill the gap in financing.

In *Heart of Peoria*, DPZ proposed a biomedical research campus located along West Main Street. They concluded that the West Main Street corridor offered "both a central location and ample opportunities for the nearby development of services and amenities that would be necessary to support this kind of campus" (Duany and Plater-Zyberk 2003: V.10) During the spring 2010 term, the students recommended that a business incubator/research campus be located in the district between Adams and Jefferson streets. The Oak and State Street corridors could be developed as mixed-use retail and civic centers for the district, using the existing warehouses for business incubator facilities combined with housing and retail functions.

DPZ cautioned that "the most common approach to developing a research campus is the suburban model: a relatively isolated cluster of buildings located on some wide-open stretch of university campus or on a greenfield site in the suburban fringe," which "would neither offer the attractions of an urban setting to the researchers and staff, nor would the resulting development bring the same benefits to the community and the immediately surrounding neighborhoods" (Duany and Plater-Zyberk 2003: v.10). The students reasoned that a research-business incubator "urban campus" could be a model for redevelopment that would bring both activity and investment interest to the area. The campus would provide facilities for retraining workers in emerging fields such as green technologies and biomedicine as well as incubator buildings for startup enterprises.

As companies become successful, a portion of the profits would be used to maintain and support new initiatives in the district.

The essential concept of synergy is to create "town-and-gown" superregional partnerships with Bradley University, the University of Illinois, Illinois Central Community College, and local and regional businesses and medical centers. The campus portion of the scheme is organized around a pedestrian quad. The main entrances to key buildings face the quad, with secondary courts that serve as public space within each block, offering a place for researchers and visitors to meet that is relatively insulated from the noise and activity of the busy streets.

New mixed-use buildings in the district generally will be three to five stories high, with pedestrian-oriented retail stores at street level. Oak Street is designated a commercial-retail corridor featuring adaptive reuse of existing warehouses. The blocks bounded by Persimmon, Maple, and Harrison Streets are designated a Mixed Office Retail (MOR) district. This area will define the southern boundary of the district and create a transition for development beyond it. The redevelopment of Oak Street and the research campus itself will remove conditions and uses that have created concern in the past. In addition, the presence of people and businesses on the street will increase safety and reduce crime in the area. The street enclosure created by the civic center buildings, along with the midblock dropoff points, will provide traffic calming that will also help insulate the neighborhood from the activity and traffic of Adams Street to the north.

Two key buildings were proposed in the spring 2009 master plan: (1) SynergiCenter, an all-glass pavilion located on Adams, will be a node for

SynergiCity and the iconic gateway to the public plaza. It will be used for exhibitions and events in the district and will provide access to development below the plaza. (2) SynergiTower, a high-rise building, will create a vertical landmark for the district and develop continuity on the skyline with the existing high-rise towers in the CBD to the north.

The study *Heart of Peoria* discouraged adding high-rise buildings and instead recommended building horizontally. Even within the studio, there was disagreement about the role of high-rises. In their final 2009 master plan, the students decided that high-rise buildings could be used as landmarks and to consolidate multiple functions in a smaller footprint, but they should be restricted to the civic center. In the 2010 master plan, a high-rise hotel was proposed that bordered the outfield of the minor league baseball stadium and complemented the transportation node at the convention center.

Parking is contained in courtyards and beneath buildings, where grade changes permit access. This strategy maintains the continuity of the street edge lined with businesses, as well as providing additional opportunities for retail activity in alleyways that also function as service streets. In-fill projects in the Arts and Culture Transect will be crucial to the completion of the historic urban fabric and provide an appropriate connection between the CBD and the proposed arts center to the north and the City Center Transect to the south.

SUSTAINABLE PLANNING

To mitigate flooding problems, the students proposed two possible solutions. In the spring 2009 master plan, they developed a landscaped levee along the river and routed a transportation corridor there as well. This solution diverts automobiles, trucks, and trains away from the district along the river. An earthen landscaped "berm" shields the traffic — both visually and audibly — from residents of the district. The majority of the riverfront would then be developed as a sustainable ecological public park and wetland biome (plate 5).

Sustainability and water treatment was of even greater concern with the development of the spring 2010 master plan, which conceived the entire district as an eco-friendly "living machine," using a variety of aquatic plants and microorganisms to filter and treat gray water and rainwater from the Warehouse District before recycling or discharging it into the river. The students used a combination of filter strips located along streets and alleyways, as well as bioswales — landscape elements designed to remove silt and pollution from surface and runoff water — located along the river. A retention basin located in the "front yard" along the river would temporarily capture runoff water and help to abate flooding. In both master plans, native plants, grasses, and rain gardens located throughout the district were proposed to filter pollutants and transform a significant portion of the park into an ecologically diverse prairie/wetland.

CIVIC CENTER

The spring 2009 master plan called for redeveloping State Street into a pedestrian-only civic center corridor extending from Adams Street to the park. In this scheme, the proposed civic center featured urban public space defined by an infrastructure of new, mixed-use buildings that provided retail space at the ground level with commercial space at the upper levels (plate 6).

The spring 2010 master plan rejected closing any major streets. Instead, students proposed developing alleyways as interior pedestrian and service streets lined with mixed-use business-residential buildings. The civic center was redefined by expanding the existing police station and adding a fire substation. The students also proposed developing a new transportation center adjacent to the convention center, close to the downtown business district, and accessible to the Warehouse District.

The intersection of Kumpf Boulevard and Adams Street, which had been unresolved in the spring 2009 master plan, now became a large roundabout lined with business incubator buildings. The roundabout, with its large conical skylight and crescent-shaped incubator buildings, provided a formal gateway to the city and defined a sense of arrival at the end of the Bob Michel Bridge, which links East Peoria with the city of Peoria (plate 7). A pedestrian plaza was also introduced beneath the roundabout with shops and restaurants. This allowed a safe way to walk from east to west without encountering traffic or weather-related hazards.

In each scheme, the most interesting economic concept will be development of a public-private partnership among the city of Peoria, industry, and higher education to promote retraining of workers and foster the development of new, emergent technologies. This concept of "synergy" will synthesize diverse interdisciplinary groups (i.e., the Creative Class), which will collaborate to develop new paradigms for sustainable technologies and enterprises. Initially, startup funding could come from a combination of public and private sources. As businesses become established, a portion of their profits will be reinvested back into SynergiCity to provide seed money for the development of new enterprises.

This money could be used, for instance, to provide low-interest loans, to promote research, and to provide incentives to develop new sustainable technologies, among other things.

The students concurred with three recommendations for the district included in the *Heart of Peoria* (Duany and Plater-Zyberk 2003): (1) officially establish this area as a TIF district and use these resources to encourage renovation and reuse of existing buildings as well as compatible in-fill projects; (2) designate this sector a "district" in the zoning code, enabling it to be redeveloped according to a specific plan; and (3) use the incentives of a streamlined permitting process to attract investment in the plan.

Conclusion

While SynergiCity is a concept that initially was applied specifically to Peoria, it has broader implications that can be translated to other midsized postindustrial cities in the United States. It is our contention that cities must continually redefine themselves if they expect to attract and sustain new "creative capital" consisting of people, enterprises, technology, and the arts, as they must do if they are to compete at a global scale. We also believe that in order for some cities to survive, they will have to critically evaluate their resources and possibly physically contract or consolidate development into sustainable "economic incentive zones" financed through a development investment bank. SynergiCity can address urban sprawl and sustainable development of the urban core by concentrating people, goods, and services into a more compact geographic area. If it is successful, it will attract people from outlying towns and suburban communities who are seeking the amenities that a midsize to large city provides. As their circumstances change, retirees and empty-nesters may wish to live in urban communities in proximity to people of all ages, races, and incomes. They will bring experiences, skills, and expertise that will be vital to the economic and social development of SynergiCity. Young professionals and creative people will also be attracted to a redeveloped urban center. They already seek the opportunities and vitality afforded by urban environments. They are also the most likely group to be willing and able to take greater financial and personal risks where the potential for long-term rewards is greatest.

Finally, and most important, SynergiCity is sustainable in its most holistic sense. If we define sustainability as a balance of social, economic, and environmental factors, then, as we have seen, SynergiCity addresses each area. Economic development is paramount to providing a successful and sustainable infrastructure. Balancing the human-made world with the natural environment is both a requirement and desirable for livability. Social sustainability, access to resources for future generations, we believe, will be achieved as architects, planners, politicians, and others address in a comprehensive manner the issues of how to provide all residents with employment, education, affordable housing, and community services. In the final analysis, SynergiCity constitutes a model for the reinvention of a sustainable, interdependent postindustrial city as a vibrant epicenter of creativity, technical innovation, and entrepreneurship that will lead postindustrial cities into the twenty-first century.

References

Bernard, A. B., J. Bradford Jensen, and Peter K. Schott. 2002. "Survival of the Best Fit: Competition from Low Wage Countries and the (Uneven) Growth of U.S. Manufacturing Plants." NBER Working Paper 9170. Bureau of Labor Statistics. Washington, DC: U.S. Department of Labor.

BLS. 2010. "Standard Occupational Classification." Bureau of Labor Statistics. Washington, DC: U.S. Department of Labor.

Brandstetter, B., et al. 2005. "Dealing with the Shrinking City — The Debate Overview." *Berliner Debatte Initial* 16(6): 55-68.

CNU. 1996. "Charter of the New Urbanism." Available at the website of Congress of New Urbanism, http://www.cnu.org/charter. Retrieved March 27, 2010.

Couri, Dr. Peter J., Jr. 1991. "Peoria's History." September. Peoria, IL: Peoria Historical Society. http://www.peoriahistoricalsociety.org /peoria/peoindustry.html. Retrieved March 27, 2010.

Cunningham-Sabot, E., and S. Fol. 2007. "Shrinking Cities in Western Europe — Case Studies from France and the United Kingdom." *Berliner Debatte Initial* 18(1): 22-35.

Duany, A., and E. Plater-Zyberk. 2003. *Heart of Peoria.* Peoria, IL: City of Peoria Economic Development Department.

Easterling, Keller. 1991. "Public Enterprise." In *Seaside: Making a Town in America*, ed. David Mahoney and Keller Easterling. New York: Princeton Architectural Press, 48-61.

Fisher, E. O'N., and P. C. Rupert. 2005. "The Decline of Manufacturing Employment in the United

States." http://www.rupertnet.net/fr2005-12-18.pdf. Retrieved March 28, 2010.

Florida, R. 2002. *The Rise of the Creative Class: How It's Transforming Work, Leisure, Community and Everyday Life.* New York: Basic Books.

Florida, R. 2005. *Cities and the Creative Class.* New York: Routledge.

Fuhrich, M., and R. Kaltenbrunner. 2005. "The East Now in the West? Urban Development in the West and Urban Redevelopment in the East — Two Unequal Siblings." *Berliner Debatte Initial* 16(6): 41-54.

Funding Universe. 2004. "Caterpillar, Inc." In *International Directory of Company Histories,* vol. 63. St. James, MO: St. James Press.

Girot, C. 2005. "Towards a New Nature." In *Landscape Architecture in Mutation — Essays on Urban Landscape,* ed. Arley Kim, Maya Kohte, and Claudia Moll. Zurich: gta Verlag, 19-28.

Grossmann, K. 2007. "Shrinkage — Between a Stylish Taboo and Addressing the Issue." *Berliner Debatte Initial* 18(1): 14-21.

Lee, A. J. 2008, summer. "An Interview with Weiming Lu." *CRM: The Journal of Heritage Stewardship* 5(2): 1-6.

Martinez-Fernandez, Christina, and Tong Wu. 2007. "Urban Development in a Different Reality — Shrinking Cities in Australia." *Berliner Debatte Initial* 18(1): 45-60.

NACo. 2008. "Find a County." Washington, DC: National Association of Counties.

Norquist, J. 2010, May 17. Interview with the authors, Chicago.

Pallagst, K. 2008. "Shrinking Cities — Planning Challenges from an International Perspective." In *Cities Regrowing Smaller,* ed. S. Rugare and T. Schwarz, 6-16. Cleveland: Urban Infill Books.

Pallagst, K., T. Schwarz, F. J. Popper, and J. B. Hollander. 2009, November. "Planning Shrinking Cities." *Progress in Planning* 72 (4): 223-32.

Spirn, A. W. 2005. "Restoring Mill Creek: Landscape Literacy, Environmental Justice and City Planning and Design." *Landscape Research* 30(3) (July): 395-413.

USCB. 2008. "American FactFinder." U.S. Census Bureau. http://factfinder2.census.gov/faces/tableservices/jsf/pages/productview. Retrieved March 29, 2010.

WCED 1987. "Towards Sustainable Development." Chapter 2 OF *Our Common Future: Report of the World Commission on Environment and Development.* UN Document A/42/427.

Wiechmann, T. 2007, February 8. "Between Spectacular Projects and Pragmatic Deconstruction." Paper presented at *Conference on the Future of Shrinking Cities: Problems, Patterns, and Strategies of Urban Transformation in a Global Context,* Berkeley, CA.

Wolman, A. 1965, September. "The Metabolism of Cities." *Scientific American* 213: 179-190.

CHAPTER THREE

Historic Preservation

THE FOUNDATION OF SYNERGICITY

PAUL HARDIN KAPP

Cities need old buildings so badly it is probably impossible for vigorous streets and districts to grow without them.

Jane Jacobs, The Death and Life of Great American Cities

FIGURE 3.1. The Cadillac Building, designed by Wm. A. Balsch Architects and completed in 1919, in the Midtown Alley district of St. Louis, Missouri. It includes Egyptian-influenced columns and ornamental motifs and has been placed on the U.S. National Register of Historic Places. (Courtesy of Paul J. Armstrong)

WHAT IS THE FIRST STEP IN MAKING SYNERGICITY? Historic preservation. It is the foundation and initial step to redeveloping the postindustrial district in the American city. Rehabilitating the existing buildings, streets, and open space is not only practical; it is sustainable both from an economic and environmental point of view. It creates an aesthetically pleasing environment that utilizes the best attributes of the district — its sense of place. Within the context of the postindustrial district, historic preservation is best defined as the adaptive use and rehabilitation of existing historic (and even not-so-historic buildings) and structures, transforming them for new and pertinent uses that will facilitate Urban Metabolism and economic activity. Historic preservation of the postindustrial district can achieve an all-encompassing change in the perception of the district from a once industrial and now neglected area of the city to a new, sustainable, and viable economic engine for the city (fig. 3.1).

Historic preservation provides significant eco-nomic benefits for redevelopment. It often provides the critical momentum for urban redevelopment to occur. It is financially feasible, and it produces readily appreciable results. Preservation allows developers and entrepreneurs to concentrate their efforts in small areas of a postindustrial district in a strategic manner. Historic preservation provides both small-scale project opportunities and large-scale policy tools to make development a reality in postindustrial districts. Redeveloping the city's neglected postindustrial districts can restore livability to the moribund downtown, and the city can become vital and productive again. This is the essence of historic preservation at the urban level. Postindustrial districts in cities are the obvious place for the healing process in cities to begin; they are inherently intact, and they are adaptable. These districts are comprised of robust buildings that were built to last by previous generations. They are built with craftsmanship that can rarely be duplicated today. When it is done correctly, historic preservation in commercial development recognizes the built heritage as a tangible and valuable asset.

Historic preservation provides significant environmental benefits in SynergiCity. Along with high-craft industrial buildings, which were built before the Second World War, are often comprised of old-growth timbers, high-quality masonry (brick, ashlar stone, and rubble), and cast iron and steel. In today's economy, the craft-based building methods and materials used for turn-of-the-century buildings are expensive and, consequently, tend to be reserved for the restoration of landmark historic buildings. Because their materials and robust structures often make them too valuable to discard, existing buildings should be maintained and transformed for new uses whenever possible. In order for SynergiCity to begin in postindustrial districts, the current policy of developing urban areas must change from one that views the postindustrial district as a collection of abandoned and underutilized buildings to one that views the district as a granary of older, rehabilitated existing structures and new buildings that can provide a variety of economic uses for a diverse group of entrepreneurs.

It is important to remember what the noted urban theorist Jane Jacobs said fifty years ago in her landmark book *The Death and Life of Great American Cities,* where she made a compelling case for the need of "aged" buildings in the American city." For her, there was a difference between "old" buildings and "aged" ones. "Old" conveys the idea of the expensive museum-piece restoration building; while "aged" she defines as "the good lot of plain, ordinary, low-value old buildings, including some rundown old buildings" (Jacobs, 1961, 187). She felt that these buildings provided the needed venue for the diversity of uses and the wide array of enterprises that allow cities to be not only economically viable but also interesting to experience. From an economic point of view, this approach is particularly useful in the postindustrial district, which already has enough density of building stock and infrastructure to be transformed into something useful again. Preservationists have always seen the benefits of transforming entire districts of a historic city; specifically, preservationists have been successful in redeveloping central business districts, commonly referred to as "Main Street Projects." Through the past 30 years of redeveloping Main Street, preservationists have learned that redevelopment does not happen immediately; in fact, it is a long and arduous process that begins with small concentrated project redevelopment efforts and leads to an eventual completion of the entire district. The key to redevelopment is developing a successful economic balance that allows both the small developer and the large-scale developer to work together toward the common goal of historic rehabilitation and adaptive use. As Jacobs's description implies, using "aged" buildings should be one way for diverse group of entrepreneurs to thrive and become productive. This balance is the key to making SynergiCity happen.

The challenge in using "aged" buildings is finding ones that are spatially flexible so as to be easily adaptable. The inherent flexibility for adaptability found in historic warehouses and factories make them a logical choice for new businesses to use. They possess the best attributes of both aged and new: lower rents and flexible use. As Jacobs (1961) so eloquently stated, "Old ideas can sometimes use new buildings. New ideas must use old buildings" (Jacobs, 1961, 188). She was clearly ahead of her time; 35 years after *The Death and Life of Great American Cities* was published, preservationists in the 1990s began to take note that historic resources not only have cultural value but also economic value.[1] These districts of intact buildings, underutilized infrastructure capacity, and distinct architectural character can be an important part of the economic development of cities, especially in postindustrial districts.

Preservationists have long recognized that preserving the built heritage inevitably leads to preserving the environment. In 1978, the late Supreme Court justice William J. Brennan Jr. stated it best in the landmark *Penn Central Transportation Co. et al. v. New York City Co., et al.*: "Historic conservation is but one aspect of the much larger problem, basically an environmental one, of enhancing — or perhaps developing for the first time — the quality of life for people" (quoted in Mays 2003: 183).

This is especially true when the postindustrial district is transformed into SynergiCity. Brownfield remediation is addressed, and planners, architects, and developers take stock of what the district can offer — useable space that is built out of quality materials located adjacent to the central business district of the city.

Reusing materials in place through adaptive use of existing buildings is an obvious way to keep building debris out of landfills. Currently, one-third of all debris in waste accounted for in municipal landfills is debris from demolition (Orange County, N.C. Office of Solid Waste Management 2010). Were the amount of debris from a historic warehouse or factory demolition taken into account, that amount would surely increase.

Utilizing existing industrial buildings and capitalizing on their material value is but one way

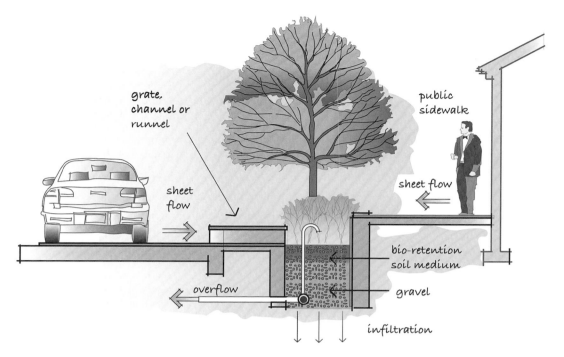

grate,
channel or
runnel

public
sidewalk

sheet
flow

sheet flow

bio-retention
soil medium

overflow

gravel

infiltration

FIGURE 3.2. Rendering of sustainable urban infrastructure improvements with filter strip plantings to filter gray water and prevent runoff. (Courtesy of U.S. Pipe/Wheland Foundry and LA Quatra Bonci Associates/Edward Dumont)

historic preservation in postindustrial cities is an environmental solution; utilizing the existing infrastructure that supports these buildings is another. In most twentieth-century industrial cities, especially in the Midwest, wide streets and alleys, broad sidewalks, and substantial water and sewer lines supported these districts. The underutilized and abandoned factory or warehouse often has accompanying it the underutilized street, railroad line, and waterfront. Like the abandoned buildings, these resources are in place and have been paid for and depreciated by the municipality. The broad streets found in the postindustrial districts can once again become viable not only for automotive traffic but, most notably, for pedestrian use. The abandoned rail line can be reused for mass

transit; even the waterway can shuttle people across areas of the city. All this begins to present a new sustainable solution for transportation in the city that reuses the existing infrastructure of the postindustrial district. In order for historic preservation to fulfill its ultimate sustainable potential in SynergiCity, every element of the district must be revitalized — the historic (and not-so-historic) buildings, the existing streets, plazas, rail lines, and waterfronts. But we must do more than simply restore historic infrastructure; we should consider ways in which it can be transformed to become effective systems for environmentally responsive solutions for the city. Storm sewer lines need to be reworked to effectively dissipate or reuse storm water. Rain gardens and filter strips are just two

ways of ecologically containing and filtering gray water that can be recycled for nonpotable uses (fig. 3.2). Waterfronts and ports should be restored in ways that allow the natural habitat to become part of the urban environment. Biomass fuel can be used in existing cogeneration plants, such as the one in Lowertown in St. Paul, Minnesota. Building new infrastructure does not have to be the inevitable answer for postindustrial redevelopment; historic infrastructure in most midwestern cities was built to last and can be retrofitted for new uses with sustainable systems and materials.

Adding to the sustainable benefits of preserving the postindustrial district are the intangible aesthetic benefits that come with the patina of age. "Character," an often difficult element to describe, is something that historic preservationists care deeply about, and once restored it becomes highly marketable. Cobblestone or brick streets, continuous brick facades with large windows and steel structures, such as water tanks, conveying systems, and even smokestacks, provide environments that are distinctive and interesting to experience. Despite the fact that these districts often possess immense buildings, they often are built at a human scale that promotes pedestrian movement more than vehicular movement. All of this often provides visually interesting areas in which to work and live (fig. 3.3).

The abandoned postindustrial districts have always been an attractive venue for innovation in cities, and part of the reason is that these areas were usually affordable to either purchase or lease. But affordability is only one aspect of their success; more and more occupants and developers are recognizing their environmental benefits. Located in or near central cores of American cities, their loca-

FIGURE 3.3. Redevelopment of the New Orleans Warehouse District has maintained the historic character of the street with cobblestone pavers and ornate street lamps. (Courtesy of Paul J. Armstrong)

FIGURE 3.4. Artist's studio in the Murray Building in the Warehouse District of Peoria, Illinois. Artists are often the first to move into large warehouses and revitalize former industrial districts. (Courtesy of Paul J. Armstrong)

tion has broad appeal for entrepreneurs and city dwellers who wish to leave the automobile behind and walk and bike more. City dwellers throughout the United States are taking note of what the city has to offer and are deciding to play a part in it and have a more active urban lifestyle. Rehabilitated postindustrial districts present a distinctive choice in urban living. Aesthetically, these aged buildings possess great character; their streets are pedestrian friendly, and they engage significant waterways that were originally an integral part of industrial operations in these districts but now can become a recreational amenity. These attributes — historic architectural character, humane sidewalks, and

distinct waterfronts — enhance the quality of life in cities, which is a major factor for attracting both talent and investment to cities today. When all of these attributes are taken into consideration during the planning and design process, the perception of the postindustrial district begins to change from a collection of abandoned buildings and streets to an actual place with both a purpose and an identity — a SynergiCity.

The positive perception of change in the postindustrial district has in the past been accomplished by the artistic vanguard, who have been primarily attracted to postindustrial buildings because they provided affordable space to either rent or purchase

(fig. 3.4). As artists flourish in these spaces, entrepreneurship begins to happen that leads to economic and social yields for the entire district. When considering all of the benefits that postindustrial redevelopment can offer — economic, environmental, and aesthetic — another benefit becomes apparent: the ability to provide an environment in which diverse entrepreneurial ventures can coexist and support each other. In redeveloping historic postindustrial districts and transforming them into SynergiCity, it is important to reconsider Jacobs's idea in *The Death and Life of Great American Cities* about the need to mix "yields."

High-Yield, Middling-Yield, Low-Yield, and No-Yield

When looking at reinventing the postindustrial city, it is important to remember some of the aspects of vibrant American cities that Jacobs wrote about fifty years ago. It is easy to dismiss her ideas as being obsolete or as having been hashed out through the past five decades by generations of urban planners, architects, developers, social scientists, and so on; but when one revisits these ideas in the context of the redeveloping of decayed postindustrial districts, many of Jacobs's ideas cannot be so readily dismissed. In chapter 10 of *The Death and Life of Great American Cities*, she identifies four types of income-producing business ventures that are required for a city district or street to thrive: high-yield, middling-yield, low-yield, and no-yield. Jacobs was very straightforward in defining "yields" as simply being the yield or economic profitability produced by a specific business or social venture. "High-yield" is self-explanatory; these are businesses and industries that are profitable and employ a large number of people of varying skill sets. "Middling-yield" refers to predominantly service-based businesses, perhaps architects and engineers or lawyers and accountants, all of whom provide a vital service and typically employ a limited number of people. "Low-yield" refers to restaurants and boutiques, corner stores, and small retail. "No-yield" can be best described as the public service contribution to the city — parks, recreational facilities, and cultural and educational facilities. Jacobs argued that "No-yield" is vital for a society to exist. "No-yield" can also describe the creative involvement in the postindustrial district; it may not be financially profitable, but necessary all the same. This includes artists' studios and galleries but also the music hall, the dancing school, and the local playhouse. "Middling-yield" and "low-yield" businesses, such as antique shops, exotic restaurants, and art studios, were dismissed as part of fringe culture fifty years ago; now, they are considered integral facets of the urban experience and are places people want to go and enjoy. Today, these business ventures help define heritage tourism in large cities and small towns throughout the country; most of us expect to experience these businesses in older buildings, not in commercial strip shopping centers, suburban malls, or office research parks (Rypkema 1998). A healthy mix of all yields is necessary for a city district to thrive. Although it is conceivable to create a new city district of new buildings that embraces economic diversity found in older mixed-yield districts, it is highly unlikely due to the high cost of new construction. Moreover, "aged" buildings in a city district have an intangible asset: a "grit" that is best described as character from age. They provide a distinctive identity that is not easily replicated and differentiates one city district from another (plate 3). City districts need to have some "grit" in order for people experiencing them to feel connected to the place and its history.

THE OFFICE RESEARCH PARK

During the past fifty years, innovation-based enterprises moved away from urban industrial districts. Cities and regional authorities planned and built places that separated high-yield enterprises from middling, low-, and no-yield ones. At the time Jacobs was writing *The Death and Life of Great American Cities*, a new type of urban design typology was being developed: the office research park. The objective for this new development typology was to provide talented people with the space needed to produce at the highest yield possible. Large tracts of forest land, such as North Carolina's Research Triangle Park or Boston's Route 128, were developed for stand-alone buildings in office parks built to suit high-tech companies such as IBM and Burroughs. Businesses, state governments, and municipalities all shared common goals and motives in these developments. For government leaders, the incentive was to capture the economic and intellectual windfall of the leading research universities in their region. They wanted to keep the best and the brightest newly graduated research talent in areas like Raleigh-Durham, North Carolina. They were also interested in having successful companies such as IBM relocate significant portions of their operations and invest in their regions as well. It is important to understand that the success of these parks was the result of their proximity to major research universities, not because they were inherently designed to spark entrepreneurship. It can be said that research parks design is actually a hindrance to entrepreneurship.

That hindrance can be best described as the automobile. Research parks were built solely around the use of the automobile; they were built adjacent to highways and were surrounded by acres of surface parking on cheap undeveloped land. Occupants of these parks became isolated and were bound to only do what the park was built for. Where could one do the routine chores of the day such as pick up dry cleaning or visit the dentist? Not in the research park. Where could one enjoy exotic cuisine or visit a boutique? Not in the research park. And where could chance encounters occur where possible fruitful business ideas could flourish? Not in the single-purposed research park. Anyone who wanted to enjoy any of the mundane but necessary experiences of everyday living would have to drive in an automobile to urban areas where these businesses were located, most often in historic areas of the city.

Planners and developers of research parks recognized this problem 20 years ago, as a new generation of skilled talent began to complain about the lack of service (and life) found in the research park. Developers began to build into research parks restaurants, day care facilities, walking and biking paths, and social spaces; all of this was intended to introduce other uses and business services into the park. But these efforts have produced lackluster results. The Research Park of the University of Illinois in Champaign, Illinois, is a good example of these newer and "more diverse" planning initiatives. Located literally in a green field (actually on a one-hundred-acre tract that was originally used as experimental agricultural land), this park was built in 2001 to promote collaboration with high-tech engineering and computer companies, large-scale manufacturing (such as Caterpillar and John Deere), and the university's College of Engineering and College of Agriculture, Consumer and Environmental Sciences. The park was planned with both the concepts of "new urbanism" and "sustainability" in mind. Along with its eight buildings, it has biking/running paths, ponds for indigenous fauna and wildlife, and a high-tech hotel and conference center with a moderately upscale restaurant. After its first decade in service, it's difficult to call the park a success. As of 2011, the park continues to be subsidized by the University of Illinois; space has not been completely filled, and tenants have come and gone. Moreover, the region has yet to see the economic activity it was led to believe would happen after the park became fully operational.

There are many reasons for this park's underwhelming performance. Many of them are outside the realm of architecture or historic preservation, but one problem is the park's lack of a mixture of high-, medium-, low-, and no-yield enterprises. Entrepreneurship greatly benefits from what is available in places that have economic diversity. Creative people are not always productive in single-use districts, and it is becoming apparent that successful collaboration that results in productive economic ventures does not always come from one group of like-minded people; it can come from a number of different-minded ones. Office buildings are not always where innovations occur. As former Andy Warhol Museum director Tom Sokolowski wryly observed: "great art was never created in a museum" (Ravensbergen 2008). The rehabilitated and reinvented postindustrial city can be the place where diverse economic activity can occur and where innovation can happen.

Today, innovation or creativity is not necessarily relegated to the university campus or the research park. As Richard Florida notes in the *Great Reset,* today's economy is based on creativity, and creativity flourishes in dense urban areas. Moreover, Florida states that the new workforce of the innovation economy will become more mobile, basically going where they are needed; if this is true, then the anonymous places found in the research park seem to offer a dismal future for the next generation of innovators and perhaps not the best use of public and private funds (Florida 2010). The next factories of innovation should be located in the place of first factories of innovation—the postindustrial landscape of our cities. Postindustrial districts such as Peoria's warehouse district are ideal places for this to happen—for the new innovation economy to emerge from the old and for ideas to emerge from a mixing of yields: SynergiCity.

Small Projects Leading to Big Ideas: Preservation and Project Phasing

With the immense amount of unused and neglected buildings and streets that survive, the challenge of reinvention of the postindustrial district is daunting. Where does one begin the long journey from derelict factories for low-tech industrial production to the twenty-first-century factories of innovation? The answer is simple: preservation. The field of historic preservation has three effective tools for redevelopment: a system for identifying buildings and districts for rehabilitation, the National Register of Historic Places; a methodology for redeveloping historic resources, the Secretary of the Interior's Standards for Rehabilitation; and an incentive for redevelopment in federal, state, and in

some cases local rehabilitation income tax credits. Together, these tools retain the valuable historic and cultural assets of our built environment and can reinvigorate depressed historic areas of cities. More important, historic preservation development refocuses private investment into areas of the city with existing and often robust infrastructure. For the developer, it brings the best bang for the buck; it allows new commercial, manufacturing, and residential space to be developed in a quicker and more cost-effective manner. Finally, historic preservation development provides a feasible and practical way to phase development. Noted historic preservation economist Donovan Rypkema (1998) reiterates Jacobs's assertions about redeveloping "aged" districts but also proposes a simple and direct way of implementing redevelopment by stating that preservation is often an effective early step in downtown revitalization:

> The creation of a National Register historic district is, nevertheless, a frequent early action taken in a community's economic development strategy—particularly in the downtown. Why is this? There appear to be two reasons: 1) National Register status permits the use of the historic rehabilitation tax credit which can substantially improve the economic return for an individual investor; and 2) being awarded National Register listing gives a community self-confidence and a sense of unique character and presents the opportunity to begin planning the economic future of the community.

The preservation-based strategy for postindustrial redevelopment is not new and has been successfully implemented in the Midwest; successful redevelopment has occurred in a number of midwestern cities, but one city truly stands out when it comes to successfully redeveloping its postindustrial heritage: Saint Paul, Minnesota. The Lowertown District redevelopment was the brainchild of Saint Paul mayor Frank Latimer, who realized that the abandoned and decayed lower industrial section of the city was in dire need of redevelopment. In 1974, Latimer created the Lowertown Redevelopment Corporation. Through the tireless work of its long-term director, Weiming Lu, an initial investment of a $10 million grant from the McKnight Foundation has produced nearly a billion dollars of urban redevelopment, turning the Lowertown Warehouse District into Saint Paul's Urban Village.

Lowertown was not a grand large-scale urban development project; it started small, with private developers adapting former warehouse buildings such as the Market House condominiums and Artspace, who developed the Tilsner Warehouse into the Tilsner Artists' Cooperative. Market House, developed in 1983, was one of the first warehouse buildings in St. Paul to be converted into loft condominiums (fig. 3.5). The building has a central atrium and large rooftop deck with 58 units within the residential portion of the building. The Tilsner Artists' Cooperative was developed when the building was in an advanced state of decay; windows were broken, the roof leaked, and many regarded the building as a haven for derelicts. But the hulking Richardson Romanesque masonry building had a robust structure, and its nearly 140,000 square feet of usable space was rehabilitated at a total project cost of $6.5 million — $46 per square foot. The adaptive use of this warehouse added 66 live/work units to Lowertown for artists and entrepreneurs. Today, Lowertown boasts over 2,000 residents, most of whom are artists and entrepreneurs. There are restaurants, markets, and boutiques, all of which are

FIGURE 3.5. The Market House Condominiums in St. Paul, Minnesota, directly to the north of the St. Paul Farmer's Market and one of the first warehouse renovations in the historic Lowertown redevelopment district in 1983. (Courtesy of Paul J. Armstrong)

within walking distance, and the entire district is lively. The success of this incremental development, which spanned a period of 30 years, has now led to a broader vision for what Lowertown can be. In 2004, the Lowertown Redevelopment Corporation commissioned Zimmer Gunsul Frasca Architects of Seattle to produce an "urban village" document for the next stage of Lowertown's development. The plan calls for linking the predominantly artists' district to the Bruce Vento Nature Sanctuary, redeveloping the riverfront into a public and environmentally sensitive park, and the construction of an intermodal light rail transit system that will connect Saint Paul with neighboring Minneapolis using the old Union Depot as the terminal station.

Currently, the transit line is being built, and it would not have been possible without the successful historic adaptive-use warehouse initiative (Lu 2010).[2] Lowertown proves that phasing of small projects based on a larger, regional vision can produce successful outcomes. It also demonstrates how preservation can be the catalyst for the redevelopment.

The redevelopment of the American Tobacco Historic District in Durham, North Carolina, is another outstanding example of the benefits of phased development gained by combining historic buildings with new uses (fig. 3.6). American Tobacco is a registered historic site with roots in the American Tobacco Factory established in the 1800s. The American Tobacco Campus is located

FIGURE 3.6. Aerial view of the American Tobacco Historic District in Durham, North Carolina.
The American Tobacco campus is an outstanding example of a phased development that adapts historic buildings to new uses.
(Courtesy of Belk Architecture)

beside the Durham Bulls Triple-A baseball park, adjacent to the new 2,800-seat performing arts center and bordered by the highly traveled state route 147. The campus features an on-site YMCA, public green space, biking trails, and five restaurants. American Tobacco is home to some of the most prominent businesses in the region, including the nationally recognized public broadcasting station WUNC Radio. The area continues to undergo renovation and eventually will include 380 residential units, additional commercial office space, and 40,000 square feet of retail and restaurants. Its design and landscaping has collected industry awards for Best Mixed Use Development, Best Renovated Commercial Property, and Best Redevelopment Project. The combination of historic buildings with modern urban chic is unlike any office space in the Raleigh-Durham Research Triangle (American Tobacco 2010).

Preservation + Sustainability = SynergiCity

Sustainability was not yet a buzzword in American culture when Jane Jacobs and Donovan Rypkema wrote about rebuilding and preserving cities. Both in the late 1950s and the early 1990s the price of oil was affordable, and these writers were more concerned about preserving historic cities than environmental sustainability. But historic preservation supports the broad goals of sustainability far beyond energy conservation. It can be fair to say that "preservation is the ultimate recycling" of materials and buildings. Historic warehouses and factories have inherent material value and energy embedded in them. Materials discarded from streets and buildings once considered suitable only for landfills — old bricks, stone pavers, large timbers, and heavy wood planks — are now regarded as valuable and marketable resources for reuse. This can be seen in the Peoria Warehouse District, where an ice cream factory was transformed into live-work units and a milk can factory has been redeveloped into office space (fig. 3.7). All of this has proven to be highly successful and indeed sustainable.

Postindustrial rehabilitation is not the typical "gut" renovation, in fact, when it has been done successfully it transforms the existing space for a new use while simultaneously highlighting the architectural qualities that were inherent from its previous use, such as the tall spaces, use of old-growth timbers for structure, and quality masonry work. Moreover, they are virtually indestructible; the Murray Warehouse in Peoria is an example of this; originally built as a warehouse for storing whiskey, its concrete frame structure has only been minimally altered (partitioned off into artists' lofts by its developer), and despite multiple roof failures and leaky windows, the structure remains sound.

Architecturally, the tall floor-to-ceiling heights are also a significant attribute of these structures; not only are these spaces aesthetically pleasing, they also allow retrofitting for new mechanical, electrical, and plumbing systems to occur in a straightforward manner and have been part of the aesthetic for warehouse rehabilitation redevelopment for the past three decades. But more important, warehouse and industrial redevelopment demonstrates disassembly and reassembly design methodologies that have become a significant strategy for sustainable design. Butler Square in the Minneapolis Warehouse District is a nationally recognized example of disassembly and reassem-

bly design (plate 10). Originally built in 1906 for the Butler Brothers Company, a mail-order firm, the eight-story brick and timber frame warehouse was rehabilitated into Historic Butler Square in two phases, first by developer Charles Coyer in 1972 and then by James Binger in 1979. In both phases, the center sections of floors were removed in order to create two large skylight-lit atriums. The atriums became prime marketing points for leasing office spaces. Removing a limited amount of space and materials increased the real estate value of Butler Square. Today, Butler Square is credited with being the catalyst for the redevelopment of the Minneapolis Warehouse District.

Reusing and refurbishing historic material and components of warehouses and factories is now considered an attractive, if not sexy, aesthetic in midwestern cities. Nowhere is this truer than the new Iron Horse Hotel in Milwaukee's Fifth Ward. Located across the Milwaukee River from the new Harley-Davidson Museum, this former firehouse has been transformed into an upscale, edgy hotel centered on the Harley-Davidson motorcycle enthusiast (plate 11). The deep brown finish of the large oak beams, the painted black brackets and supports, and the exposed brick walls set the right tone for the motorcycle patron who is decked out in black motorcycle leather jacket and chaps and enjoying the finest French wines. Here postindustrial is high-end, responding to an ever diverse American aesthetic of both design and architecture. But whether it is designing with the industrial fire doors of the Iron Horse Hotel or designing new live-work units that retain the original walk-in refrigeration vaults of the old Sealtest Ice Cream Factory in Peoria, it is very clear: valuable building materials are remaining in redeveloped industrial buildings and not ending

FIGURE 3.7. Office interior of the former Sealtest Ice Cream Factory in the Peoria Warehouse District, developed by Pat Sullivan of the JP Companies, recycles old materials with new functions. (Courtesy of Paul J. Armstrong)

up in the landfill. This point cannot be overstated; old-growth timbers, massive masonry walls, and large steel components can no longer be removed and discarded; they should be reused. This is where preservation and sustainability ideas converge.

Reusing valuable materials and building components does not need to end at the building; in fact, the same reuse thinking should occur at the urban scale as well. Most postindustrial districts were built with a robust infrastructure in order to accommodate industrial operations. The streets of Peoria, Rockford, Milwaukee, and Saint Paul are quite wide, and some of them still retain their railroad tracks and cobblestone surfaces. These features can add to the overall character of the redeveloped district. Abandoned rail lines in the large alleys of Peoria or Milwaukee can once again be reused for transport, thereby reducing the need for the automobile. All of these ideas are both preservation based and sustainability based and can contribute to making an environment that is dynamic and memorable to experience.

Historic preservation values and sustainability converge in SynergiCity. It is in the postindustrial districts where material waste from construction can be minimized and infrastructure can be reinvented to improve the environment. Furthermore, it will be in the massive warehouses, with their two-foot exterior masonry walls, that the argument will be made that preserved historic buildings are more energy efficient. Architects and engineers will employ mechanical systems that utilize the thermal mass of the masonry walls for heating and the tall ceilings for cooling. Windows will be retrofitted with interior storm window systems that reduce their draftiness. All of this is already happening where postindustrial redevelopment is occurring.[3]

Social Capital and Historic Preservation: Bringing Creative Capital to SynergiCity

In "The People of Preservation: Preservationists as Social Capital," the concluding chapter of *Buying*

Time for Heritage, J. Myrick Howard points out the important role of preservation in building social capital in places. He refers to social capital as the building of social networks and the reciprocity and trust that arise from them. Social capital fuels the innovation economy through interpersonal relationships and idea-sharing dialogue between entrepreneurs and visionaries. Through his 30-plus years as executive director of Preservation North Carolina, Howard has come to the realization that preservation builds social capital. He states that the preservation of historic districts and historic cities is essentially a visionary endeavor. It requires a leap of immense faith and a tremendous amount of creativity. For Howard, there is nothing more powerful than the end result — the before-and-after picture of a rehabilitated building, street, and district. It is both tangible and conclusive.

This backward-forward vision coupled with a risk-taking spirit makes the preservation community a natural partner with the creative-entrepreneurial community. In historic places, more often than not, these two groups are one and the same. Both groups often share common goals: to make the most of the resources that are available and to live and work in a meaningful and dynamic environment. The potential of the social capital that preservationists bring to the table should not be dismissed by municipal governments; instead, it should be embraced. Historic preservation is a civic-minded, community-building endeavor (Howard 2007).

In order for historic preservation to make an impact in SynergiCity, preservationists will need to bring their talents and vision to the planning table and work hand in hand with economists, planners, architects, landscape architects, engineers, and government officials. They must realize

the environmental challenges of brownfield remediation and strive to strike a balance between the needs of a city's urban systems and natural systems. Furthermore, preservationists will need to look beyond their traditional role of interpreting history through the lens of the built landscape and begin to see that historic resources can have great economic productive potential as well. Historic preservation has long been a field that values the historic environment as a cultural resource; now it is time for it to value the historic environment as an economic one as well.

Preservationists will also need a firm understanding of real estate development and should understand the market forces and objectively assess the scope of work required in rehabilitating a historic building, street, or district. They will need to understand how to quantify risk and to phase work in a progressive manner. Furthermore, preservationists need to do more than use policy tools; they need to attract investors and develop markets that can sustain redevelopment. Typically, this process begins by matching the right occupant to the right building. This was the case in the development of Midtown Alley in St. Louis, in which the developer targeted a specific business market — creative firms such as advertisement agencies, commercial photographers, and graphic designers — as tenants for the district. These firms were well suited for the building space in Midtown Alley. They were entrepreneurs who wanted historic character in their workspace, moderate overhead, and proximity to downtown. Once an initial market of similar creative-work-based businesses was established, other businesses, services, and amenities soon followed to serve them. Restaurants relocated in Midtown Alley and then condominiums, and now retail is beginning to relocate there. This was a gradual process, but it started with strategic marketing to the right type of tenant. Through gradual small-area development and targeting business enterprises, a critical mass of business activity occurs. This critical mass will strike a balance between high-income-producing entrepreneurship and lesser, but equally critical, ones. Through historic preservation, a balance between old and new will happen along with a balance between the high-tech business and the corner coffee shop or boutique. SynergiCity will become more than a new industrial park; it will become a community. Unlike the research parks of the past, innovation districts will emerge where economic productivity, living, and socializing happen simultaneously.

City planners, municipal economic development officials, and mayors should take the opportunity for postindustrial transformation seriously. Although investment in these types of projects is incremental and often complex, the final results are compelling. Examples can be found throughout the United States; in Edenton, North Carolina, before Preservation North Carolina undertook the conversion of the Edenton Cotton Mill into 35 live/work units in 1996, the assessed tax value of the 2,000-square-foot factory was $840,845; today the tax value is more than $5 million (Howard 2007). The city of Baltimore, Maryland, assessed the abandoned 52-acre postindustrial tract in Westport at a mere $99,000; beginning this year, Turner Development will invest over a billion dollars into it (plate 16). And there are indirect cost benefits for municipalities to consider as well (Turner 2010). Redeveloping abandoned factories instead of demolishing them redirects tons of construction debris away from landfills, and underused infra-

structure becomes once again productive. The cost savings in these two indirect benefits are immeasurable. Historic preservation can make SynergiCity happen, and as a result of focusing on the economic, environmental, and aesthetic benefits of the postindustrial district, a much more sustainable outcome will happen: a new community.

Notes

1. In *Economics of Historic Preservation: A Community Leader's Guide*, Donovan Rypkema identifies himself and other like-minded preservationists as part of "the revisionist school" in historic preservation, a new breed of preservationists so labeled in the early 1980s by real estate expert Richard Roddewig, who were motivated as much by the economic benefits of historic preservation as by the cultural benefits (Rypkema, 1994, p. 12).

2. Telephone interview with Don Miles, FAIA, principal-in-charge of the Urban Village Vision, by the author. The decision to design environmental and cultural features in Lowertown, such as the riverfront park and a winter garden, were based on surveys by the Lowertown Redevelopment Corporation of Lowertown residents who had moved into rehabilitated warehouses. This market-based research demonstrates that the success of the preservation development brought about a need for larger civic projects for Lowertown such as parks and greenspace.

3. The National Trust for Historic Preservation has proven that retrofitting historic buildings reduces energy use by up to 29%.

References

American Tobacco. 2010. "American Tobacco IS Downtown Durham's Entertainment District!" "About Us," website of American Tobacco, www.americantobaccohistoricdisttrict.com/about-us.html. Accessed January 16, 2012.

Florida, R. 2010. *The Great Reset: How New Ways of Living and Working Drive the Post-crash Prosperity*. New York: Harper.

Howard, J. M. 2007. *Buying Time for Heritage: How to Save an Endangered Historic Property*. Raleigh, NC: Preservation North Carolina.

Jacobs, J. 1961. *The Death and Life of Great American Cities*. New York: Random House.

Lu, Weiming. 2010, June 23. Interview with Paul H. Kapp and Paul J. Armstrong.

Mayes, Thompson. 2003. "Preservation Law and Public Policy: Balancing Policies and Building an Ethic." In Stipe 2003, 158-84.

Orange County, NC. Office of Solid Waste Management. 2010. "Construction and Demolition Debris." Available at the website of Orange Country, NC, www.co.orange.nc.us/recycling/candd.asp. Accessed January 16, 2012.

Ravensbergen, D. 2008. "Be Nice to the Creative Class." Available at thetyee.ca/Views/2008/08/05/CreativeClass/ Accessed January 17, 2012.

Rypkema, D. D. 1998. *The Economics of Historic Preservation: A Community Leader's Guide*. Washington, DC: National Trust for Historic Preservation Press.

Stipe, R. E., ed. 2003. *A Richer Heritage: Historic Preservation in the Twenty-First Century*. Chapel Hill: University of North Carolina Press.

Turner, P. 2010, August 10. Interview with Paul H. Kapp.

CHAPTER FOUR

Creating Urban Metabolism

PAUL J. ARMSTRONG

URBAN METABOLISM, ORIGINALLY PROPOSED IN 1965, is a model to facilitate the description and analysis of the flows of the materials and energy within cities (Wolman 1965). It offers benefits in the study of the sustainability of cities by providing a unified or holistic viewpoint to encompass all of the activities of a city in a single model.

Urban Metabolism can be classified into the following three types:

1. *On a national or regional scale*: In this type of study the material exchanges between an economy and the natural environment are analyzed. Indicators are calculated in order to assess the level of resource intensity of the system.

2. *Corporate material flow analysis*, or along an *industrial supply chain* involving a number of companies: The goal of material flow analysis within a company is to optimize the production processes in such a way that materials and energy are used in the most efficient manner (e.g., by recycling and reduction of waste). Companies that implement a material flow analysis can use the results to improve their operations costs and environmental performance.

3. In the *life cycle of a product*: This is another term for the life-cycle inventory step of life-cycle assessment.

Urban Metabolism can be used as a *quantitative* measure of the "health" of a city: A city "who is whole," with respect to physical, social, and economic factors, is presumably a healthy city. Where these factors are deficient indicates an "ailing" city. It also can be a *qualitative* indicator of livability. The term *quality of life* is used to evaluate the general well-being of individuals and societies. According to ecological economist Robert Costanza, "while Quality of Life (QOL) has long been an explicit or implicit policy goal, adequate definition and measurement have been elusive. Diverse 'objective' and 'subjective' indicators across a range of disciplines and scales, and recent work on subjective well-being (SWB) surveys and the psychology of happiness have spurred renewed interest" (2008).

A livable city—suitable for human living—is one that is in balance such that all of its parts and resources contribute to its inhabitants' quality of life. One method of rating cities is the Creativity Index (Florida 2002). This is a composite measure that is based on four indices for the most current year available: the Innovation Index (1999), High-Tech Index (2000), Gay Index (2000), and Creative Class (1999). In the United States, Madison, Wisconsin, ranks highest among the regions with 250,000 to 5,000,000 people. Several other Midwest cities are ranked in the top 50, including Lincoln, Nebraska (19), Rockford, Illinois (24), Appleton-Oshkosh-Neenah, Wisconsin (27), and Peoria, Illinois (35). Mercer's Quality of Living Index (Mercer 2011) uses 39 criteria, including political and economic stability, health care, educational opportunities, culture, recreation, hygiene, safety, and public transportation. While European cities dominate the top tier of ranked cities, San Francisco (30), Chicago and Washington, D.C. (both at 43), New York City (47), and Seattle (48) round out the top 50 cities for quality of life, with scores of 99.8 or better (Mercer 2011). In 2010 the rating also identifies the cities with the best eco-ranking based on water availability and drinkability, waste removal, quality of sewage systems, air pollution, and traffic congestion. In this survey, seven U.S. cities with scores of 126.6 or higher, such as Honolulu (2), Minneapolis (6), Pittsburgh (13), Washington, D.C. (23), Boston (25), Philadelphia (34), and St. Louis (43), rank among the top 50 cities worldwide for eco-living (Mercer 2010).[1]

The City Who Is Whole

In his essay "Architecture as Medicine," Daniel Willis (1999) uses the modern hospital to draw analogies to architecture. Whereas the hospital is often perceived as a "machine for healing," studies in modern medicine indicate that the attitudes and beliefs of patients have a significant impact on their ability to recover. Willis points out that modern hospitals, due to their infrastructures of complex technology and systems, share many attributes with other highly mechanized building types. They run on a system of "abstract time of twenty-four hour sameness" in which the functions of the hospital, like the patient, are objectified. He argues that hospitals, like other building types, can create an "authentic sense of place" by rejecting "machine metaphors" for deeper physical and aesthetic attributes that actually may be more beneficial to healing than efficiency (Willis 1999: 4-5).

In a sense, the modern hospital, functionally as well as socially, resembles a modern city in its programmatic and technological complexity. It assembles several familiar functions, such as housing, education, technology, restaurants, offices, and institutions, into a single complex. Thus, its *metabolism of operational flows and strategies* may be compared to the metabolism of a city, where the flows of information, technology, economy, and social life must all be integrated (plate 14).

The mind-body dilemma in medicine also can be compared to the function-aesthetics problem in architecture: "Both dichotomies," writes Willis, "are comprised of abstract concepts" that are "artificial creations . . . with their own peculiar histories and origins" (Willis 1999: 9-10). Thus, he argues, the "form follows function" dictum of modern architecture, in which aesthetics become[s] the rational outcome of functions, must be questioned based on the limitations of its own representational system—as Jorge Silvetti (1977) eloquently argued in his essay "The Beauty of Shadows."[2] Likewise, the presumed rational order of the city, which is often the result of the integration of complex functions and systems, does not necessarily translate directly into quality-of-life.

Comparisons of cities to the human body have been made since the time of Vitruvius. Le Corbusier viewed the city hierarchically in anthropomorphic terms with an administrative civic "head," a mixed-use "body" of retail and housing, and service and industrial "appendages." Modern architects and urban designers have tended to view the city as a mechanism in which the parts must function together efficiently for the benefit of the whole; thus, architecture and, more pointedly, zoning become "machines for healing" the city. But machine metaphors, predicated largely on a functionalist approach, obscure the more nuanced and authentic issues of place-making.

Leon Krier (1984) criticizes mechanical functional zoning as "the most effective means in destroying the infinitely complex social and physical fabric of preindustrial communities." He proposes that the city should reintegrate main urban functions into urban quarters (districts) of limited territorial size in which residence, work, and leisure should be located within walking distance. For example, Soulard Square in St. Louis is an established community with a farmers' market, restaurants, small shops, residences, and churches all situated in a compact, walkable neighborhood.

A more useful analogy, according to both Krier (1984) and Christopher Alexander and his colleagues (1987), is an organic model of urban growth as a process of incremental transformations through time. A well-planned city is "whole," and the purpose of responsible city planning is "to heal the city." Alexander's overriding rule is that "every increment of construction must be made in such a way as to heal the city. . . . Every new act of construction has just one basic obligation: It must create a continuous structure of whole around itself."

Postindustrial cities in the United States have been diagnosing and treating their "ailing" commercial infrastructures for several decades, with mixed results. Urban renewal programs in the United States during the 1960s, for example, gave little attention to preserving the fabric of older neighborhoods or to the significant displacement of the poorer residents. Since then, many smaller-scale cities, such as Peoria and Milwaukee, have had to rely on a handful of industries to sustain their aging manufacturing bases. Enticing new industries and the jobs they create continues to be a major economic and political goal. However, bringing new businesses and industries into postindustrial communities extracts a price. For example, Caterpillar Corporation, which has its headquarters in Peoria, is a major Fortune 50 company that manufactures and markets heavy industrial earth-moving equipment throughout the world. The financial health and well-being of the city of Peoria is directly tied to Caterpillar's financial growth and continued vitality. The city also believes that in order to continue to grow and prosper, it will need to attract more Fortune 50 companies like Caterpillar, rather than foster its own creative capital of talent, technology, culture, and enterprise. This problem is not unique to Peoria, since many postindustrial cities are competing for the same limited pool of companies. Furthermore, the harder that cities compete with one another by offering lucrative incentives such as tax breaks, land for development, and pro bono services, the more likely they are to bankrupt themselves in the process.

Admittedly, the role of architecture as built environment to "heal" a city in a holistic sense is limited. As Weiming Lu, past president of the Lowertown Development Corporation in St. Paul, observes, "physical renewal does not bring social regeneration" (Lee 2008). However, buildings do have a lasting impact on the urban environment in that they give form to the city, define its streets and paths, create scale, and house vital functions. In short, architecture gives order to the city and its inhabitants and, in turn, is given meaning through the rituals of daily life. Thus, as Alexander points out, the city is an *organic composition* whose processes of its planning and growth are integral to its health and metabolism.

Sustainable Development

The concept of urban metabolism also provides a means of understanding the sustainable devel-

opment of cities by drawing an analogy with the metabolic processes of organisms. As Alexander et al. (1987) observe: "When we look at the most beautiful towns and cities of the past, we are always impressed by a feeling that they are somehow organic. This feeling of 'organicness,' is not a vague feeling of relationship with organic forms. It is not an analogy. It is instead, an accurate vision of a specific structural quality which these old towns had . . . and have. Namely: Each of these towns grew as a whole, under its own laws of wholeness."

The parallels between organic growth of cities and sustainable processes also are strong: "Cities transform raw materials, fuel, and water into the built environment, human biomass and waste" (Decker et al. 2000). In practice the study of an urban metabolism (in urban ecology) requires quantification of the inputs, outputs, and storage of energy, water, nutrients, materials, and wastes. This enables planners, developers, and design professionals to determine strategies that will create projects that are better suited to diverse urban and natural ecosystems.

Urban metabolism can be defined as "the sum total of the technical and socio-economic processes that occur in cities, resulting in growth, production of energy, and elimination of waste" (Kennedy et al. 2007). The metabolism of an ecosystem, for example, involving the production, via photosynthesis, and consumption, by respiration, of organic matter is often expressed by ecologists in terms of energy. A few studies of urban metabolism have focused on quantifying the embodied energy in cities, while others have more broadly included fluxes of nutrients and materials, and the urban hydrological cycle.

Sustainable development must "meet human

needs while preserving the environment so that these needs can be met not only in the present, but also for future generations" (United Nations 1987). Lu contends that "urban development is most successful when there are natural areas nearby, where people can escape the city for a quiet walk or a moment of reflection" (Lee 2008). Many postindustrial cities in the Midwest region of the United States were developed along water transportation systems, which provided sources for potable water as well as routes for the transport of goods and services. Today, protection of these natural resources is vital to the ecology of both the cities and the region. Consequently, many cities have become environmental stewards by protecting their watersheds and developing environmental strategies to mitigate the effects of flooding, erosion, and pollution. In Peoria, the Illinois River is a resource that is used for transportation and recreation. The Warehouse District lies in the floodplain of the river and can be inundated during heavy rains and seasonal flooding. In addition, the bluffs on which both Peoria and East Peoria are situated create a natural watershed to the river. Filtering and treating gray water before it reaches the river is essential to maintaining the water quality for now and into the future.

The Third Ward in Milwaukee is bounded by Lake Michigan to the east and the Milwaukee River to the west. Consequently, water and effluents that enter the river also are carried directly into the lake. For more than three decades, the city of Milwaukee has been working in partnership with the University of Wisconsin–Milwaukee in the study of its transportation corridors, urban redevelopment, and natural environments. Most recently, it is carefully examining its natural watersheds and engineering infrastructure of distribution systems and is taking measures to revitalize its waterways with environmental safeguards. Shoreline along the Milwaukee River and Lake Michigan once used for industrial purposes is now being ecologically reclaimed for recreation and natural habitats.

Even the largest of the Great Lakes presents a fragile ecosystem under intense ecological pressure. Open to international shipping, Lake Superior is continually threatened by invasive species carried by large ships. As a port city, Duluth, Minnesota, must always be vigilant for pollutants and nonindigenous invasive species that threaten the quality of its water, fish, and wildlife habitats, as well as its economy (plate 13).

Sustainable development ties together concern for the carrying capacity of natural systems with the social challenges facing humanity. As early as the 1970s the term "sustainability" was employed to describe an economy "in equilibrium with basic ecological support systems" (Stivers 1976). Ecologists have pointed to *Beyond the Limits* (Meadows et al. 1992), which explores how exponential growth interacts with finite resources, and presented the alternative of a "steady state economy"—defined by Thomas R. Malthus (1803) as an economy of relatively stable size—in order to address environmental concerns.

During the 1990s, St. Paul and Duke Energy Generation Services developed Ever-Green Energy, a wood-fired combined heat and power (CHP) cogeneration facility to produce clean and efficient energy for the Lowertown District. According to its website, CHP is a process that generates both electricity and heat at the same time. Steam from the turbine generator that creates electricity is used to heat water rather than being released into the atmosphere and lost. The biomass fuel used in the St. Paul facility is clean wood waste generated in the Twin Cities metro area. This CHP process extracts more usable energy from the fuel than creating heat or electricity alone, so it is much more efficient. Ever-Green Energy (2008) claims that by using renewable energy, the CHP plant simultaneously produces 25 megawatts of electricity and up to 65 megawatts of thermal energy.

Large quantities of wood waste are generated in the Twin Cities metro area annually, resulting in storage and disposal problems. The CHP plant turns approximately 280,000 tons of this renewable resource into green energy annually, replacing about 60% of District Energy St. Paul's use of coal and oil and significantly reducing carbon dioxide, sulfur dioxide, and particulate emissions. The Ever-Green Energy CHP plant demonstrates that addressing the problem of energy in a sustainable and cost-effective manner will produce multiple cost savings that can be passed on to the consumer. It is just one example of how sustainable infrastructures can be developed.

The field of sustainable development can be conceptually broken into three constituent parts: *environmental sustainability, economic sustainability,* and *sociopolitical sustainability*. The three building blocks of economic sustainability are *information, integration*, and *participation*. In sustainable development everyone is a user and provider of information. Developing economies, therefore, need to change from old sector-centered ways of doing business to new approaches that involve crossdisciplinary coordination and the integration of environmental and social concerns into all development processes. Furthermore, broad public participation in decision-making is a fundamental prerequisite for achieving sustainable development (Allen 2007).

According to A. M. Hasna (2007: 48), "sustainability is a process which tells of a development of all aspects of human life affecting sustenance. It means resolving the conflict between the various competing goals, and involves the simultaneous pursuit of economic prosperity, environmental quality, and social equity—famously known as three dimensions (triple bottom line)—with the resultant vector being technology."

As pointed out in chapter 2, the first step in sustainability is preservation and adaptive reuse of existing buildings. This is not preservation in the historical or interpretive sense with the goal of freezing a building or place in time. Rather, it is a pragmatic response to using what already exists (provided it's serviceable) and razing only those buildings that cannot be saved.

Banbury Place in Eau Claire, Wisconsin, is a good example of adaptive "recycling" of buildings on a limited budget (plate 8). With more than 1,900,000 square feet of floor space, this former tire factory is a unique multiuse, multitenant facility located on a scenic site along the banks of the Eau Claire River (Banbury Place 2009). It is Eau Claire's best known industrial landmark. Banbury Place accommodates a mixture of light industrial manufacturing, commercial warehousing, service, retail, public/private offices, self-storage, and luxury warehouse-style residential apartments. It offers a wide range of on-site amenities, creating a vibrant activity center that facilitates the networking of tenants. Compared to many high-end warehouse renovations, Banbury Place is far more basic. For example, many of its original glazed openings, each filling an entire structural bay, have been replaced with smaller stock windows. And some openings have been filled in altogether with concrete block, thereby diminishing the authentic industrial character of the complex. Interior details and finishes are inexpensive and standardized to such a degree that one cannot distinguish one building from another internally, which makes way-finding and orientation difficult. However, by keeping renovation costs to a minimum, Banbury Place remains an affordable live/work environment for its tenants.

Milwaukee has been the headquarters of Harley-Davidson, Inc., a manufacturer of motorcycles, since 1903 (Harley-Davidson 2010). The Harley-Davidson brand is widely respected and has developed a dedicated following among motorcycle enthusiasts. The 130,000-square-foot Harley-Davidson Museum, located on Walker's Point in the Fifth Ward, is a popular tourist attraction. The Iron Horse Hotel, which also is dedicated to Harley enthusiasts, is housed in a renovated firehouse whose original industrial structure, materials, and character have been preserved and reinterpreted in new elements and details (plate 11). In contrast with Banbury Place, no expense has been spared. One could say that the Harley-Davidson brand defines Milwaukee's postindustrial renaissance by presenting a product and an image that is quality driven and appeals to a broad clientele of blue-collar workers and white-collar professionals alike. In other words, the clientele of the Iron Horse, who also are likely to own Harleys, have come to expect high-style design from a company that promotes motorcycles at the "cutting edge" of design and performance.

Pat Sullivan, a "hands-on" developer and partner in the JP Companies in Peoria, reuses just about every material in his buildings. He does not limit his efforts to renovating buildings but also addresses the street by recycling pavers. In this more sustainable scenario, buildings and materials are salvaged, recycled, and repurposed for new applications. A general theme of all postindustrial redevelopment, therefore, is the integration of old and new. This applies to the adaptive reuse of existing warehouses in Minneapolis into edgy, high-tech lofts and businesses, as well as the development of new, modern condominiums built shoulder-to-shoulder with historic buildings in Milwaukee and St. Paul, Minnesota.

Creative Class versus Creative Capital

In *The Rise of the Creative Class*, Richard Florida (2002) notes how at Carnegie Mellon University students were casually "recruited" by a high-tech company based in Austin, Texas. Their recruiting methods were low-key and unconventional: "hanging out" with prospective candidates was preferred to formal interviews, reflecting both the philosophy of company and the generational mindset of its employees. He also notes that one of its "star" recruits from Carnegie Mellon sported spiked multicolor hair, body tattoos, and multiple piercings. "What a change from my own college days," he muses, "when students would put on their dressiest clothes and carefully hide any counterculture symptoms." Clearly, hiring employees that "fit in" to a corporate mold was not what this company wanted.

But what piqued Florida's interest most was the fact that young, talented professionals were leaving Pittsburgh and moving to Austin. Florida had personally witnessed Pittsburgh's own transformation as a postindustrial city, yet it could not create the same quality of life for these professionals that Austin promised. In lieu of professional sports teams, museums, or high-art cultural activities, they are choosing cities such as Austin as a place to live and work because they have a culture that appeals to a young "creative class": a thriving music scene, ethnic and cultural diversity, fabulous outdoor recreation, and great nightlife. Most important, such cities are more affordable than many U.S. cities located on the west and east coasts.

So why can't Pittsburgh, or any other up-and-coming postindustrial city for that matter, compete with Austin or Silicon Valley for the "best and brightest" people? Florida concluded it is not simply jobs, as many economists would argue, but quality-of-life benefits that draw the creative class to unlikely places. Another reason is that despite high ratings for quality of life, Pittsburgh consistently ranks as one of the worst performing U.S. cities in terms of poverty, crime, employment, income, and housing abandonment (Hollander et al. 2009). This paradox also plagues many other postindustrial cities. Safety, along with quality of schools, ranks among the highest concerns for people moving back into central cities.

However, like Pittsburgh, many postindustrial cities in the Midwest have much to offer, including affordability. New technologies do not have to be developed elsewhere when the educational and economic resources are already present, waiting to be tapped. Yet, even in Milwaukee's vibrant Third Ward, creative talent is leaving for Chicago because that is where the creative class seeks opportunity.

Not all creative talent leaves postindustrial cities. In fact many talented people seek opportunities in such cities because they are affordable and they *do* offer certain lifestyle choices they desire. Jassen

Johnson is a founder and partner of Renaissance Development Associates in St. Louis, with dual M. Arch. and M.B.A. degrees. For his architecture thesis at the University of Illinois in 2002 he performed a market analysis for redevelopment of Midtown Alley in St. Louis and developed planning and architectural proposals that he has since put into action. In just eight years, Renaissance Development has developed over $80 million in projects, including WireWorks (plate 12). Jassen was able to capitalize on experience in the construction industry that he acquired working with his family and his architectural education and business acumen to create a firm that offers comprehensive development, design, and construction services. Furthermore, he markets the quality of life that his firm promotes and designs for to attract creative professionals to urban districts as the first step in creating community. For this reason, as Cindy Washington of ND Development in St. Louis explains, creative communities are not so much about attracting a particular age group as they are about people who share "a frame of mind."

Quality of life (QOL) is represented as the interaction of human needs and the subjective perception of their fulfillment, mediated by the opportunities available to meet the needs. Quality-of-life factors include (1) opportunities to meet human needs now and in the future for the built, human, social, and natural environments realized through investments of capital and time; (2) human needs, including subsistence, reproduction, security, affection, understanding, participation, leisure, spirituality, creativity, identity, and freedom; and (3) enhancement of subjective well-being (happiness, utility, and welfare) for individuals and/or groups.

The ability of humans to satisfy these basic needs arises from the opportunities available and constructed from social, built, human, and natural capital (and time). Costanza et al. (2008) identify four types of capital as a means for providing these opportunities: (1) *social capital* is networks and norms that facilitate cooperative action (Putnam 1995); (2) *human capital* is the knowledge and information stored in our brains, as well as our health and labor potential; (3) *built capital* is manufactured goods (tools, equipment, consumer goods), buildings, and infrastructure; and (4) *natural capital* is the structure of natural ecosystems. To this list we could add *technology capital*, which fosters the development of new technologies in biomedicine, ecology, and informatics. All forms of capital are investments that generate flows of benefits. For example, the benefits of natural capital are the renewable and nonrenewable goods and services provided by ecosystems. Costanza and Daly (1992) point out that "the differing characteristics of these . . . types of capital can be used to help guide policy and decision making with regard to meeting human needs." Collectively, they constitute what we refer to as *creative capital*.

If they are to attract creative talent, postindustrial cities must critically reassess their creative capital, which includes people, technology, institutions, and cultural and environmental amenities. They must identify new and emergent technologies that are being developed in their own regions and provide the incentives and lifestyle choices that will attract and keep young entrepreneurs. They need to take inventory of their physical infrastructures and protect and sustain their natural resources. Public-private partnerships must be forged among cities, businesses, and academic institutions to promote

sustainable research and development as well as educate new workers and reeducate already skilled workers for emerging opportunities.

Urban Synergy and the Transect

The patterns of redevelopment of postindustrial cities are now becoming familiar. At the initial stages of transformation, artists, countercultural types, and so-called bohemians looking for raw space and cheap rent seek out derelict buildings. Old warehouses, with their robust structures, industrial materials, high ceilings, and large unobstructed floor plates, are ideal environments for lofts and artists' studios. Ground floor spaces can be developed into galleries, restaurants, commercial, and office spaces (fig. 4.1). New startup companies and creative agencies often seek out such spaces for the same reasons as artists. Warehouses are desirable because they are adaptable to a virtually unlimited number of uses. This trend also brings in developers who see economic opportunities in transforming raw warehouse spaces into modern live/work environments. Visionary architectural and planning initiatives coupled with creative people and entrepreneurs make postindustrial areas trendy, which attracts new investment. Of course, this process also results in gentrification, which, although objectionable to some, is often the result of development of postindustrial districts and the catalyst for the redevelopment of adjacent derelict districts. The Lowertown Redevelopment Corporation in St. Paul, Minnesota, addressed this problem by creating a development bank to fill the gap in financing for projects in the district. This funding mechanism encouraged local

FIGURE 4.1. Warehouses can be adapted to many uses, for example this restaurant at WireWorks in St. Louis. (Courtesy of Paul J. Armstrong)

residents and entrepreneurs to stay and invest in Lowertown, rather than be displaced (Lee 2008).

This scenario does not happen overnight. It is a process that generally takes decades, beginning with a combination of grassroots community groups and individual initiatives, which in turn inspire new, more coordinated forms of development. Redevelopment plans for Lowertown in St. Paul, for example, began in 1979 through a public-private partnership coordinated by Weiming Lu, past president of the Lowertown Redevelopment Corporation, and former mayor George Latimer. Today, it is nearly complete with future development plans to create the Bruce Vento Conservation Area along the east bank of the Mississippi River. Redevelopment of Milwaukee's Third Ward began

around the same time. It is now the home of the Milwaukee Institute of Art and Design and has propelled development in the adjacent Fifth Ward Warehouse District.

In Minneapolis, redevelopment of the warehouse district into mixed-use lofts (fig. 4.2) and of the Gold Medal flour mills into a museum has been complemented by the addition of major new cultural buildings such as the Guthrie Theater, designed by Jean Nouvel, and Target Field, home of the Minnesota Twins baseball team.

Canal Park in Duluth is situated in a former industrial area adjacent to its famous aerial lift bridge. Today it includes the historic DeWitt-Seitz Building, a commercial-style building designed in 1909, which has been renovated so as to house re-

tail shops, office spaces, and restaurants (plate 9). With easy access to Lake Superior and a maritime museum, Canal Park attracts tourists as well as a diverse population of young and old (plates 13 and 15). New hotels and lodges share with existing buildings the rugged beauty of the lakefront.

SYNERGY

Synergy, in general, may be defined as two or more agents working together to produce a result not obtainable by any of the agents independently. The term *synergy* was refined by R. Buckminster Fuller (1975), who analyzed some of its implications and coined the term *synergetics*. The characteristics of synergy include:

> A *dynamic state* in which combined action is favored over the difference of individual component actions
>
> *Behavior of whole systems* unpredicted by the behavior of their parts taken separately, known as emergent behavior
>
> The *cooperative action* of two or more stimuli, resulting in a different or greater response than that of the individual stimuli

Synergy, therefore, *creates* urban metabolism by combining diverse resources to create an entirely new entity. In the postindustrial city, *urban synergy* includes urban ecology, preservation and adaptive reuse, and design guided by the principles of New Urbanism. *Urban ecology* is a subfield of ecology that deals with the interaction of organisms in an urban or urbanized community and their interaction with that community. Urban ecologists study the trees, rivers, wildlife, and open spaces found in cities to understand the extent of those resources

FIGURE 4.2. Bookmen Stacks Lofts in Minneapolis provides residents with upscale living in a sleek glass-and-steel high-rise building located within walking distance of the Guthrie Theater and Target Field. (Courtesy of Paul J. Armstrong)

and the way they are affected by pollution, overdevelopment, and other pressures. Analysis of urban settings in the context of *ecosystem ecology* (looking at the cycling of matter and the flow of energy through the ecosystem) may ultimately help us to design healthier, better managed communities by understanding what threats the urban environment brings to humans. Today, there is an emphasis on planning communities with an ecological design using alternative building materials and methods. This is in order to promote a healthy and biodiverse urban ecosystem.

THE TRANSECT AND THE SMARTCODE

The urban-to-rural transect is an urban planning model created by New Urbanist Andres Duany. The *transect* defines a series of zones that transition from sparse rural farmhouses to the dense urban core. Each zone is fractal in that it contains a similar transition from the edge to the center of the neighborhood. The transect is an important part of the New Urbanism and Smart Growth movements. Duany's firm, Duany Plater-Zyberk & Company (DPZ), has embodied the transect philosophy in their SmartCode generic planning code for municipal ordinances.

The SmartCode, developed by DPZ, is a model form-based unified land development ordinance designed to create walkable neighborhoods across the full spectrum of human settlement, from the most rural to the most urban, incorporating a transect of character and intensity within each. It folds zoning, subdivision regulations, urban design, and basic architectural standards into one compact document. Because the SmartCode enables community vision by coding specific outcomes that are desired in particular places, it is meant to be locally calibrated by professional planners, architects, and attorneys.

Duany promotes transect planning in lieu of traditional Euclidean zoning and suburban development in which large tracts of land are dedicated to a single purpose, such as housing, offices, and shopping, which can be accessed only via major roads.

The concept of the transect was borrowed from ecology. Ecological transects are used to describe changes in habitat over some gradient, such as a change in topography or distance from a water body. Patrick Geddes, in his Valley Section (a section of land taken from ridgeline to shoreline) of the early twentieth century, was among the first to proclaim that human settlement should be analyzed in the context of its natural region.

A major feature of transect planning is that it incorporates a variety of residential and commercial spaces into a single neighborhood. A typical neighborhood would, for instance, consist of a light commercial area with a bank, general store, pub, coffee shop, and apartments. Moving outward from the center, residential density gradually decreases, from apartments to townhouses to fully detached houses. The central area is designed to be a focus of transit and, ideally, within walking distance of any point in the neighborhood.

The Transect has six zones, moving from rural to urban. It begins with two that are entirely rural in character: *Rural preserve* (protected areas in

perpetuity) and *Rural reserve* (areas of high environmental or scenic quality that are not currently preserved but perhaps should be). The transition zone between countryside and town is called the *Edge*, which encompasses the most rural part of the neighborhood and the countryside just beyond. The Edge is primarily single-family homes. Although the Edge is the most purely residential zone, it can have some mixed use, such as civic buildings (schools are particularly appropriate for the Edge). Next is *General*, the largest zone in most neighborhoods. General is primarily residential but more urban in character (somewhat higher density with a mix of housing types and a slightly greater mix of uses allowed). At the urban end of the spectrum are two zones that are primarily mixed use: *Center* (this can be a small neighborhood center or a larger town center, the latter serving more than one neighborhood); and an urban *Core* that serves the region. Typically, the Core is a central business district.

The major advantages of the transect as an urban planning tool are (1) education—it is easy to understand; (2) coding—it can readily be translated into the familiar framework of Euclidean zoning districts; and (3) the creation of immersive environments. Transect planning is inherently synergistic, in that all of the elements of the human and natural environments must work together in the transect to create something that is greater than the sum of its parts. The transect also creates a framework to control and promote growth in certain areas; increases pedestrian life, local safety, and community identity; and provides tools to protect and restore natural environments. Transect planning cannot be applied, however, without a change to local ordinances.

New Urbanism as Catalyst

New Urbanism began as a response to urban sprawl. Its core planning principles are based on Traditional Neighborhood Development (TND) and Transit-Oriented Development (TOD). In a TND the development of a community begins with a master plan that provides a network of interconnected streets, alleyways, and convenient walking distances, all contained within a greenbelt. Neighborhoods are designed with a quarter-mile radius (a five-minute walk from edge to center). Street blocks are generally not bigger than 230 by 600 feet, with integrated building types and uses. Squares and parks are evenly distributed, with community buildings placed on prominent sites. All these are controlled by a design code that draws on the architecture of the region and regulates building use, building placement, building form, landscape, and street types.

A typical TOD is mixed-use community with an average walking distance of 2,000 feet (or 10 minutes) to a transit stop and a core commercial area. Average density for a TOD residential area is between 10 and 25 dwellings per acre (approximately 25-60 dwellings per hectare). At the center, core commercial uses must occupy at least 10% of the total area, with a minimum of 10,000 square feet (1,000 square meters) of retail space adjacent to a transit stop. Principal community buildings and services are also located in central areas. School and secondary community buildings are located at the edges, which are more automobile oriented. In these "secondary areas" residential density can go as low as six units per acre (15 units per hectare).

New Urbanism has often been applied to new suburban developments but is equally amenable to the development of inner-city cores and former industrial sites. Warehouse districts in many postindustrial cities provide ample opportunities for incorporating new buildings and planning strategies with existing buildings and infrastructures. As pointed out earlier, warehouses can be adapted to new mixed uses. When new buildings are added, they often use materials and forms that reflect the industrial character of the warehouses as well as the historical character of the city.

Typically, adaptations to existing buildings can take the following forms: (1) canopies and entrances, (2) balconies, (3) roofscapes (penthouses, green roofs, and roof decks), (4) entry and display corners (turrets, bows, chamfers), and (5) courtyards and in-between spaces. Canopies on industrial buildings were originally fabricated of cast-iron or steel and used for protective overhangs for loading docks. Today they are made of a combination of glass, steel, wood, and other materials to define entrances and protect pedestrians from the elements. The former Allen D. Everitt Knitting Company building in Milwaukee's Fifth Ward, developed by Pieper Properties, uses glass and steel curtain walls, canopies, and balconies to add architectural interest to the cream city brick facades (fig. 4.3). The seven-story, 84,500-square-foot mixed-use commercial building has 71,000 square feet of office space and 13,500 square feet of retail space (Weiland 2008). The bold porte cochere of the Iron Horse Hotel in Milwaukee is fabricated from concrete, wood, and steel. Its industrial character recalls Milwaukee's blue-collar heritage and its reinvention as a technology-driven city. Balconies are conventionally associated with residential architecture. While some are integrated with the facades and structure, many balconies are fabricated from lightweight materials and physically attached to the structure. In Milwaukee's Third Ward, attached balconies that projected over streets became so prolific that design codes were developed to regulate them.

Many cities are mandating the use of sustainable materials and performance standards. Chicago, for example, is promoting green roofs that are habitable. In Minneapolis, roof decks on warehouse loft buildings create upscale outdoor spaces for residents. Architect Jim Shields adaptively reused an old terminal building to create the upscale Marine Terminal Lofts in Milwaukee's Third Ward by adding penthouse condominiums above the existing terminal building. These glass pavilions, which overlook both the street and the Milwaukee River, become illuminated "light boxes" at night and highlight activities on the roof. In Peoria, the entrances of many warehouses address the corner using turrets, rounded corners, and chamfers. Ceramic tiles, limestone, and granite are used for ornamental arches, capitals, and cornices.

New Urbanism encourages the use of courtyards and "in-between" spaces to promote a sense of place and community. The alleyways in Peoria's Warehouse District, for instance, are more akin to internal streets than narrow alleys and can easily accommodate services, pedestrians, and secondary business entrances. In St. Paul, space in between buildings is used for pedestrian circulation through blocks and outdoor dining for restaurant patrons (fig. 4.4).

However, public spaces such as "pocket parks" and the like should not be considered in districts where safety is a factor. St. Louis's Midtown is an urban corridor that links the University of St. Louis to the downtown commercial core. Historically, it

FIGURE 4.3. The former Allen D. Everitt Knitting Company building in Milwaukee's Fifth Ward at Walker's Point, developed by Pieper Properties. (Courtesy of Paul J. Armstrong)

FIGURE 4.4. New multifamily housing in Lowertown, St. Paul, Minnesota, provides the semipublic courtyards and in-between spaces promoted by New Urbanism. (Courtesy of Paul J. Armstrong)

was a vibrant commercial and entertainment district oriented toward the automobile. During the mid-1950s tracts of land were cleared for mid-rise low-income housing. When these buildings were demolished in 1998, the area once again became desirable for redevelopment.

Midtown Alley is a three-by-six-block area that is being redeveloped by Renaissance Development Associates in partnership with DN Development. Instead of creating community space at street level, they opted to develop rooftop decks where people could gather informally without safety concerns. As Jassen Johnson of Renaissance Development observed in an interview, the primary things that bring people together initially in any community are "animals and food." He also recognizes the importance of brand recognition and place-making. Hence, the name Midtown Alley has historical associations that resonate with the community, and his company sponsors social events such as marathons and streetfests that bring people together in large numbers several times each year.

When its planning principles are applied strategically to existing urban districts, New Urbanism actually can be a catalyst for the metabolism of cities and regions. Doug Kelbaugh (1997) argues that "New Urbanism entails more than simply recycling old planning principles and practices, but represents a new and total attempt to find a unified design strategy for an entire region which can be applied to inner city and downtown neighborhoods." For example, in instances where warehouse districts are adjacent to the central business districts, the vitality created in these developments can help to reenergize the downtown as well as adjacent districts. Cities and urban districts that are well designed should be memorable as well as livable. Consequently, they are places where people *want* to live. As Leon Krier has observed, the modernists failed "to make towns and villages . . . that people want to come from" (Andersen 1991). Today, vernacular forms help define place, and classicism judiciously applied to civic and institutional structures once again conveys a sense of tradition and permanence.

New Urbanism is often criticized for creating elitist "designer suburbs" that try to "reclaim the earlier suburban ideals of democracy and community, lost through the invasion of the masses" (Leung 2003). But when its principles have been applied to brownfield sites in the inner cities, they have often been hailed as noteworthy alternatives to unworkable high-rise low-income housing projects and derelict slums.

If New Urbanism promotes a shift from "yards to parks" that emphasizes collective space over individual space in suburban communities, then one can imagine a similar shift toward community and neighborhoods in urban areas as well. Both new and existing architecture can be used to define "public" and "in-between" spaces. Existing streets can be reinforced by aligning buildings to the sidewalks without setbacks in order to create continuous edges and unified streetscapes. Public squares can occur at corners or on entire blocks where buildings have been removed. Secondary community spaces can be introduced in pedestrian ways between buildings or in courtyards. Other urban amenities such as open-air markets and public parking can occupy spaces reclaimed from underutilized areas, such as those under overpasses and bridges.

In *The Death and Life of the American Street*, Jane Jacobs looked closely at the attributes for successful neighborhoods in the 1960s and used her research to argue compellingly "for the rediscovery of dense, tried-and-true urban vitality" (Andersen 1991). Since many warehouse districts already have an existing infrastructure of roads, services, and buildings, they are not tabula rasae. They also have a midrise scale that is appropriate for developing pedestrian-oriented neighborhoods. Development sizes of new buildings also can vary according to site sizes, which vary according to the pattern of private land ownership. Infill buildings can be added wherever increased density is required. Green spaces can be preserved along lakes and rivers to control flooding, filter gray water, and provide natural biomes for wildlife and recreation. Furthermore, warehouses can be built up vertically because they are structurally robust to begin with. Consequently, the land use patterns in urban postindustrial districts can be significantly reduced relative to suburban development.

Conclusion

The postindustrial city is a combination of old and new. It is a blend of existing buildings, which are adapted for a variety of mixed uses, modern loft-type buildings, which employ a combination of industrial and high-tech materials, and cultural, civic, and historical buildings.

Postindustrial cities are reinventing themselves by creating urban synergy through private and public partnerships that develop strategies for sustainable development that attracts new forms of creative capital. They are embracing New Urbanism and planning strategies, such as TND and TOP, to address public transportation needs and design guidelines for creating pedestrian-oriented neighborhoods. With greater emphasis on ecology, postindustrial cities are becoming environmental stewards who protect natural resources and watersheds by creating sustainable biomes for recreation and wildlife habitats. And they are reclaiming former brownfield sites for future sustainable redevelopment.

The organic model of the city suggests that it is always in flux. Consequently, its growth and contraction must be anticipated and planned. A healthy city is a livable city that functions efficiently and is scaled appropriately for people and their activities. Yet it must be adaptable for present needs and future opportunities. It must be economically, environmentally, and socially sustainable. Applying the principles of New Urbanism, such as Transect Planning and the SmartCode, enables planners, developers, and architects to holistically design sustainable urban districts and neighborhoods in former industrial buildings and sites that balance the requirements of ecology, economy, and society. Synergy creates livable cities with healthy metabolisms that foster opportunities for new enterprises and technologies to flourish and provide the lifestyle choices and amenities that will attract a new creative class. As the city prospers, it will generate "regional metabolism" that will affect and benefit other nearby communities. As a result, its own urban metabolism will be increased and sustained by the synergistic effects of its creative capital of human talent, social enterprises, cultural institutions and amenities, built environments and products, natural resources, and emerging technologies interacting at multiple scales regionally and nationally. Just as the "Sun Belt" cities prospered during the high-tech boom, so too can postindustrial cities in the Midwest prosper by attracting a diverse group of creative people, new enterprises, and emerging technologies that are drawn to the reinvented postindustrial city and the quality of life it offers.

Notes

1. Muskat, Oman (48), was the only Middle Eastern city on Mercer's Top 50 eco-cities ranking. Mercer is a for-profit company, and Oman is an oil-rich country that is not known for being environmentally conscious. Mercer's eco-city ranking system calls for "water availability, water potability, waste removal, decent sewage treatment facilities, as well as limited air pollution and traffic congestion," according to their 2010 eco-city news release. Both the city and the country face a serious freshwater shortage and rely heavily on desalination processes to meet their needs. See Laylin (2010).

2. According to K. Michael Hays (1998), Silvetti conjoins the discourse of realism with the general tendency of architectural theory in the 1970s to look to (post)structuralist studies of language as a possible paradigm for architectural thought. He develops a theory of architectural production, which he calls "criticism from within," through which he aims to expose the fundamental mechanisms by which elements of the language of architecture are lifted out of their historical context and recombined.

References

Alexander, C., H. Beis, A. Anninou, and I. King. 1987. *A New Theory of Urban Design*. New York: Oxford University Press.

Allen, W. 2007. "Learning for Sustainability: Sustainable Development." Available at the website Learning for Sustainability.net: Helping People Collaborate and Innovate, http://www .learningforsustainability.net/susdev/. Retrieved June 18, 2010.

Andersen, K. 1991. "Is Seaside Too Good to Be True?" In *Seaside: Making a Town in America*, ed. D. Mahoney and K. Easterling. New York: Princeton Architectural Press, 42-45.

Banbury Place. 2009. "Banbury Place: A Historic Restoration." Available at the website of Banbury Place.com, http:///www.banburyplace.com/. Retrieved June 19, 2010.

Costanza, R., and H. E. Daly. 1992. "Natural Capital and Sustainable Development." *Conservation Biology* 6(1): 37-46.

Costanza, R., B. Fisher, S. Ali, C. Beer, L. Bond, et al. 2008. "An Integrative Approach to Quality of Life Measurement, Research, and Policy." *S.A.P.I.E.N.S.* 1(1): 17-21. Available at Surveys and Perspectives Integrating Environment & Society, http://sapiens .revues.org/169. Retrieved June 21, 2010.

Decker, H., S. Elliott, F. A. Smith, D. R. Blake, and F. Sherwood Rowland. 2000. Energy and Material Flow through the Urban Ecosystem. *Annual Review of Energy and the Environment* 25: 685-740.

Ever-Green Energy. 2008. "Ever-Green Energy: Success Story." St. Paul: Ever-Green Energy. Available at http://www.evergreen-energy.com/. Retrieved June 19, 2010.

Florida, R. 2002. *The Rise of the Creative Class and How It's Transforming Work, Leisure, Community and Everyday Life.* New York: Basic Books.

Fuller, R. B. 1975. *Synergetics: Explorations in the Geometry of Thinking.* In collaboration with E. J. Applewhite. With an introduction and contribution by Arthur L. Loeb. New York: Macmillan.

Harley-Davidson, Inc. 2010. "History: From 1903 until Now." Available at Harley-Davidson USA, www .harley-davidson.com/en_US/Content/Pages /H-D_History/history.html. Retrieved July 10, 2010.

Hasna, A. M. 2007. "Dimensions of Sustainability." *Journal of Engineering for Sustainable Development: Energy, Environment, and Health* 2(1): 47-57.

Hays, K. Michael. 1998. Introduction to "The Beauty of Shadows," by Jorge Silvetti. In *Architecture Theory since 1968*, ed. Hays. Cambridge, MA: MIT Press, 262.

Hollander, J. B., K. M. Pallagst, T. Schwarz, and F. Popper. 2009. "Planning Shrinking Cities." Chapter 4 of *Shaken, Shrinking, Hot, Impoverished and Informal: Emerging Research Agendas in Planning*, ed. H. Bianco and M. Alberti, *Progress in Planning* 72: 223-32.

Kelbaugh, D. 1997. *Common Place: Toward Neighborhood and Regional Design.* Seattle: University of Washington Press.

Kennedy, C. A., J. Cuddihy, and J. Engel Yan. 2007, May. "The Changing Metabolism of Cities." *Journal of Industrial Ecology.* doi:10.1162/jiec.0.1107.

Krier, L. 1984. "Critique of Zoning." In *Leon Krier: Houses, Palaces, Cities,* ed. Demetri Porphyrios, 32-33. London: AD Editions.

Laylin, T. 2010, June 22. "Mercer's Oman Eco-City Ranking Suspect." Available at the website of Green Prophet, Portland, OR, Marylhurst University, html:///www.greenprophet.com/2010/06 /mercer-muscat-oman/. Retrieved July 20, 2010.

Lee, A. J. 2008, summer. "An Interview with Weiming Lee." *CRM: The Journal of Heritage Stewardship* 5(2): 1-6.

Leung, H. 2003. *Land Use Planning Made Plain.* 2nd ed. Toronto: University of Toronto Press.

Malthus, T. R. 1803. *An Essay on the Principle of Population.* 1st ed. (1798), with excerpts from 2nd ed. (1803). With an introduction by Philip Appleman and assorted commentary on Malthus edited by Appleman. Norton Critical Editions. New York: Norton.

Meadows, D. H., D. L. Meadows, and J. Randers, 1992. *Beyond the Limits: Global Collapse or a Sustainable Future.* London: Earthscan.

Mercer. 2010. "2010 Quality of Living Worldwide City Rankings—Mercer Survey." Available at the website of Marsh Mercer Kroll, http://www.mercer.com /summary.htm?idContent=148670. Retrieved June 18, 2010.

Mercer. 2011. "Mercer Quality of Living Survey— Worldwide Rankings, 2011." Available at the website of Marsh Mercer Kroll, http://www.mercer.com/ qualityoflivingpr#city-rankings. Retrieved January 28, 2012.

Putnam, R. D. 1995. "Tuning In, Tuning Out—The Strange Disappearance of Social Capital in America." *PS* 28(4): 664-83.

Silvetti, J. 1977. "The Beauty of Shadows." Reprinted in *Architecture Theory since 1968*, ed. K. M. Hays (1998). Cambridge, MA: MIT Press, 262.

Stivers, R. 1976. *The Sustainable Society: Ethics and Economic Growth.* Philadelphia: Westminster Press.

United Nations. 1987, December 11. *Report of the World Commission on Environment and Development.* General Assembly Resolution 42/187.

Weiland, A. 2008, October 17. "CRE Spotlight: Momentum Continues at Walker's Point." *BizTimes. com.* Available at BizTimes.com, http://www .bixtimes.com/news/2008/10/17/cre-spotlight -momentum-continues-walkers-point. Retrieved June 20, 2010.

Willis, D. 1999. "Architecture as Medicine." In *The Emerald City and Other Essays on the Architectural Imagination*, 1-22. New York: Princeton Architectural Press.

Wolman, A. 1965. "The Metabolism of Cities." *Scientific American* 213(3): 179-90.

FIGURE 5.1. The Eastern Market in Detroit is a popular destination. The comprehensive redevelopment plan for the market and its surrounding district is embodied in the title "Eastern Market 360." (Courtesy of Laura Mann)

CHAPTER FIVE

The Socioeconomic Opportunities of SynergiCity

LYNNE M. DEARBORN

The Promise of SynergiCity

Cities support a large number of interlinked human institutions and provide the physical context within which much of the world's population lives and works. To support city habitation, the quality of life offered to all urban residents, regardless of their socioeconomic standing, should be a critical consideration in rethinking urban redevelopment models for the "creative age" (Florida 2002). Quality of life depends not only on opportunities to build wealth and maintain employment but also on the attributes of the built environment, measures of physical and mental health, and opportunities for education, recreation, leisure time, and a sense of social belonging (Gregory 2009). Broadly examining the SynergiCity concept allows consideration of the urban system as a whole to understand and address the complex problems many cities face, particularly declining industrial cities.

Cities that are in physical, social, and economic decline offer fertile ground for reimagining urban form, distribution, and infrastructure, to creatively rethink and address the "wicked problems" (Rittel and Webber 1973) present in these environments. To be sure, issues of social equity, educational opportunity, and qualities of place must figure prominently in this reimagination, as should attributes of quality of life. Implementation of the SynergiCity concept in Rust Belt cities must recognize the underlying social inequity that currently undergirds postindustrial development. Likewise, addressing and strengthening the inherent qualities of place must be central in the application of the SynergiCity concept in medium-sized Midwest cities. In addressing issues of social equity in the application of the SynergiCity concept for urban redevelopment, this chapter will first briefly provide context for the idea of social equity in urban redevelopment and will then examine several ongoing redevelopment efforts that address social equity, economic opportunity, and sense of place. An analysis of efforts in two cities — Detroit's Eastern Market District redevelopment (fig. 5.1) and Boston's Dudley Street Initiative — offers lessons from successful bottom-up, community-based efforts that build on local strengths that can be applied to the SynergiCity concept to fully realize its potential.

The chapter concludes with three primary lessons for SynergiCity:

1. *Equitable urban design and architecture.* Urban redevelopment should incorporate a process that promotes involvement of all stakeholders in a meaningful way in creating the plan for redevelopment and the resulting physical interventions.

2. *Safeguard the local population.* It is necessary to guard against socioeconomic changes in the urban environment that result in informal eviction of lower income residents who may no longer be able to afford higher rents and decreasing affordability of local businesses as they begin to cater to a more affluent set of neighborhood consumers.

3. *Environments that educate.* As environments are redeveloped, they need to do more than provide for utilitarian functions. Environments should be designed so that they illustrate physically and socially sustainable development patterns. These environments may visibly demonstrate waste and water recycling or social inclusion of all generations through meaningful opportunities for involvement.

Historical Socioeconomic Patterns in the Industrial City

The social, economic, and political histories of industrial midwestern cities underlie their current physical forms. The layouts of these cities result from patterns of urbanization generated in response to the Industrial Revolution. In these cities a new social hierarchy, headed by an entrepreneurial class of industrial capitalists, developed and transformed urban physical, economic, and political structures. Patterns of socioeconomic segregation and assumptions about exploitable human labor underpinned the urban forms that these cities developed. Opportunities presented by this development came at substantial social and physical costs, as workers were forced into strictly controlled living and working conditions that were dominated by a new industrial environment. The power structures implicit in the socioeconomically segregated industrial city were exacerbated, particularly in the United States, as suburbanization resulted in ever greater distances between those in the middle and upper classes and those in the industrial working classes. Over the last three decades transformation from an industrial-based to an informational-based economy has intensified the socioeconomic divide, as well as the physical decline of many midwestern industrial cities.

The conditions of decline present in many cities are beyond singular, quick-fix solutions. Cities face complex problems resulting from a layering of decades of changing demographics, technological transformation, and a shifting and increasingly global marketplace. While the results of urban problems are visible physical decay, the threads of these problems run much deeper and are not just physical in nature. Thus purely physical solutions,

while they may present a glimmer of hope as fresh, clean additions in areas of decay, ultimately fail to spark long-term and lasting change because underlying structural problems remain. The conditions present are not simply physical, not simply local, and not simply solved with more money (Keating and Krumholz 1999). They are complex, with linked social, political, economic, and physical dimensions that overlap at multiple scales. They impact not just the local neighborhoods of central cities but also adjacent neighborhoods, city districts, whole cities, regions, and states. Therefore, the solutions cannot be simple, or singular.

Some cities, such as New York, seem to be eternally resilient and able to remake themselves as a whole even while retaining pockets untouched by economic, social, and physical renaissance. Other historically industrial U.S. cities have spent decades remaking themselves and only now have begun to demonstrate progress in addressing these complex and multidimensional urban problems. Those that demonstrate success, such as Philadelphia and Pittsburgh, have built on their physical, social, and economic strengths and the opportunities they present. Rather than using public funds in public-private real estate partnerships that generate spectacular developments and provide a new high-profile façade for the downtown (Krumholz 1999), these cities have "use[d] that money to invest in local assets, spur local business formation and development, better employ local people and utilize their skills, and invest in improving quality of place" (Florida 2010: 84). Furthermore, Philadelphia, recognizing that long-term prosperity in the informational age requires an increasing population of college graduates, has taken important steps to build an alliance of city government, foundations, and private and educational institutions that support

city residents returning to school to earn a degree (Florida 2010).

Even in cities and city districts that continue to struggle with complex endemic social, economic, and physical challenges, ongoing redevelopment efforts that address social equity, economic opportunity, and sense of place offer examples of successful bottom-up, community-based efforts that build on local strengths. These redevelopment efforts are offered in distinct opposition to mega real estate ventures, such as festival marketplaces and sports stadiums, which have promised comprehensive urban renaissance but mostly have provided negligible economic spillover for city residents. Efforts that have been successful in addressing the complex problems facing U.S. industrial cities as they attempt to redevelop have addressed issues of social and economic equity through local economic development that has created new jobs for unemployed local residents and provided net tax increases to cities (Krumholz 1999). Over the past 30 years, these two development paradigms — spectacular downtown real estate development and local economic development — have been deployed to address the complex challenges of urban redevelopment in U.S. cities. The two paradigms offer very different processes, as well as different physical and socioeconomic redevelopment outcomes.

Issues of Redevelopment

Planners and designers have attempted to engage urban problems throughout history. Rittel and Webber (1973) suggest that planners historically conceptualized such problems as "tame" or simple and addressed them in a straightforward manner. In addressing many urban problems of the past, this approach improved conditions for many people, for example, reducing epidemics of water and airborne disease. However, this kind of simple conceptualization of urban problems and their solutions also played a role in the complexity and intensity of urban problems that exist today. Rittel and Webber use the term "wicked" to describe the type of complex problems that planners and designers encounter in urban environments. In using this label they mean to suggest that the complexity of the problems is vexing and without a clear or easy solution. Accordingly, development of suburbs and single-use zoning has solved the problem of unhealthy urban environments by providing improved quality of life for those who could migrate to the suburbs, thus improving their condition. However demonstrating the complexity of the issue, it heightened problems for those who were left behind (Cisneros 1996).

The complicated and protracted troubles left in the wake of past planning and development efforts have stymied those who recognize their complexity (Man-Neef 1991). Several authors have suggested that viable solutions to complex problems depend on how the problem is framed (Krumholz 1999; Rittel and Webber 1973; Schon 1987). Viable solutions also are contingent on an analysis of the strengths and opportunities a particular city's physical and social environments present. Detroit, widely recognized as one of the most economically and physically traumatized U.S. industrial cities in our day, is clearly distressed but also offers strengths and opportunities. Its current complex challenges are rooted in its historical cultural segregation and animosity between African Americans and Caucasians and the resulting race riots of 1943 and 1967; its 1970s downtown real estate development focus on the spectacu-

lar Renaissance Center; and its physical fabric of sprawling detached single-family homes developed in the age of the automobile. The historical and current strengths of the Detroit region, to name a few, include a metropolitan area population of 4.2 million, a world-class airport, the educational and research potential of two nearby major universities and numerous local educational institutions, some of the world's most advanced engineering technology, a creative spark represented by its historical and current progressive music scene, and at present a great deal of vacant urban land (Florida 2010). Rebuilding Detroit, given its challenges and assets, will take time and creative, community-based, bottom-up development processes that must be bolstered by city and state policies that support neighborhood-based, small-scale redevelopment efforts within a frame of comprehensive regional development.

Woven through the history of Detroit, as well as other U.S. industrial cities, is the undercurrent of social inequality and social exclusion. Although Detroit had a "large and prosperous black middle class [and] higher than normal wages for unskilled black workers due to the auto industry" (Fine 1989: 32), African Americans felt dissatisfaction with Detroit's social conditions even before the 1967 riots. They felt discriminated against in regard to policing, housing, employment, spatial segregation within the city, mistreatment by merchants, shortage of recreational facilities, quality of public education, access to medical services, and the way President Lyndon Johnson's war on poverty operated in their city (Fine 1989). Following massive white flight of the 1960s and 1970s, which hollowed out the city's core and concentrated disadvantaged populations within the city, the conditions have continued to deteriorate, and dissatisfaction has grown as a result

of ineffective redevelopment strategies. Recurrent patterns of spatial and social inequity plague many cities that have, like Detroit, chosen not to focus on their inherent strengths or to support job creation, improved education, and small-scale, resident-driven development. Even strategies that are local and neighborhood-based must be implemented carefully, lest gentrification make an area unaffordable to its low- and moderate-income residents.

Attracting middle- and upper-income households back to city neighborhoods is a common urban redevelopment strategy. Diversifying the income range of city dwellers to include households with more disposable income offers one way to maintain the economic health of cities and to increase a city's tax base (Betancur 2002). However, this should be accomplished while securing a place for low- and moderate-income residents in their own neighborhoods. The first step in avoiding various pitfalls that isolate and exclude on the basis of social and economic characteristics is to recognize the benefit of supporting a diverse urban population. The second step is to develop a comprehensive strategy that addresses social and economic equity concerns. The next section examines two case studies that demonstrate strategies for accomplishing this second step.

Creative Economy and Social Equity

The restructuring of urban fabric that has accompanied macro-scale economic changes over the last decades of the twentieth century has exacerbated urban social inequality by creating and maintaining patterns of social and spatial exclusion. The persistence of spatial segregation, poverty, homelessness, urban crime, and neighborhood change through gentrification have been set within a debate about the "worthiness" of those who have been marginalized by these changes (Thorns 2002). Such gentrification within former warehouse and industrial districts generally follows after pioneering artists take up residence. Without specific policies and strategies to safeguard the affordability of these districts, these artists often are displaced from these districts as traditional developers use public and private funds to transform them into mixed-use villages, as Gillem and Hedrick note in chapter 7.

In order to rectify structural forces that undergird inequalities, there is a need to change the way economic and social opportunities are structured and wealth is generated (Thorns 2002). Although economic and social systems have evolved to utilize human creativity as never before, we are failing to engage the opportunity of the so-called creative age to uniformly "raise living standards, build a more humane and sustainable economy, and make our lives more complete" (Florida 2002: xiii). Rather than solving the myriad structural inequalities that exist, the creative economy has tended to amplify social and economic inequality by failing to recognize and address "externalities" (Florida 2005: 171) such as increased housing costs, economic displacement, traffic congestion, and stress. Direct confrontation of these externalities at the beginning phases of development through comprehensive planning and government support is needed. The following two case studies, Detroit's Eastern Market District Redevelopment and Boston's Dudley Street Initiative, highlight creative solutions that build on local strengths to recognize and address structural inequalities. The degrees to which comprehensive planning and local government support have been or could be beneficial to the bottom-up, community-based efforts will be discussed.

Case Study 1: Detroit's Eastern Market

As noted, Detroit is widely recognized as one of the most distressed cities in the United States. Even given this notoriety, "a more organic grassroots kind of redevelopment is taking place" in Detroit (Florida 2010: 80). However, such redevelopment, "left to its own devices will neither realize the promise [of innovative, wealth-creating productivity] nor solve the myriad social problems" (Florida 2005: 171) present in a city like Detroit. This case study will highlight the redevelopment of the Eastern Market and its surrounding district to illustrate efforts to address social, spatial, and economic inequity in Detroit. This redevelopment effort, spearheaded by the Eastern-Market Board and the market's director, builds on three of Detroit's existing strengths: underutilized historic building stock, activist residents and nonprofit leaders, and plentiful vacant land. First, central to the plan is the Eastern Market, a public market facility that has provided city residents with access to the agricultural bounty of the region since 1891 (Johnson and Thomas 2005). Second, the plan develops linkages between the Eastern Market vendors and merchants, the city of Detroit (who owns the market's assets), and the greater community of residents and local nonprofit organizations. Finally, the plan employs new strategies to redevelop large tracts of vacant land in neighborhoods adjacent to the market by creating a system of linked denser urban villages with networks of open space usable for agricultural production, recreation, and rebuilding a healthy urban ecosystem.

In the pre–World War II era, the Eastern Market grew to be one of the largest farmer's markets in the United States, where fresh produce was delivered for resale to wholesalers, retailers, and the general public. However, following World War II, with the advent of prepackaged foods and the modern supermarket, the nature of the Eastern Market and the surrounding district changed. Fewer members of the general public shopped at the market, and more wholesalers and large-scale food processors located in the area. In the recent past, the Eastern Market has become known to the general public as an important hub for the southeastern Michigan food distribution industry rather than a farmer's market serving the public throughout the week. The comprehensive redevelopment plan for the market and its surrounding district, which is embodied in the title "Eastern Market 360°," is to transform the liveliness of Saturday morning at the market into a vitality that extends throughout the week. In addition, the overarching strategy underpinning the reinvigoration of the market and its district is to help rebuild the region's local food system by creating facilities and strategies that help increase both the *supply* of and the *demand* for healthy food. This philosophy, related to the international "slow food" movement, links to grassroots efforts across the United States and particularly in Michigan and Wisconsin. However, the Eastern Market's bottom-up strategy to focus on developing and promoting the local food system is unique in urban redevelopment, even when compared to redevelopment in St. Louis's Soulard Market district (fig. 5.2) where its renaissance was kindled by the return of middle-

and upper-income citizens in the 1970s (Rowley 2010).

In Detroit, this redevelopment strategy grows not only out of the desire to reinvigorate the urban environment through redevelopment but also out of a very real need for residents of the city's neighborhoods to gain access to fresh, healthy foods in a city with a surfeit of convenience and liquor stores and without a single major grocery store (Clynes 2009). As the recession of the early twenty-first century has battered Detroit, the inability of residents to locate and afford healthy food has increased, and the goals of the Eastern Market redevelopment have solidified around strategies to increase access to healthy food while simultaneously establishing a foodcentric creative district that supports "foodie entrepreneurs" and associated startup businesses (Gentile 2009).

The Eastern Market 360° Plan is based on physical construction and reconstruction, but the purpose of the expanded and improved facilities at the market is to help redevelop Detroit's local food system, with the Eastern Market as its hub (fig. 5.2). While the market is already part of the system's retail, wholesale, and food processing functions, the redeveloped market will also provide nutrition education, grower training, organic waste composting facilities, specialty food production, and incubation of small food businesses (Kavanaugh 2009). Aspects of the 360° Capital Improvement Plan that specifically address social and economic equity and quality of life for Detroit's low-, moderate-, and middle-income residents include the plan's focus on improving public health by increasing supply and demand for nutritious food and on expanding district business activity. The plan calls for adding the Market Hall Education Center Complex and

FIGURE 5.2. The Soulard Square Market in St. Louis, Missouri, was founded during the 1970s and serves as a prototype for neighborhood urban markets today. (Courtesy of Paul J. Armstrong)

for greater utilization of the wholesale market to get food into underserved areas of the city. Thus, expanding these facilities and programs will increase access for all to knowledge about improving nutritional health and healthier cuisine and how to prepare it. Increasing district business activity includes expanding the retail farmer's market operation beyond Saturdays, increasing special events opportunities, incubating food-related businesses, and adding appropriate mixed-use development to increase customer traffic and economic vitality (Eastern Market Corporation 2009). This goal incorporates corresponding increased opportunities for job creation and income-earning possibilities for local residents.

One other important initiative in the redevelopment of the Eastern Market campus is a partnership with the nonprofit Greening of Detroit to create the Detroit Market Garden adjacent to the campus. Detroit Market Garden will be the city's first production-focused small-scale farm, where a variety of fruits, vegetables, and cut flowers will be grown and harvested for sale in the Eastern Market District (Eastern Market Corporation 2007). This market garden will also act as a demonstration for local low- and moderate-income gardeners to highlight intensive planting strategies and the use of hoop houses to extend Detroit's growing season to 11 months. The garden will also produce starter plants and offer them to local gardeners. Through

FIGURE 5.3. DSI-Youth Farming Project, Detroit, August 2010.
(Courtesy of Sunita L. Karan)

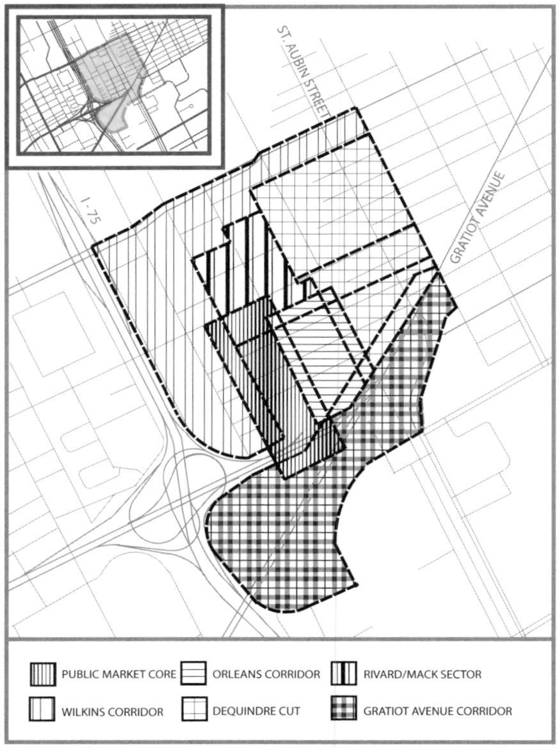

FIGURE 5.4. Map of Eastern Market District Redevelopment
Area of Detroit, highlighting the six redevelopment subareas.
(Courtesy of Charles Dana)

these strategies the market garden will facilitate more productive household and community gardens within the city, increasing low-cost access to healthy fresh food and possibly resulting in small-scale, high-yield urban farms (fig. 5.3).

The redevelopment of the Eastern Market Campus is intended to increase the facility's market share within the regional food network and to strengthen an important anchor that can help transform the historic core of Detroit using a food focus. The redeveloped Eastern Market Campus is the centerpiece of a plan to redevelop the Eastern Market District, an area bounded by Interstate

Route 75, St. Aubin Street, and Gratiot Avenue and at this time somewhat cut off from adjacent areas (fig. 5.4). The primary initial strategy employed within the Eastern Market District Redevelopment Plan is to simplify zoning in the area; this would eliminate current conflicts between different sets of regulations and organizations such as city zoning, the Eastern Market Historic District, the Urban Renewal Area, the Empowerment Zone, and the Recreation Department Area, to name a few. This strategy would in turn lead to an increase in the area's mix of uses and would allow greater connectivity to other neighborhoods (Kavanaugh 2009).

The proposed rezoning would eliminate purely industrial zones in favor of zones that will increase the density of business uses and expand areas devoted to residential and mixed-use residential and business. The plan seeks to balance opportunities for economic development within the district while maintaining the area's "authentic grittiness" in order to attract more creative people to live, work, visit, and invest in the district. Further, the plan seeks to create a mixed-use, mixed-income neighborhood that improves the business climate and enlivens streets and public spaces through the careful blending of housing options and businesses that respect the "food identity" of the district. Finally, the plan seeks to enhance connectivity within the area and between it and other parts of the city so that traffic flow will be improved for vehicles, cyclists, and pedestrians and so that major corridors will develop a unique sense of place while providing pleasant experiences (Chan Krieger Sieniewicz Architecture & Urban Design 2008).

Within this comprehensive redevelopment plan the Eastern Market plays three roles: (1) the hub of a robust local food system, (2) the heart of a compelling business district, and (3) the keystone to adjacent viable and sustainable neighborhoods (Eastern Market Corporation 2009). The market also becomes the centerpiece of a socially, economically, and physically sustainable redevelopment initiative. This initiative builds on the strength of a locally diverse agricultural asset. It leverages existing facilities and infrastructure in the renovations and additions to the district. The redevelopment plan's improved connectivity to the rest of the city through the rails-to-trails transformation that is proposed for the Dequindre Cut area, as well as the reconnecting of street grids to surrounding neighborhoods, offers the potential of easy access to jobs, food, and housing. The plan focuses on energy efficiency and small-scale energy production. It promotes the development of small, local, independently owned businesses. Addressing the fact that some city residents may have difficulty getting to the market, the plan also incorporates initiatives to bring fresh food from the market into other city neighborhoods through collaborations with local food banks and through the "AM Market Fresh Farm Stand," which is a cooperative effort to get products from the growers at Eastern Market into a wide variety of venues throughout the region,

including convenience stores in inner-city neighborhoods (Eastern Market Corporation 2009). Finally, the motivation at its heart is to improve the physical and economic health of all of Detroit's residents.

This case study of the Eastern Market has highlighted nonprofit-driven, neighborhood-level planning and redevelopment, which has as its centerpiece a neighborhood anchor and urban historic landmark. Although the motivation for the plan is a broad concern for improving residents' health and access to healthy food citywide, the plan relies relatively little on comprehensive city planning and policy changes. Nonetheless, it has great potential to spur new development around the market because it incorporates support for job creation through new food-based businesses with its incubator and economic development support and because it develops a mixed-use district and creates conduits to move goods from the district into the larger city. The next case study, the Dudley Street Initiative, conversely illustrates a redevelopment strategy that has been strengthened and made more effective as a result of city-level policy initiatives and changes.

Case Study 2: The Dudley Street Initiative

The one and a half square miles of the Dudley Street Neighborhood within the Roxbury and North Dorchester sections of Boston (fig. 5.5) had a population of 12,000 in its core area in 1990 (Medoff and Sklar 1994). While this number represents a population only half what it was in 1950, it is substantially larger than the 125 residents who currently

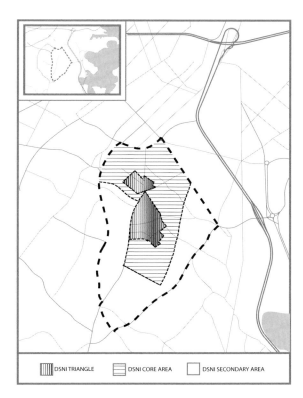

FIGURE 5.5. Map of Dudley Street Neighborhood Initiative Area in Boston. (Courtesy of Charles Dana)

live in Detroit's Eastern Market Redevelopment Area. To understand redevelopment that has occurred under the Dudley Street Initiative beginning in 1984, it is necessary to take several steps back in Boston's post–World War II development history.

At the end of World War II, Boston was in the midst of severe fiscal decline, with the total assessed valuation of real property having fallen about 30% between 1930 and 1960 and with only one private office building having been built in the city in that same time period. From 1950 to 1960 Boston's population decreased by 13% as white, middle-class residents moved from the city to the suburbs. In the same decade the number of jobs in the city also declined by 10% (Krumholz and Clavel 1994). Understanding the impact of these economic conditions on their investments, business and corporate communities mobilized to elect a succession of two probusiness mayors who would be supportive of a vigorous redevelopment agenda to sustain the growth strategy of the city's private business and real estate interests. John Hynes, mayor from 1949 to 1959, and John Collins, mayor from 1959 to 1968, successively enacted policies and redevelopment schemes that paved the way for large-scale developments like the Prudential Center and urban renewal schemes like the West End clearance project.

These efforts, dubbed the "New Boston," exacerbated poverty by draining the city of working-class manufacturing jobs and drastically reducing the supply of housing affordable to working-class and low-income families. Fried (1972) documented the negative impact on the more than 2,600 working-class West End families who lived in that area prior to its clearance, one of the first massive federally funded urban renewal endeavors in the country. Such large-scale "slum" clearance projects generally targeted socially cohesive working-class neighborhoods in desirable locations near downtown. Cleared land was then made ready for redevelopment by the increasingly influential business community.

During Collins' administration, a group of particularly influential business leaders, known as the Boston Coordinating Committee, "persuaded the state and the city to create a 'superagency,' the Boston Redevelopment Authority (BRA), which combined the city's planning and urban renewal functions" (Krumholz and Clavel 1994). The BRA's

urban renewal program cleared around 25% of the city's land area, sharply reducing affordable rental housing. To spur development of large-scale office towers and luxury housing downtown in cleared areas, Collins offered tax concessions and other incentives. This promotion of upscale office development continued with the administration of Boston's next mayor, Kevin White.

The pattern of redevelopment implemented in Boston between 1950 and 1984 created economic prosperity for some but left a majority of poor and working-class residents unemployed or underemployed and in competition for an ever-decreasing number of low-cost rental units in the city. These inequitable conditions paved the way for a more socially conscious political and development agenda, which many Bostonians hoped for when they elected Ray Flynn mayor in 1983. Flynn had been a progressive city council member who "was always introducing bills to protect tenants from condo conversions and rent increases" (Krumholz and Clavel 1994: 134). The Flynn agenda attempted to share prosperity between downtown businesses and the working-class and poor residents and neighborhoods through development linkage, inclusionary zoning, rent control, and control of condominium conversions.

The Flynn administration also developed a property disposition process that favored neighborhood-based non-profit development corporations (CDCs). The intention was to give neighborhood residents the ability to set the development agenda. At the same time the Flynn administration put measures in place to nurture and support development by CDCs, building development capacity, packaging available subsidies, and working to get long-term affordability guidelines in housing

guaranteed by FHA, Fannie Mae, and HUD. Flynn also campaigned to get banks to invest in the city's neighborhoods by commissioning a study of disinvestment measures among Boston's banks (e.g., redlining, discrimination, and disparity in lending terms). The Dudley Street neighborhood and surrounding areas of Roxbury and Dorchester had suffered large-scale disinvestment during the probusiness mayoral administrations of Hynes, Collins, and White. Concurrent with the final years of the White administration and the beginning of the Flynn administration, service providers and leaders in the Dudley Street neighborhood began to meet and organize in response to negative conditions. In the midst of White's more proneighborhood political agenda, the Dudley Street Neighborhood Initiative was taking shape.

The Dudley Street area was home to successive groups of immigrants who relocated from ethnic neighborhoods in the old part of Boston. From the late 1800s through the 1950s, the neighborhood sustained a mix of ethnic and immigrant groups, including Irish, Italian, and African Americans. Latinos and Cape Verdean immigrants became a significant part of the Dudley population during the 1960s and 1970s (Medoff and Sklar 1994). As a result of urban renewal "slum" clearance in some neighborhoods and gentrification in other neighborhoods, African Americans and a variety of Latino groups removed in the renewal process moved to the Dudley Street neighborhood. By 1990 the neighborhood's population had a concentration of Latinos (30%) and of non-Hispanic blacks (50%) that included Cape Verdeans. The Latinos were a mix of Puerto Rican, Dominican, Honduran, Guatemalan, Cuban, and Mexican. The non-Hispanic black population was composed primarily of African Americans and Cape Verdeans, each making up about 25% of the Dudley core area population.

This mix of English, Spanish, and Portuguese (Cape Verdean) speakers initially came together in the 1980s around the issue of illegal dumping of garbage. Decades of disinvestment in the neighborhood, resulting from redlining by banks and insurance companies and lack of maintenance by absentee landlords, resulted in large tracts of vacant land and abandoned structures. In addition, BRA's urban renewal plans for the neighborhood led to tensions, speculation, and one of the highest arson rates in the country (City of Boston Arson Prevention Commission 1986; Medoff and Sklar 1994). By the late 1970s, the heart of the Dudley neighborhood had "approximately 840 vacant lots covering 177 acres of land" (Medoff and Sklar 1994: 32). This desolate landscape of weedy vacant lots became a dumping ground for trash, old cars, and construction debris, resulting in unhealthy and intolerable conditions for residents. However, it took the impetus of an alliance of service providers, a private foundation, and community organizing to bring residents together to fight for resident-directed redevelopment.

In early 1981, a number of neighborhood organizations, service providers, and a church came together to form a coalition focused on neighborhood crime issues but did not generate much momentum. Later that year one of the involved groups, La Alianza Hispana, a Hispanic social service agency, commissioned an in-depth planning study by MIT students titled *From the Ground Up*. This document emphasized the "potential asset" in the neighborhood's large tracts of vacant land and suggested putting vacant land in a trust for future

housing and other development. In 1984, again with technical support from MIT's Department of Urban Studies and Planning, a strategic planning conference was organized for community stakeholders and activists. Shortly after this conference, the director of La Alianza Hispana contacted the Riley Foundation, one of Massachusetts's larger charitable trusts, seeking funds to replace carpet in the organization's facilities.

This initial contact was the catalyst that eventually moved Dudley community stakeholders and activists forward to organize the Dudley Advisory Group. This group set the boundaries of a Dudley Street Neighborhood core area and secondary area (fig. 5.5) and attempted to create and put a governance structure in place for what it called the Dudley Street Neighborhood Initiative (DSNI), a coalition to build community consensus toward an overall plan of action for the core area. At a community-wide meeting to announce the formation of the coalition and ostensibly to elect board members, some of the 200 community residents who attended challenged the legitimacy of the proposed board (mainly members of the Dudley Advisory Group) because they felt that a majority of the board should be neighborhood residents. This was a turning point when neighborhood residents began to claim ownership of the renewal process in their neighborhood. Eventually a board structure was approved that included a majority of neighborhood residents.

With initial funding and assistance from the Riley Foundation, the DSNI began fervent community organizing, first around the neighborhood illegal dumping issues. Once they got action from City Hall and the mayor's office to stop the illegal dumping, they moved on to the next issues, ad-

dressing other neighborhood quality-of-life concerns. These organizing activities also worked to unify diverse residents and neighborhood business owners, as they were brought together in the common pursuit of making the neighborhood better in the present while also creating excitement about plans for longer term renewal.

To break the pattern of outsider agency domination and to empower residents in making decisions about the redevelopment of their neighborhood, the DSNI effectively made a bargain with the city that the city would cease selling off vacant land until the people of the neighborhood were able to complete a comprehensive redevelopment plan and exercise community control over the future vision for their neighborhood (Dudley Street Neighborhood Initiative 2008; Medoff and Sklar 1994). Funding from a number of philanthropic foundations, along with an impressive record of neighborhood unity and grassroots organizing victories, allowed the DSNI to hire a consultant to engage the community in a bottom-up, participatory planning process to arrive at a shared vision for the neighborhood. The city's public facilities office somewhat reluctantly agreed to take a secondary role in this process, to make relevant data available for the planning process, and to review and evaluate existing city policy to understand what might need modification in order for the community to achieve its goals. The DSNI board worked with the planning consultant's team to develop a vision for the neighborhood's future and to identify neighborhood assets. The board's vision included "low-density, mixed-income housing with owner and renter occupancy, back-yards and open space; a mix of retail stores and light industry with significant local ownership; and expanded community services with particular emphasis on the youth and elderly" (Medoff and Sklar 1994: 100). A planning committee made up of residents and experienced development professionals was charged with broad development responsibility, as well as review of activities within the larger planning process. Subcommittees chaired by board members and made up of resident members of the DSNI were responsible for working with the consultants in four key areas: housing, economic development, human services, and land use/planning. Residents were primary, active participants in the planning process, which continued for nine months. The consultants worked to encourage the residents to see new opportunities in their neighborhood.

The next parts of the planning process, in mid-1987, included a series of design *charrettes*, in which architectural consultants and students worked with residents to translate resident descriptions into visual representations. The most significant theme that grew out of this process was the vision that continues to guide DSNI's management of physical and social neighborhood improvements to this day. The revitalization of the Dudley Street Neighborhood into a "sustainable urban village" (Meyer et al. 2000: 1), which combines housing, shopping, open space, and a multiuse community center, guides a range of decisions about future development that will bring "not just quality affordable housing, but quality of life" to the neighborhood (Medoff and Sklar 1994: 108).

Since the completion of *The Dudley Street Neighborhood Initiative Revitalization Plan* (DAC International 1987), many physical improvements have taken place in the neighborhood. "More than half of the original 1,300 vacant parcels have been transformed into over 454 new quality affordable homes, community centers, a Dudley Town Common, a community greenhouse, parks, play-grounds, [community] gardens, parking lots, an orchard, and allied public spaces" (Urban Strategies Council 2007). Figure 5.6 shows the formerly vacant lots that have been transformed into a community garden, as well as a renovated triple-decker, typical of housing in the neighborhood prior to redevelopment.

Many of these efforts have been completed through partnerships with other organizations that have similar goals and ideals. In keeping with the history of this grassroots movement, neighborhood residents continue to guide development through the DSNI board and committees and engage with other nonprofit and for-profit developers to complete physical improvements. Today, the DSNI primarily focuses its efforts in three areas: community economic development, resident leadership, and youth opportunities and development.

Sustainable economic development in the Dudley Street community focuses on "generating home-grown economic power" (Meyer et al. 2000: 7) via local ownership and control and local circulation of dollars engendering more living-wage jobs for residents. Continuing resident leadership necessitates efforts to cultivate leaders from among residents of the neighborhood; the DSNI believes cultivating new leaders prevents existing leaders from becoming entrenched and offers new life for the neighborhood in organizing, planning, and implementation. The DSNI's efforts focused on youth address a critical, long-term concern in the Dudley Street Neighborhood: lack of opportunities for the neighborhood's youth to develop into the next generation of leaders. The DSNI has an extensive series of programs focused on youth development, involving efforts to support youth in organizing activities that contribute to the neighborhood, youth entrepreneurship, and postsecond-ary education, including the youth urban farming project developed on vacant land within the neighborhood. With its current focus on socially sustaining programs, DSNI and the Dudley Street Neighborhood are looking ahead to a promising future. Solid community organizing has built a grassroots redevelopment process that has at its heart socially equitable development outcomes that offer improved quality of life for neighborhood residents. The DSNI's efforts are particularly concerned with offering a better quality of life to the neighborhood's low- and moderate-income, ethnically and racially diverse residents who were for so many decades treated as second-class citizens of the city of Boston.

Lesson for SynergiCity

The lessons these two case studies offer for SynergiCity are as much about process as product; they both describe processes and outcomes that are more equitable than what has become business as usual in the redevelopment of many cities in the United States. These efforts illustrate redevelopment initiated by a nonprofit entity in the case of Eastern Market in Detroit and citizen-initiated redevelopment in the case of the DSNI in the greater Boston area. In both cases, the initiators had something other than financial profit as the primary motivator. And because they have controlled the process, they have been able to maintain focus on socially equitable outcomes, even as they have engaged, or may in the future engage, for-profit developers to take on pieces of the larger plan. While these two efforts are not primarily motivated by financial gain, we can draw three important lessons from them that can be applied to any redevelop-

FIGURE 5.6. The Dudley Street Neighborhood Initiative Revitalization Plan in Boston has transformed formerly vacant lots into community gardens and spearheaded renovation of existing multifamily housing in the neighborhood. (Courtesy of Sunita L. Karan)

the city of Boston in the late 1970s. The BRA was preparing to bulldoze sections of an urban neighborhood that was home to more than 12,000 people without regard for the needs or desires of those people or consideration of what would happen to them if their neighborhood was cleared.

Boston mayors and city council members listened and responded to powerful business interests in the city at the expense of working-class and low-income city residents, who were denied a voice and were left in ever more perilous economic, social, and physical conditions. The first lesson for SynergiCity should be incorporating a process and products that could be characterized as Equitable Urban Design and Architecture. It is more inclusive of diverse voices and offers the opportunity to tap the creative potential of the two-thirds of the workforce who are currently outside the creative sector (Florida 2005) by bringing them into the process of redevelopment. This lesson opens redevelopment to organic, bottom-up, community-based efforts. These efforts must be supported by local government policies and processes, as the Dudley Street case shows. But it also can be facilitated by university-based community design efforts in partnership with resident- and nonprofit-led efforts. Some for-profit developers are making an effort to involve local residents in development decisions. However, unless local citizens see themselves as partners, they will most likely not view such efforts as equitable.

ment effort, whether for-profit or nonprofit, to create more socially equitable processes and products that offer new economic viability for urban neighborhoods and their residents.

PROMOTE EQUITABLE URBAN DESIGN AND ARCHITECTURE

The first lesson offered for SynergiCity is the need for a process that involves all stakeholders in a meaningful way in creating the plan for redevel-

opment and the resulting physical interventions. The professionals involved in this process must work to move resources, political power, and political participation away from business elites who have frequently benefited from public policy and redevelopment and toward the needs of middle, moderate- and low-income people (Krumholz and Clavel 1994), who are often deprived of basic quality of life by redevelopment. Illustrating such a reversal of process and product, the DSNI case study describes what was considered a "throwaway" in

SAFEGUARD THE LOCAL POPULATION

The second lesson responds to Florida's concern for the "externalities of the creative age" (Florida 2005: 171). As a city works to create the environment that will attract creative workers and as a consequence attract companies involved in the creative economy, it may prompt gentrification as an area becomes more desirable. When wealthier people buy property in a less-prosperous community, the average income increases and average family size decreases. Gentrification may reduce industrial land use when an area is redeveloped for commerce and housing, as the Eastern Market Redevelopment case study illustrates. The gradual transformation of industrial buildings to mixed-use residential and commercial can reduce available industrial, living-wage jobs. Gentrification of areas as a result of redevelopment also often results in the informal economic eviction of lower-income residents, because of increased rents, house prices, and property costs. Such socioeconomic changes often spawn new local businesses that cater to a more affluent base of consumers and decrease affordability of goods and services for less wealthy residents.

While it can be desirable to attract a more economically diverse population to neighborhoods through the redevelopment process, if the promise of the creative age is to be realized, no one can be left unconsidered or suffering negatively through the redevelopment process. The lesson about safeguarding the local population suggests that the SynergiCity concept must incorporate, among other things, the means to support a diverse series of affordable housing options. This can be accomplished, as the Dudley Street case shows, through linkage and inclusionary zoning policies and support for neighborhood-based CDCs through local policy initiatives, and through the deliberate inclusion of housing choices that will appeal to a diverse socioeconomic population. In the case of the DSNI, the resident-directed nonprofit development corporation was one important vehicle for the development of an appropriate array of affordable housing choices. Likewise, the support of several philanthropic foundations was critical to maintaining housing affordability and promoting appropriate economic development for the neighborhood, the other component that must be considered. Economic development that creates new jobs for the local population and provides a net tax increase to support basic infrastructure and services is a critical component to safeguard the quality of life of the local population. Development incentives must be carefully structured so that they do not relinquish tax revenues that are greatly needed to support city infrastructure and services (e.g., fire, police) and public goods like financially sound public education systems.

CREATE ENVIRONMENTS THAT EDUCATE

The final lesson that these case studies offer for the SynergiCity concept has to do with the need for redeveloped environments to do more than provide for utilitarian functions. Both case studies feature physical and social environments that educate present and future generations about ways to reverse the negative consequences of current development patterns. The Eastern Market offers components of the physical environment that educate local urban gardeners about intensive planting techniques, methods to extend the local growing season, and organic waste composting—all means to increase garden yield for households, often of limited means, that will benefit from greater access to healthy food that they grow themselves.

The Eastern Market likewise demonstrates an environment that intends to produce 15% of its energy from renewable sources (solar panels and biogas generation) and to increase comfort while reducing energy needs by introducing passive heating and cooling schemes. The Eastern Market development also offers more traditional learning environments such as classrooms and teaching kitchens that will be used to educate local residents about nutritious foods and how to prepare them.

The DSNI illustrates a social environment that educates neighborhood residents, and youth particularly, about their talents as leaders and their value within the neighborhood social network. The DSNI's programs to foster resident leadership in adults and youth demonstrate to residents their worth in the community. This is critical to community participation and contradicts many messages that low-income minority adults and youth receive from the broader social environment about their lack of value vis-à-vis middle- and upper-income urban area residents. Like the Eastern Market, the DSNI also provides support for more traditional forms of education through its youth scholarship program and the neighborhood mentoring activities of those youth who are scholarship recipients. The Dudley Street Neighborhood redevelopment likewise also includes aspects of the physical environment that educate with regard to equitable and resource efficient development through reuse of existing housing and additions of new affordable housing and through the local urban farms and community gardens that now exist on vacant land in the neighborhood. These aspects demonstrate careful and equitable use of resources that benefit low- and moderate-income residents by supporting basic needs for a healthy living environment.

The planners, architects, and landscape architects who work on this kind of development effort must conceive of environments, like those presented here, that not only amply satisfy functional needs but go beyond them to educate all who experience the environment about development options that have a smaller resource footprint and promote an equitable social arrangement.

The Socioeconomic Opportunities of SynergiCity

This chapter has demonstrated that with some very deliberate efforts, the SynergiCity concept offers incredible socioeconomic opportunities for cities and the broad social and economic spectrum of urban residents. As Florida (2002: xiii) points out, no one is going to succeed in modifying the social and economic system "to complete the transformation to a society that taps and rewards our full creative potential" without taking careful and deliberate actions that target the entire population. Such a modified social and economic system will need to recognize the worth and potential contribution of all citizens. It will need to nurture the potential contributions of those who are not yet part of the "creative class." Conditions to nurture creative contributions will require that planners, policymakers, politicians, educators, architects, urban designers, and developers come to terms with embedded structural inequalities and work to reverse those inequalities through changes in public policy, education, and the built environment. With such

changes in place, the socioeconomic promise of SynergiCity can be broadly realized.

References

Betancur, J. J. 2002. "Can Gentrification Save Detroit? Definition and Experiences from Chicago." *Journal of Law in Society* 4(1): 1-12.

Chan Krieger Sieniewicz Architecture & Urban Design. 2008. *Eastern Market District Economic Development Strategy*. Cambridge, MA: Eastern Market Corporation.

Cisneros, H. G. 1996, December. "The University and the Urban Challenge." In *A Collection of Essays*. Special issue, *Cityscape* 1-4: 1-23.

City of Boston Arson Prevention Commission. 1986. *Report to the BRA on the Status of Arson in Dudley Square*. Boston: Boston Redevelopment Authority.

Clynes, M. 2009. "Fresh, Fresh, Exciting: Near East Side Dwellers Get Boxes of Green Goodness." Available at the website of Issue Media Group, www.modeldmedia.com/features/freshfood20209 .aspx. Accessed February 8, 2010.

DAC International. 1987. *The Dudley Street Neighborhood Initiative Revitalization Plan*. Boston: DSNI.

Dudley Street Neighborhood Initiative. 2008. "DSNI Historic Timeline." Available at the website of Dudley Street Neighborhood Initiative www.dsni. org/timeline.shtml.date. Accessed June 10, 2010.

Eastern Market Corporation. 2007. "Detroit Eastern Market."

———. 2009. "Eastern Market: Redeveloping America's Largest Public Market." Detroit: Eastern Market Corporation.

Fine, S. 1989. *Violence in the Model City*. Ann Arbor: University of Michigan Press.

Florida, R. 2002. *The Rise of the Creative Class*. New York: Basic Books.

———. 2005. *Cities and the Creative Class*. New York: Routledge.

———. 2010. *The Great Reset: How New Ways of Living and Working Drive Post-crash Prosperity*. New York: HarperCollins.

Fried, M. 1972. "Grieving for a Lost Home." In *People and Buildings*, ed. R. Gutman, 229-48. New York: Basic Books.

Gentile, M. 2009. "Saturday Morning Marketing: Entrepreneurs Use Eastern Market to Grow." Available at the website of Issue Media Group, www .modeldmedia.com/features/easternmarket20209 .aspx. Accessed February 8, 2010.

Gregory, D. 2009. "Quality of Life." In *The Dictionary of Human Geography*, ed. D. Gregory, R. Johnston, and G. Pratt, 606-7. Malden, MA: Blackwell.

Johnson, L., and M. Thomas. 2005. *Detroit's Eastern Market: A Farmers Market Shopping and Cooking Guide*. 2nd ed. Detroit: Wayne State University Press.

Kavanaugh, K. B. 2009, March 17. "Eastern Market Plan Calls for $50M in Investment over 10 Years." *Model D*, Development News sec., www.modeldmedia.com/devnews/emkt36018309 .aspx.

Keating, W. D., and N. Krumholz, eds. 1999. *Rebuilding Urban Neighborhoods: Achievements, Opportunities, and Limits*. Thousand Oaks, CA: Sage.

Krumholz, N. 1999. "Equitable Approaches to Local Economic Development." *Policy Studies Journal* 27(1): 83-95.

Krumholz, N., and P. Clavel. 1994. *Reinventing Cities: Equity Planners Tell Their Stories*. Philadelphia: Temple University Press.

Man-Neef, M. A. 1991. *Human Scale Development: Conceptions, Applications and Further Reflections*. New York: Apex Press.

Medoff, P., and H. Sklar. 1994. *Streets of Hope: The Fall and Rise of an Urban Neighborhood*. Boston: South End Press.

Meyer, D. A., J. L. Blake, H. Caine, and B. W. Pryor. 2000. *Program Profile: Dudley Street Neighborhood Initiative*. Columbia, MD: Enterprise Foundation.

Rittel, H. W. J., and M. M. Webber. 1973. "Dilemmas in a General Theory of Planning." *Policy Sciences* 4: 155-69.

Schon, D. A. 1987. *Educating the Reflective Practitioner*. San Francisco: Jossey-Bass.

Thorns, D. C. 2002. *The Transformation of Cities: Urban Theory and Urban Life*. New York: Palgrave Macmillan.

Urban Strategies Council. 2007. "Boston's Dudley Street Neighborhood Initiative and Dudley Neighbors, Inc." Unpublished summary. Urban Strategies Council. Available at www.urbanstrategies.org/programs/econopp /slfp/documents/DSNIDNIDesc507.doc. Accessed January 6, 2012.

CHAPTER SIX

Restoring Urbanism in U.S. Cities

JOHN O. NORQUIST

SynergiCity as Prototype

Peoria, Illinois, is the very symbol of the midwestern American city. "But will it play in Peoria?" was the question vaudeville show producers asked themselves before launching a nationwide show tour. Now the phrase is used as inside-the-Beltway shorthand for whether an issue with appeal to Washington, D.C., elites can also appeal to the average middle-class American. However they've played politically, federal programs and policies have significantly impacted Peoria and other U.S. cities.

This book's lead authors, Paul Hardin Kapp and Paul J. Armstrong, researched Peoria, Illinois. In chapter 2 they describe Peoria as a potential "Synergy City": a city that embraces its complexity, diversity, and connectedness to create a fertile and attractive environment for economic and cultural development. A nineteenth-century river town and farm service center with an industrial sector led by heavy equipment manufacturer Caterpillar, the greater Peoria area has enjoyed a steadily prosperous economy in much of the postwar period. The city's

population was about 113,000 in 2000 (2000 U.S. Census) and peaked at around 127,000 in 1970. The 2010 census indicates that the population, at around 115,000, is rising again. The five-county metropolitan population has continued to grow and now exceeds 375,000. Peoria resembles many other Midwest cities, some with modestly growing metropolitan areas, others experiencing stagnant or declining city populations. Toledo, Ohio, Racine, Wisconsin, Evansville, Indiana, and many other cities share this situation. Each has also experienced decentralization of its population and decline in its downtown and central neighborhoods. Large Midwest cities like St. Louis, Buffalo, Milwaukee, Detroit, Pittsburgh, Cincinnati, and Cleveland have also lost significant population to their expanding suburbs. In all cases the reasons for decline are complex.

Overall reduced growth in nationwide manufacturing explains part of it. But Midwest industrial cities should be cautious about writing off their manufacturing sectors. Much of the service sector growth in the last decade was debt-leveraged real estate and banking activity that is now shrink-

ing relative to manufacturing. Furthermore, many manufacturing processes are quieter and safer than those of the past and can be allowed and encouraged in urban neighborhoods like Peoria's River Warehouse District. Form-based code that encourages mixed uses, including live/work units, can serve as a great setting for the synergy the authors advocate (fig. 6.1).

Development: The Impact of the Automobile

Richard Florida's writings promote development that attracts the well-educated professional class. He cites examples like New York City's Soho with its condos, art studios, and chic shops converted from warehouses and factories. Soho is now mostly housing, galleries, and shops, with few industrial activities. Yet we should remember that it was Soho's urban industrial atmosphere that helped attract artists and hipsters in the first place. Craftsman, artists, and artisans can fit nicely with

FIGURE 6.1. The Soulard neighborhood in St. Louis, Missouri, incorporates a residential, retail, and restaurant mix that enhances the character of the district and animates the streets. (Courtesy of Paul J. Armstrong)

small-scale manufacturing. Milwaukee's Third Ward warehouse district includes galleries, pricey condos, shops, and restaurants but still retains the wholesale produce commission, machine tool shops, and even a small-scale steel producer (plate 14). In the 1960s Milwaukee tried to remove most of what had been a lively Italian neighborhood.

Housing was removed to make room for suburban-style industrial lots. The old buildings left were to be designated a "combat zone" for porn shops and gentlemen's clubs. Fortunately, the city ran out of money and ran into resistance from property owners before the job could be completed. When I became mayor in 1988, the plan had shifted to

rehabilitation and renovation. Property developers were already creating Milwaukee's version of Soho. To facilitate the transition to housing and galleries, the city was seeking to move the produce commission to a remote site. The argument was that the morning truck movements and hustle and bustle of Commission Row were incompatible with residential living. I opposed this plan, and the commission merchants stayed. I felt that turning the mixed-use Third Ward into a condo ghetto was as mistaken as the earlier attempts at making it into an industrial zone. The Third Ward has prospered since, adding over 2,000 new residents while retaining much of its industrial character.

In addition, old Midwest cities like Peoria have suffered from federal and state programs and local policies that undermine urbanism and population density while subsidizing and encouraging decentralization, which is often referred to as sprawl. For example, the interstate highway program subsidizes grade-separated highways that facilitate fast long-distance travel by motor vehicle. Connecting distant metros by express roads holds benefits for travelers, and interstates hold a practical utility that makes great sense in rural areas with low costs per acre and few if any existing structures to remove. But in densely populated and built-out cities, the roads are expensive, can undermine property values, and disrupt the efficiency of existing street networks. The large grade, separated highway undermines one of the fundamental assets of cities: location efficiency. If two people hold similar jobs and one person walks across the street to work and the other drives 25 miles, their value to the economy is the same, but their cost is not. The government rewards the longer, energy-consuming trip with a large subsidy and ignores the value

FIGURE 6.2. In Midtown Alley in St. Louis, the developer targeted a specific business market, such as advertisement agencies, commercial photographers, and graphic designers, as tenants to create a critical mass of "destination businesses" for the district. (Courtesy of Paul J. Armstrong)

of the short walk. Federal policy should support economic value without disadvantaging compact urban development served by energy-efficient transit, as Harvard economist Ed Glaeser has argued persuasively ("Why the Anti-urban Bias?," *Boston Globe*, March 9, 2010).

The clear and oft-stated goal of federal transportation policy is to reduce congestion. This narrowly focused objective clashes with the very purpose of cities as a gathering spot for commerce and cultural interaction (fig. 6.2). Let's face it: successful cities become congested because people choose to be in them. Cities like New York, Portland, Oregon, and San Francisco, with vibrant economies and high real estate values per square mile, experience congestion. However, it is not just traffic congestion but also people, money, and job congestion. Cities like Detroit and Buffalo, with shrinking economies and low real estate values, have low congestion. They also may have low congestion because they are crisscrossed with freeways. In one way the freeway building in Detroit and Buffalo has succeeded in achieving the stated goal of government policy, as delineated in the Highway Capacity Manual and AASHTO Geometric Design of Highways and Streets ("Green Book") of the American Association of State Highway and Transportation Officials (AASHTO). The AASHTO system would rate Detroit quite highly; the Green Book lists the following levels of service:

A = Free flow
B = Reasonably free flow
C = Stable flow
D = Approaching unstable flow
E = Unstable flow
F = Forced or breakdown flow

By this measure, congestion is no longer much of a problem for Detroit. While cities like New York City and San Francisco suffer from congestion ratings of E and F, Detroit enjoys almost free-flowing traffic. So while federal and state transportation agencies value low congestion, the market, as measured by real estate prices, values places with high levels of congestion.

Cities are beginning to understand that focusing narrowly on moving traffic on big roads is counterproductive. In 1975 New York City's West Side Highway fell down. The expressway, built in the 1930s, was literally at the end of its design life of 40 years. The elevated roadway blocked views of the Hudson River from Chelsea, Tribeca, and the Battery. The neighborhoods wanted their views back. They wanted to reconnect with the river. After a struggle that lasted more than a decade the decision was made to replace the expressway with a surface thoroughfare, West Street. It paid off in higher real estate values, more development, and more jobs. Similarly, San Francisco and Portland eliminated freeways and gained population, jobs, and housing. In Milwaukee we sought the elimination of the Park East Freeway on the north end of downtown. After a decade of struggle we opened McKinley Boulevard in 2003. It replaced the freeway and is the now a lucrative site for development. Manpower Inc., a Fortune 500 corporation, moved from the suburbs to a site adjacent to the boulevard. Thousands of new housing units have been added to the neighborhood, and traffic distribution has actually improved without the freeway. Many millions of dollars worth of development has occurred along the corridor. One cautionary note: Milwaukee County, which owned almost 90% of the land under the Park East Freeway, encumbered the right-of-way with "community benefits" restrictions on developers, contractors, and landowners that have slowed development in the right-of-way itself. Adjacent properties have surged in value, but the social restrictions have, in my opinion, been a drag on redevelopment.

Traffic that is just moving through cities without visiting holds little or no value for the city, while traffic that is moving to a destination within the city can hold great value. Traffic congestion is a bit like cholesterol. There is both good and bad cholesterol, and cholesterol levels need to be managed, not eliminated. Trying to defeat congestion without considering the nature of particular traffic can generate collateral damage that can severely hurt a city's vitality. Peoria and many other cities removed on-street parking to free up room for through traffic. With the same objective, they have also converted two-way streets to one-ways. Both these actions hinder shoppers' ability to conveniently visit downtown retailers. Jefferson and Adams are the main north-south streets in downtown Peoria. They should be the bustling centers of Peoria's commerce and civic life, but instead they are devoted to moving cars during Peoria's very brief commuter rush period. The threat of congestion was also addressed by the construction of Interstate 74, a giant structure built through downtown. Peoria's one-way pairs and I-74 are clear examples of infrastructure serving the government's narrow-minded battle against congestion even though there is little congestion to be concerned about.

Zoning versus Form-Based Coding

Another example of a policy that undermines urbanism is the application of strictly separated-use zoning to cities. Such zoning was promoted by the federal government starting in 1931 in an executive order issued by President Herbert Hoover. Having served as administrator of the U.S. relief effort to help a devastated Europe recover at the end of World War I, Hoover felt that U.S. cities, like those in Europe, were crowded and dirty and needed to spread out and separate commerce from housing. Although his order was more exhortatory than mandatory, its underlying intent remains embedded in many federally created policies and programs, including the two huge federal guaranteed secondary mortgage markets, Fannie Mae and Freddie Mac, as well as the Department of Housing and Urban Development's 21(d) capital subsidy program for multifamily rental housing. Separate-use zoning has undermined the value of existing neighborhoods and had the effect of mandating new development to be separated into pods, with housing, retail, and office uses strictly separated. This confounds efforts to build a traditional Main Street with apartments built above storefronts. Luxembourg architect-planner Leon Krier compares experiencing the traditional city to eating a delicious chocolate cake, properly assembled from ingredients and carefully baked. He then describes U.S.-style suburban sprawl as like the ingredients of the cake; the sugar, water, cocoa, flour, and baking powder are spread over the kitchen counter and then consumed separately. Not very tasty! It is, Krier says, the complexity, connectivity, and diversity of the properly assembled city that are most enjoyable.

Many federal and state policies have encouraged sprawl and undermined urbanism, but market and demographic forces, as described by Chris Leinberger in *The Option of Urbanism: Investing in the American Dream*, have begun to favor urban places. As household sizes shrink, demand increases for urban forms such as apartments and townhouses. Young adults seeking greater social and job opportunities prefer urban living. Urbanism is more popular, so now would seem to be a good time to change rules and policies that discourage it.

In Milwaukee, as mayor from 1988 to 2004, I set out to reform coding and zoning to encourage mixed uses in commercial and retail corridors (fig. 6.3). The code reforms adopted in Milwaukee "legalized" urban forms like apartments or offices above shops. Setback requirements for buildings were adjusted to encourage construction of buildings along sidewalks and closer to streets. I encouraged city planners to do the same in newer portions of the city, where setbacks from streets had been set as deep as 100 feet, often with no provision for sidewalks.

In some older portions of the city, zoning overlays had been imposed on commercial streets in the 1950s and 1960s that made existing buildings nonconforming use and thus condemnable for the purpose of eventually widening streets. This had the effect of undermining property owners' ability to attract capital to repair or improve their property, as banks and title insurance companies held no interest in assuming risk in property likely to face condemnation. For example, one of Milwaukee's east-west thoroughfares (National Avenue) is 54 feet wide — wide enough for two moving lanes in each direction plus a lane on each block were three and four stories. As a result, the lot sat vacant for 35 years until we relaxed the off-street parking requirement. A four-story mixed-use building was constructed almost immediately after the change. Cities all over America have unnecessarily repressed their own real estate development with counterproductive parking requirements. Don Shoup, a UCLA economist, wrote a book about it, *The High Cost of Free Parking.* He discourages local officials from requiring parking and instead urges them to leave that decision to property owners and their tenants — according to Shoup, most medium and large U.S. cities underprice on-street parking. In addition, they not only have parking regulations that undermine the value of the city but wastefully invest taxpayer funds in underutilized publicly owned parking.

All of these interventions — oversized streets, separated uses, and parking minimums — derive from an attitude that undervalues urbanism. Fortunately, the current markets do place a higher value on urbanism (fig. 6.4).

FIGURE 6.3. Milwaukee's Third Ward uses form-based codes to create a mix of uses that contribute to livability. (Courtesy of Paul J. Armstrong)

side for parking. The City Council of Milwaukee, at the request of the Public Works Department, in 1962 imposed a setback on the south side of the street that would create a travel surface of 72 feet, thus providing room for two additional lanes. If this policy had been carried to completion, three miles of buildings collectively worth many millions of dollars would have been removed to speed up traffic on National Avenue. Instead, we repealed the nonconforming-use setback and legalized the avenue's existing dimensions.

The Problem of Parking

Another counterproductive encumbrance on urban property is off-street parking regulation. Water Street runs along the west side of Milwaukee's City Hall. In the early 1960s off-street parking requirements were imposed on private property on Water Street. A building with a frontage of 19 feet had been lost to fire. The new ordinance required seven off-street parking spots on the lot, even though it was only 70 feet deep and the other buildings on the

A New Urban Policy

At the end of World War II, the United States was triumphant and undamaged by war. Many of the cities of Germany and Japan — Hamburg, Dresden, Berlin, Tokyo, Hiroshima, and Nagasaki — lay in near total ruin. America had won, and Germany and Japan had lost. U.S. cities had produced much of the war material that fueled the Allied victory. No city was more productive on either side of the battle lines than Detroit, which produced tanks, jeeps, artillery, aircraft, ammunition, and firearms. At war's end Detroit had nearly 2 million people, a

vast streetcar system, quality housing, and a vibrant downtown. It was a well-planned city with the Woodward Plan, named for Augustus Woodward, modeled after the L'Enfant plan of Washington, D.C. Its radiating streets carried motor vehicles and served as trunk routes for a vast streetcar system. After World War II the plan was ignored, a system of freeways was built, and the streetcars were removed.

How did this work out for Detroit? Today all the cities of Germany and Japan are rebuilt, while Detroit, having lost more than half its population, looks as though it was Ground Zero for World War II. Other industrial cities have also suffered, usually not to the extent of Detroit, but enough to appear in dire need of repair. Pittsburgh, Buffalo, Gary, Indiana, St. Louis, and Cleveland all lost half their populations between 1950 and 2000, and many medium- and small-sized industrial cities shrank as well.

There are, of course many reasons that U.S. cities deteriorated in the post–World War II period. New technology, particularly the automobile, changed travel patterns in a way that undermined the supremacy of downtowns as centers of commerce. In addition, as America prospered, many citizens freely chose to enjoy their prosperity in larger houses on larger lots outside the city. Yet a significant part of the decline of U.S. cities can be traced to U.S. transportation and housing policies that distorted markets and pushed decentralization far beyond where market forces alone would have

FIGURE 6.4. Condominiums along the Milwaukee River in Milwaukee's Third Ward bring vitality to the river. (Courtesy of Paul J. Armstrong)

taken it. The federal government and, by extension, state governments subsidized and otherwise encouraged, through regulation, nonurban forms of development.

Since the Great Depression, municipal organizations like the U.S. Conference of Mayors and the National League of Cities have frequently called for a Federal Urban Policy. This is a good example of the oft-repeated caution "Beware what you ask for." Let's assume that by policy they mean federal programs that benefit cities, particularly city governments. Revenue sharing, federal block grants, disaster relief, Homeland Security grants, energy grants, housing programs, and most recently stimulus funds are all programs that have provided cash to local governments. Some programs currently exist; others have been canceled. Revenue sharing, enacted under President Richard Nixon, was ended under President Reagan. While federal aid to cities is often discussed, it might surprise people to know that cities actually get little of their revenue from the federal government. In most years it's less than 5%, and the biggest share of that is assistance to public housing residents.

While not a major source of discretionary revenue, the federal government, from the nation's founding, has had a powerful impact on cities both for good and ill. Perhaps the most beneficial federal contribution to cities is the U.S. Constitution and especially the Bill of Rights. Individual freedom is important to the culture and economy of cities. Another great federal contribution to U.S. cities is the guarantee of free commerce among the states without restrictions or tariffs. In many other ways the federal government has undermined cities. Changing the federal antiurban rules and policies to allow or even encourage urbanism would only help cities.

More successful cities will, in turn, also help America. More compact, complete, and well-connected development will save energy and add efficiency to the American economy. Urbanism also brings social benefits to communities. As it says in the preamble to the Charter of the New Urbanism:

> The Congress for the New Urbanism views disinvestment in central cities, the spread of placeless sprawl, increasing separation by race and income, environmental deterioration, loss of agricultural lands and wilderness, and the erosion of society's built heritage as one interrelated community-building challenge. (www.cnu.org/charter)

For cities, states, and certainly the federal government, it is the right time to address that challenge.

PART II

Sustainability in SynergiCity

CHAPTER SEVEN

Making Postindustrial Cities Livable

MARK L. GILLEM

WITH VALERIE HEDRICK

THE AMERICAN CITY IS IN THE FINAL STAGES OF a major transformation. The services sector has largely replaced manufacturing. This shift has left vacant industrial facilities, brownfield sites, and nearly empty rail yards. Jobs have migrated to homogenized edge cities without the perceived environmental and sociocultural baggage of the industrial city. In this chapter, we will analyze two primary strategies that are being used to make postindustrial cities livable. First, environmental damage that has pushed capital to the suburbs must be mitigated. To address the contamination left over from the industrial era, postindustrial cities have embarked on aggressive restoration programs. Brownfield sites, where smokestack industries and rail yards once stood, have been cleared and built on. The second strategy is perhaps more challenging. To attract capital and residents, postindustrial cities need to be made livable through appropriate public investments. Postindustrial cities must at-tract postindustrial workers whose previous options have been the office towers, shopping malls, and subdivisions of suburbia. To draw private development that supports social equity, environmental sustainability, and livability, postindustrial cities need to reinvent themselves by restoring damaged landscapes and building vibrant public realms. They can do this through a variety of strategies, but our focus is on transforming unsightly freeways into urban parkways and parks that are magnets for redevelopment.

In the first section of this chapter, we focus briefly on the transformation from industry to services in developed countries and highlight the spatial ramification of this change. In the second section brownfield redevelopment is the focus, and four case studies show how cities across the United States are transforming rail yards and industrial zones into livable districts. These districts initially attract a vanguard of artists who can see the benefit of and seek the low cost of living in rejuvenated warehouses and former industrial buildings. These artists are followed by developers who oftentimes use public and private funding to transform the districts into vibrant mixed-use urban villages. In the third section, the focus turns to parkways and parks. Three case studies show how investments in the public realm make postindustrial cities more livable. We conclude by highlighting a few common themes in this transformative process.

From Industry to Services

What do Americans make anymore? It seems that, apart from cars and construction materials, more and more goods are produced in developing countries like China and Vietnam. With their low labor costs and lax environmental regulations, these countries have a distinct advantage over developed countries when it comes to producing things. As a result, cities in the United States and in many developed countries are solidly in a postindustrial era. These cities, and the countries they are in, no longer exist as centers of manufacturing; rather, they are now centers of service-related industries. In G8 countries, for example, the shift is profound. The precursor to the G8 started as an organization of the largest industrialized countries, but now the organization can be considered more of a meeting between the largest postindustrial countries (graph 7.1). Services are the largest sector in all of these countries, with industry and agriculture lagging far behind. This shift away from manufacturing and toward services is largely driving the transformation of cities and is leading to new models of space that support new models of economic development.

The spaces that supported industrial production are now open for transformation. Sociologist Mark Gottdiener (1994) emphasizes that space is an important concept not because it promises some new form of life but because the built environment is critical to the transformation of everyday life. Built form works like a stage on which people act out their lives. It can be transformative if it supports the needs of the people it serves. Gottdiener argues that spatial forms result from the interplay between action and structure. The actions are what people do, and the structure is the sociospatial framework in which they function.

In the twentieth century, when America was an industrial powerhouse, the spatial framework of cities supported production. Industrial zones, rail yards, and even highways were built to support the making and transportation of goods. Now, with fewer goods produced in American cities, the rail yards and highways that were used to transport

those goods across an expanding nation have either found new uses or have fallen into disuse. Making these postindustrial cities livable necessitates a repurposing of these former spaces of production. Industrial areas are becoming complete neighborhoods, with housing, shopping, parks, and service-related employment areas integrated into walkable communities. Rail yards are being cleaned up and converted to mixed-use urban villages. And highways are being replaced by promenades and parkways that focus as much on pedestrians as on motor vehicles.

Redeveloping Brownfields

Since the 1950s, American developers have largely focused their efforts on greenfield development. The costs associated with infill development and environmental restoration have pushed development to the suburbs. Similarly, the incentives of inexpensive land, easy access to interstate highways, and low-cost loans have pulled development to the urban fringe. The result has been America's unique contribution to planning, known as suburban sprawl—a low-density, auto-oriented development pattern that consumes undeveloped land at metropolitan edges at the expense of infilling within the developed core. Until recently, developers largely ignored brownfield sites, commonly known as properties where the presence of contamination may complicate redevelopment (EPA 2009). The Government Accountability Office estimates that there may be up to 450,000 brownfield sites in the United States (Link-Wills 2007). Brownfields are properties that are underutilized or abandoned be-

cause of the presence of environmental contamination. In land-scarce urban areas, redevelopment and infill projects can help rejuvenate these areas. The presence of large tracts of polluted land is certainly a disincentive to development and a barrier to livability in postindustrial cities. The examples in the next section include the Pearl District in Portland, Oregon, Miami's Midtown, San Francisco's Mission Bay, and Baltimore's Westport Waterfront. They show that large portions of land need not remain underutilized but instead can become a catalyst for future urban neighborhoods.

PORTLAND: THE PEARL DISTRICT

Portland is well known for its successful development strategies. Urban Growth Boundaries limit development on prime farmland and other sensitive lands. Light rail lines connect downtown with suburbia. Streetcars navigate the urban core and link walkable neighborhoods filled with mixed-use buildings. Urban parks and plazas help make downtown Portland's density more livable. One area that has benefited from these strategies is the Pearl District, formerly known as the Hoyt Street Yards. The yards occupied a prime swath of land between the Willamette River and the downtown core and served several railroads (Hoyt Street Properties 2010). These rail lines carried people and goods and prosperity into Portland. Breweries, warehouses, and other industries also filled the city blocks of this waterfront. As railroads declined in the mid- and late twentieth century, the rail yards fell into disuse. The warehouses and industries once served by these rail lines also began to close their doors, and the area declined further. As in other cities, the area containing rail lines had a legacy of

GRAPH 7.1. Sectors' Percentages of GDP for G8 Countries, 2009. Note that services account for the largest percentage of GDP and agriculture the smallest. (Courtesy of Mark Gillem)

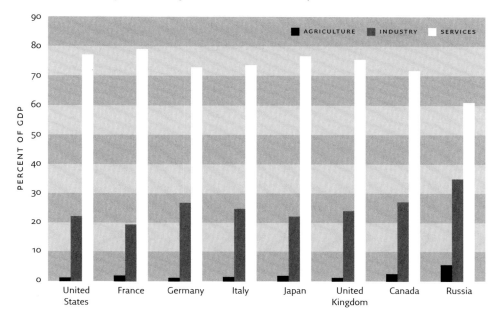

remediating both its existing, recyclable infrastructure and environmental contamination before the area could be made livable.

It took a decade to clean up the property, and in 2004, the Oregon Department of Environmental Quality issued some of the final Certificates of Completion for the property. With the contamination removed, the Pearl District is now a transit-connected urban neighborhood with a mix of retail, office, and high-end and affordable housing spaces. It is also a destination for visitors looking for restaurants, river views, and the Portland icon Powell's City of Books. The Pearl District builds on Portland's focus on sustainability—the district contains numerous buildings with silver, gold, and even platinum-level LEED certifications, featuring "green" roofs, on-site stormwater handling, sustainable or recycled building materials, water-

conserving plumbing fixtures, and energy-efficient building designs.

The initial signs of transformation started in the 1980s; artists began seeking low-rent loft space in the area's empty warehouses. This is a common theme in urban redevelopment: artists are the vanguard, and more traditional developers and their bank backers follow. The first major development occurred on a 34-acre parcel that had been the Burlington Northern rail yards. In 1997, three years after Hoyt Street Properties (HSP) purchased the site, the Portland Development Commission and HSP reached an agreement that relocated the Lovejoy Street viaduct in return for HSP's promise to include affordable housing in their development plans and to donate land for several city parks within the district. This relocation opened the entire northern end of the parcel for development as

a connected, walkable neighborhood. Included in the plans for the area was Portland's agreement to extend the streetcar line into the neighborhood and to use the availability of good public transit to encourage car-free living. In 2000, another developer, Gerding/Edlen, purchased the shuttered but still standing five-block Blitz-Weinhard Brewery and recycled it into the Brewery Blocks, a development of commercial and residential units that preserves the historic architecture of the brewery (HSP 2010).

Unlike other urban redevelopment projects, which inevitably face at least a few complaints about gentrification and the displacement of low-income residents, the Pearl District has been at least moderately successful at including affordable housing, both midrange and low-income, in the development of the neighborhood. According to the *Portland Tribune*, these buildings are not immediately recognizable as low-income or affordable housing, as they are designed to blend in with the overall aesthetic of the neighborhood (Korn 2007a, 2007b). Ironically, it is this blended-in-with-the-neighborhood aesthetic that may cause some to dismiss the neighborhood as being homogenously yuppie. The low-income housing and its residents aren't especially visible. Tommie Stallworth, a 58-year-old Vietnam veteran living in one of the affordable units, says, "It's not all about the money. It's the people. Nobody is walking around with a T-shirt saying 'I'm poor,' and nobody is walking around with a T-shirt saying 'I'm rich'" (Korn 2007a). Those who point to the mostly young, white, predominantly childless demographic of the neighborhood claim that the Pearl could become like San Francisco and Seattle, with "low capture rates in the core and no school-age kids at all in the core" (Arnold 2009), leading to a neighborhood with a college-dorm feeling. However, since 2007, the neighborhood has begun to experience a baby boom, and some developers are building the first two- and three-bedroom units in response to the changing population figures. As a result, there are plans to open a "satellite" public school in rented space in the Pearl District in 2011, hoping to attract and retain young families (Arnold 2009). And as is the case in nearly every city in America, there is always some concern about the effects of gentrification as it relates to race. "Affordable housing units in the Pearl District bring the neighborhood some income diversity; not everyone there is rich. But it hasn't brought the other diversity; almost everyone there is white" (Korn 2007b).

Rail still plays a major role in the Pearl District. In cleaned-up former rail yards, streetcars have been added to the district and have contributed to a building boom. The 7.8-mile (roundtrip) streetcar line, which opened in 2001 and cost $56.9 million to build, has spurred $2.39 billion worth of private development along the line, with over 7,200 new residences along the entire line (Carroll 2009). This can be considered the streetcar effect. This is an important element of the Pearl District's success, and it has been emulated by many communities across the United States. Developers and their bankers value the permanence of a streetcar line and are more willing to invest along the line, especially when compared to the paltry development that usually occurs along bus routes, which can be realigned with ease. Simply put, streetcars attract private investment. Within the Pearl District alone, more than 1,000 residential units have been built, along with 2.1 million square feet of mixed-use space. One tangible benefit of the streetcar is

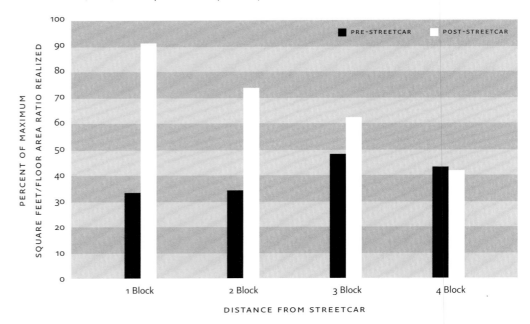

GRAPH 7.2. Before and after introduction of the Portland Streetcar Line: increases in development one, two, three, and four-plus blocks away (Courtesy of Mark Gillem)

that fewer residents need cars, and "developers are able to construct mixed-use projects with parking ratios lower than those found elsewhere in the city" (Adams and Carroll 2006).

Because they can take transit, walk to stores and work, and live in a mixed-use setting, residents living along Portland's streetcar line drive less — about 31 million miles per year fewer than their suburban counterparts — and this results in reduced congestion, improved air quality, and reduced carbon emissions (Carroll 2009). Interestingly, the streetcar effect disappears quickly as measured by the percent of maximum square footage/floor area ratio realized. This is one reason why most of the Pearl District is within four blocks of a streetcar line. After the streetcar opened, development soared along the streetcar line (graph 7.2).

The success of the Pearl District can be traced

back to several key factors. First, the artistic vanguard that moved into the area opened the eyes of the city and its developers to the potential of the district. Second, the demographic shifts occurring nationwide that are resulting in fewer families generate a new demand for urban living. Third, the district's focus on sustainability makes urban living more attractive to those who want to reduce their environmental footprint. Fourth, the district's financing model helped pay for redevelopment. Public investment in the public realm using Tax Increment Financing (TIF) helped pay for brownfield remediation, new parks, improved streets, and new transit. This rather creative (but legal) financing approach took projected revenue from future property tax increases based on planned redevelopment and used that future revenue to support bonds that generated immediate funds for redevelopment. One flaw in this approach is that the future revenue will be unavailable to pay for potentially needed city services that the new development will eventually demand (e.g., police, fire, schools, etc.). The use of TIF is usually reserved for designated urban renewal areas. But this type of financing can generate controversy, especially if it is aimed at specific private developments. In 2007, voters in Eugene, Oregon, for example, rejected a public financing scheme using urban renewal funds. The funds would have supported one private development slated for the city's dilapidated downtown core. In the Pearl District, what perhaps made the use of TIF slightly more palatable was the fact that in addition to subsidizing private development, the funds also paid for public improvements. When seen as a direct subsidy with little benefit to the public and substantial benefit to the developer, this type of financing is suspect. Rather than subsidize individual projects, municipalities may be better off paying for public realm improvements (e.g., public parks, great streets, and transit) that can benefit multiple developers and the larger public.

The Pearl District is an example of how one postindustrial city has converted valuable but underused industrial land into a vibrant mixed-use neighborhood. The Pearl District's numerous parks help make the density livable. The streetcar line gives residents transportation choices. And the development, while at times overscaled, also attempts to blend in with the historic fabric of warehouses and factories.

MIAMI: MIDTOWN

Prior to early 2001, Miami's 56-acre Buena Vista Railyard site was hardly a "buena vista" (beautiful view). It was a derelict rail yard filled with weeds and rusting metal. And it was one of the largest parcels of vacant land in Miami's urban core, adjacent to Wynwood, a working-class barrio that would one day be an arts district, the emerging Design District, and the waterfront community of Edgewater. Other than the railroad tracks, there was no infrastructure that would facilitate the reuse of this land into residential or commercial development. The property was owned by the Florida East Coast Railroad (FECR) and was being used as a storage yard for freight containers and a graveyard for rusting rolling stock (Kaplan 2008). Due to its identity as a storage yard, the area was zoned for industrial use only. Because of the low value of the industrial land, FECR appeared unlikely to consider selling the property. And, as with many industrial and railroad sites, environmental contamination made the site less attractive to residential developers than the previously undeveloped drained swampland west of the city.

So it was not until the early 2000s that redevelopment of this brownfield was even considered. The land sold for $34.4 million to New York developer Joe Cayre, whose main goal was to create connectivity between the old rail yard and the Design District, which lay across the rail tracks. Twenty-six acres of the development was sold to Developers Diversified Realty, a Cleveland-based firm that created a landscaped, low-rise retail district, called Shops at Midtown, which includes a two-story Target, a Marshall's department store, and several restaurants. In looking back at this project, it is safe to say that while the intentions were good, the execution has been troubled. "Construction delays, lawsuits, the real estate market crash, and the tanking economy have diminished the development's prospects of revitalizing the area" (Alvarado 2009). Pushing forward, however, the completed pieces of the project have already begun to improve the quality of the neighborhood by creating over 1,500 jobs and safe, healthy places to live. To make the development work, the city provided over $177 million in tax breaks. But providing tax breaks to developers, as was the case in Oregon, generated controversy. In Miami, policy-makers weighed the trade-offs and decided that the public investment would pay off in the long run.

One key factor in redeveloping this parcel was getting the land rezoned from industrial to mixed-use commercial. In addition, the property was divided into development subdistricts with maximum block sizes that would allow integration into the existing city street grid, with height and setback regulations similar to those in other high-density neighborhoods. What came out of the rezoning process was something akin to a Form-Based Code or a SmartCode. A code emerged that was based on the type of form the developers and designers wanted to achieve. These types of codes are increasingly common because they give public agencies and residents an assurance that their key goals (e.g., height, massing, use, etc.) will be met while at the same time they give designers and developers flexibility in the details of the development. Hercules, California, for instance, was one of the first major brownfield redevelopments in the United States to adopt a form-based code, and it has been successful in guiding redevelopment of its former dynamite plant. In Miami, the city and the developers worked to bring about the necessary zoning changes. In addition, both the city of Miami and Miami-Dade County worked with the developers to fund over $86 million in public improvements, including street paving, gutters, sidewalks, water and sewer lines, drainage systems, landscaping, and irrigation (City of Miami 2010).

Like Portland's Pearl District, Midtown was encumbered with environmental contamination. Because the area was known to contain arsenic from an herbicide that had been used along the tracks, as well as petroleum and lead contamination, the original purchaser of the property, Kimley-Horn and Associates, decided to forgo the standard site assessment and remediation process and have the entire site designated a brownfield site. From there, environmental restoration plans were integrated into the land planning and civil design components of the project (Department of Civil and Environmental Engineering 2010).

In 2008, when the project stalled due to a combination of the global economic slump, weather-related construction delays, lawsuits, and an overbuilt condo market in Miami, arts organizations in nearby Wynwood took advantage of some of the then-vacant spaces in Midtown Miami to house temporary art exhibitions, drawing foot traffic into the uncompleted spaces. This has lent the developing Midtown neighborhood some of the borrowed chic of the slightly more established Wynwood art district, an ironic twist to the original vision that Midtown Miami would drive the revitalization of the surrounding districts. Of course, the development benefits from its adjacency to this preexisting design district, but this actually reinforces a concept initially articulated by Richard Florida: that the "creative class" is and will be a key constituency that will drive redevelopment of postindustrial cities (Florida 2002).

Largely absent from Midtown Miami is any attempt at mixed-income or affordable housing.

Midtown Miami might have started with a vision of a diverse, transit-oriented neighborhood, but it has morphed into a satellite of Miami Beach. The "transit" part of "transit-oriented" has not materialized either. What has been built is a set of high-end high-rises full of well-heeled, young, commuting hipsters, chic restaurants, some shopping, and 3,000 parking spaces, all built around a kind of New York City theme (the logo for Midtown's website is graphic that looks like a New York City subway token), with significant public infrastructure funding going to the developer.

Phase 1 of Midtown Miami — three towers of high-rise luxury residences, a total of 908 residential units — is complete. Outdoor gathering spaces in these high-end buildings include fireplaces and rooftop swimming pools with views of downtown and Biscayne Bay. All of this residential luxury sits atop ground-level retail and restaurants. Retail and restaurant space, according to Suzanne Schmidt at Kreps/DeMaria, the public relations firm representing Midtown Miami, occupies a total of 660,000 square feet. Office space comprises 60,000 square feet. There are 3,000 parking spaces included in this development so far. According to Schmidt, the demographic of Midtown Miami "mirrors the demographic and vibe of the Wynwood Arts District and the Design District: young, hip, more than 50% gay . . . many young professional couples and artists who have migrated from Miami Beach" (2010). The residential property in Phase 1 has a 95% occupancy rate at present, with a mix of owners and renters. Unfortunately, the proposed streetcar line that figured prominently in the original vision for Midtown Miami has not been constructed. Schmidt points out that "everything in phase 1 is right here, in walking distance, so there really hasn't

been a need for it yet." Despite the lack of affordable housing or transit connections, Midtown is an example of the type of public-private partnership needed to make postindustrial cities more livable. New housing, parks, and shops occupy a former rail yard and brownfield site, and the transformation has helped turn an underutilized land asset into a thriving new district.

SAN FRANCISCO: MISSION BAY

According to historian Nancy Olmstead, Mission Bay's history is full of "dreams and schemes [that] have been a traditional part of this landscape ever since the 1850's when speculators sold waterlots in Mission Bay, in anticipation of the city's growth" (2007). Over the years, those lots, marked by poles driven into the shallow waters of Mission Bay, became dry land through the dumping of millions of cubic yards of fill. Later, a horsecar line that followed the track lines of the railroad carried passengers to the iron- and steelworks at Potrero Point. Worker housing sprang up along the horsecar line. In the 1860s version of affordable housing, a worker could buy a 25-by-75-foot lot for "ten dollars in gold and small monthly payments."

After it was completely filled in, Mission Bay was an industrial area and rail yard for nearly a century. The 303-acre site that had been home to the Southern Pacific Railroad now hosts high-end condos, biotech firms, a 43-acre campus of the University of California San Francisco, and 41 acres of waterfront and public parks (King 2000). The eventual build-out calls for 6,000 housing units (to date, 3,126 housing units have been built), including 1,700 affordable homes, 4.4 million square feet of commercial space, 500,000 square feet of retail space, a new public school for 500 students, a new public library, and new fire and police stations (San Francisco Redevelopment Agency 2010). This green, walkable, city-within-a-city is connected to nearby areas by the Mission Creek Bikeway, the soon-to-be-built Blue Greenway from China Basin to Candlestick Point, and the Third Street Light Rail line, connecting Mission Bay to the rest of San Francisco. A short distance away, on Fourth Street, is the Caltrain station that allows Silicon Valley professionals an easy commute to the Redwood City, Sunnyvale, Santa Clara, and San Jose.

While the neighborhood is attracting residents from all over the Bay Area and has received praise for its focus on green technology, sustainability, and beautiful waterfront views, the escalating prices and the changing demographics of the area have attracted some controversy. The real estate blog Curbed SF casts a hip and sarcastic eye on neighborhood news and issues, including those involving the latest prices and features of the redeveloped Mission Bay. An entry touts a one-bedroom condo in Arterra, "the LEEDiest of all condo buildings in San Francisco. Monthly rent, green pride baked in: $2300" (Wang 2010). These prices are certainly well above what would be considered affordable by those who previously occupied the eastern neighborhoods of San Francisco. In San Francisco, the median income is $55,000; for African-American households, it's $44,000. Using standard mortgage calculators, the annual income required to purchase the lowest priced, market-rate unit in the new developments is $175,000. Sustainability should be more than a technological solution. If infill buildings with recycled carpet, low VOC paint, and energy-efficient appliances force low-income families into developments at the suburban fringe, then the concept of sustainability is demeaned. Some, including San Francisco city superintendent Sophie Maxwell, question whether the area really needs more market-rate housing: "We're building for people who aren't here," says Maxwell (Redmond and Hirsch 2007). Adjacent to Mission Bay's green buildings and high-end condos are the blue-collar neighborhoods of Bayview and Hunter's Point. Redevelopment of Mission Bay into an upscale, green, transit-oriented community, populated by mostly white, affluent, high-tech workers, brings with it prosperity and environmental revitalization. But it also contributes to the out-migration of a predominantly African-American, blue-collar population. Like other brownfield redevelopments, Mission Bay has struggled with affordability, phasing, and environmental remediation. And like other projects, the effort has involved public-private partnerships to make the financing work. It remains to be seen if Mission Bay will become an upper-middle-class enclave that turns its back on the history and diversity of the city.

BALTIMORE: WESTPORT WATERFRONT

For most of the nineteenth century, the waterfront at Westport served as both a bucolic getaway spot for Baltimoreans and a convenient place south of the city for industrial uses. By 1920, industrial uses and rail yards had mostly taken over the area. By the 1970s, the entire waterfront west of Hanover Street was either industrial or regarded as wasteland, including a large automobile graveyard that the city removed in 1978 (Chalkley 2006). Despite this attempt at cleanup, the area remained mostly underdeveloped. The lone holdout was a glass factory. In 2004, when the Carr-Lowrey glass factory went bankrupt, developer Patrick Turner purchased the parcel of land on which it had produced bottles since 1889, and the parcel was rezoned to allow Turner to begin plans for Westport Waterfront (fig. 7.1).

After the adjacent Baltimore Gas & Electric land was purchased, work began in December 2009 on the first phase of the development, using American Recovery and Reinvestment Act funding, as well as TIF, to help pay for infrastructure and shoreline reconstruction. This 52-acre, transit-oriented, mixed-use development, when completed, will contain 2,000 residential units, two hotels, 300,000 square feet of retail, and 2 million square feet of office space (Galef 2010). The site will also contain extensive open spaces, including pedestrian and bike trails, plazas, an esplanade, and two piers for kayak and rowing-crew launches (Ruggiero 2010). Westport's existing stop on the Baltimore light rail line will become a hub for a multimodal transportation system that includes sidewalks and bike paths (Galef 2010) connecting Westport to the rest of Baltimore (plate 16).

Environmental challenges in this project involved identifying and removing materials such as asbestos and oil tanks, as well as mitigating contaminated soil and groundwater, all of which are common to many brownfield redevelopments. Unique to Westport was "the developer's desire to create a soft 'green' edge, via tidal wetlands restoration, at the waterfront, [rather than] the paved and sealed bulkhead treatment typically required with the redevelopment of a former industrial site" (Galef 2010). The developer has leveraged this concept as a key marketing point. But the use of parks and green space to attract investment is not a new

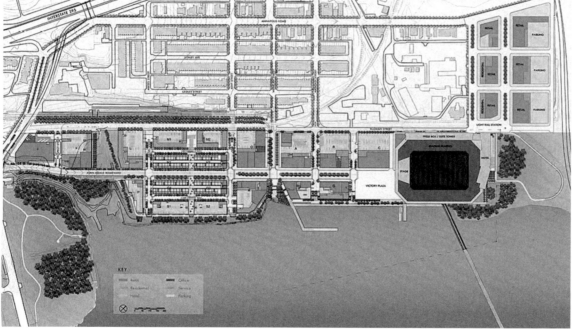

Figure 7.1. General view and site plan of Westport Development, Baltimore. (Courtesy of Turner Development)

marketing concept. Central Park in New York is perhaps the most prominent example. And the green will not stop at the water's edge. In a press release on Turner Development's website, Turner says that the builder of Westport's housing units "will offer green sales upgrades: energy-efficient appliances and light-fixtures and heat-recovery systems. All this will come with an 'affordable' price tag starting at around $300,000" (Pfaeffle 2010). In an area of Baltimore where the 2006-2010 median household income was $39,386, it becomes clear that $300,000 will not be affordable to the current residents of Westport.

However, Tom Chalkley argues that Turner's "vision of an upscale, eco-friendly waterfront has achieved an almost unheard-of degree of consensus among the most disparate interest groups that ring the water." Catherine Fennell, the former development director for the city's Department of Housing and Community Development, says that "Turner started early. Usually, [developers] wait until they have all their approvals before they start working with the community. . . . The project will go more smoothly than it would have, if he'd come in and tried to ram it down their throats" (Chalkley 2006). Turner believes that when his vision for Westport is completed, there will be new jobs in commercial buildings he is developing that will replace the industrial jobs that have left and the new housing, including designated affordable housing, and the diverse, green, walkable urban village with waterfront views and public open space, will be a better place for all of its residents, longtime and new. This is a tall order for the postindustrial city.

Replacing Freeways

A livable city is a walkable city, with spaces scaled for the human being: sidewalks, streets that can be crossed safely, daylight between buildings, and appropriately scaled outdoor "living rooms" of well-planned parks that connect citizens to the natural environment. But in the post–World War II era, many cities allowed such pedestrian concerns to take a backseat to the desire to move cars through and around the city at high speeds, unfettered by stoplights and crosswalks. Those roads, such as the Embarcadero Freeway in San Francisco, Park East Freeway in Milwaukee, and Harbor Drive in Portland, Oregon, all gave the best views in the city to the drivers of the fast-moving automobile, cut pedestrians off from their waterfronts, and created perpetually shadowy places beneath their elevated sections. The volume of traffic on these congested corridors eventually led to city planners to a crossroads: whether to widen, improve, and expand these highways or tear them down. The three case studies presented in this section show that livable cities can thrive without freeway spurs running through them and that reconnecting the city to its waterfront can lead to a renaissance in the urban core.

SAN FRANCISCO: THE EMBARCADERO FREEWAY

Planners and engineers in the 1950s conceived a grand plan for the City by the Bay. They envisioned elevated freeways encircling the city and, with federal funding, began an ambitious construction program. But their ambitions were thwarted by a public averse to the idea of turning San Francisco into a highway with a city in the middle. They did, however, get a few sections built, including the Embarcadero Freeway. This double-decker concrete viaduct, built in 1958, despite public resistance, funneled heavy traffic from the Bay Bridge into the city. Although originally designed to take a turn inland and head west past Aquatic Park, all the way to the Golden Gate Bridge, residents convinced the Board of Supervisors to end the freeway at Broadway (King 2004). In passing between the historic Ferry Building and the foot of Market Street, the freeway cut off the City by the Bay from its namesake bay and hid the iconic building, a survivor of the 1906 earthquake, from view "behind a dark wall of car exhaust and noise." The area overshadowed by the elevated freeway fell into blight and remained cut off from the rest of the city. Gridlock also became a problem because traffic on San Francisco's freeways and city streets was funneled directly onto and from the Embarcadero Freeway at various points.

Even before the Loma Prieta earthquake in 1989, which eventually led to the removal of the freeway, many in the city wanted the structure removed. In 1985, for example, the Board of Supervisors voted to remove it. Supervisor Richard Hongisto disagreed, arguing that freeway removal was "a deliberately designed traffic jam" (Preservation Institute 2010b). And in 1986, a failed referendum calling for the freeway's removal showed that a majority of San Franciscans shared Supervisor Hongisto's fears. However, on October 17, 1989, the Loma Prieta earthquake damaged the Embarcadero Freeway and the Central Freeway in San Francisco. Both freeways had to be closed while repairs were considered. To the surprise of some, gridlock did not result. The public simply drove other streets or took public transportation. Public sentiment shifted, and in February 1991, with "a ceremony that included fireworks and . . . 'Shake, Rattle, and Roll' by a group of men in Ethel Merman drag," demolition of the Embarcadero freeway began. *San Francisco Chronicle* columnist Herb Caen, for whom a section of the promenade is now named, remarked at the destruction, "You have to go to the Berlin Wall to find more jubilation over concrete being reduced to rubble" (Brown 2003).

Most of the Embarcadero Freeway had been an elevated span above the street, named the Embarcadero, rather than developable land. But the city of San Francisco spent $50 million to redevelop the street as a boulevard with wide promenades, served by antique, refurbished trolleys acquired from other cities (Preservation Institute 2010b). Immediately after the demolition of the freeway, property values along the newly sunlit Embarcadero went up 300% (Norquist 2010). Rollerbladers and office workers on lunch breaks pass each other on the wide, palm-lined promenades with views of the water and the East Bay hills beyond. Large sculptures on temporary exhibition draw tourists to take photos. Giants fans can hop a streetcar to the ballpark, or paddle their kayaks in McCovey cove, waiting to catch a home run. The Embarcadero is now the centerpiece of a rejuvenated waterfront. Cars still make their way from the Bay Bridge to various points in the city, but they do it on surface streets and along grand boulevards that have become magnets for infill development. Without question, the removal of the elevated freeway has made San Francisco a much more livable city. And, as in Portland, the streetcar effect certainly has played a role in the success of the area. Visitors from across the Bay Area can take heavy rail into the city and easily transfer to the streetcar to attend baseball games, visit museums, or enjoy other amenities of downtown San Francisco. They can also take the streetcar all the way to Fisherman's Wharf and then transfer to cable cars that access much of downtown. Residents can take the streetcar along the Embarcadero from their new homes in Mission Bay to the heart of downtown.

MILWAUKEE: PARK EAST FREEWAY

At the same time San Francisco's traffic engineers were planning to remake the city on their auto-oriented terms, their colleagues in the Midwest were planning a similar system of freeways around Milwaukee. Planned in 1952, during the postwar highway-building boom, the Park East Freeway was going to be part of a loop of freeways completely encircling downtown Milwaukee and connecting the Lake Freeway to what is now Interstate Route 794 (Preservation Institute 2010a). In 1965, property was acquired for the right-of-way and hundreds of homes and scores of businesses were demolished. In 1971 the first stretch of the freeway opened to traffic, and further land was acquired and cleared to finish the section connecting the freeway to the lakefront, bisecting Juneau Park and cutting it off from the waterfront. The threatened incursion into an existing park was the final straw that helped convince elected officials in Milwaukee to heed neighborhood activists who campaigned against the freeway's march toward the waterfront. Mayor Henry Maier effectively stopped the project in 1972 by vetoing funding for relocating utilities in the path of the proposed freeway, emphasizing the cost: "America is the only nation in the world to let her cities ride to bankruptcy on a freeway.... My city has discovered that the freeway is not free"

(Preservation Institute 2010a). As was the case with the Embarcadero Freeway, the presence of an elevated freeway, even an incomplete one, lowered property values so far that this prime riverfront property was used mainly for parking lots. The remainder of the cleared land remained vacant for 20 years, due to its designation as a transportation corridor, until the 1990s. When the state lifted that designation, the land was sold for redevelopment, and the East Pointe neighborhood emerged: condos, townhouses, small retail, and "even a supermarket with a pedestrian-friendly entrance on one side and a parking lot on the other" (OCL Blog 2008). It became "part of a revival of residential construction in downtown Milwaukee and in downtowns across the country" (OCL Blog 2008).

The Park East Freeway spur was essentially an elevated road to nowhere, given that it did not connect with the Lake Freeway and carried only 35,000 vehicles a day, compared with the mainline I-794, which carried 89,000 vehicles a day. The elevated roadway was a deterrent to redevelopment of the area for years. After all, if one had a choice, would living in the noise and pollution shadow of an elevated freeway be one's first choice? In 1999 Milwaukee's mayor, Wisconsin's governor, and county officials reached an agreement to spend federal transportation funds on removing the Park East Freeway. They recognized that redevelopment of the area required its removal. Due to the low traffic volume on the freeway, traffic engineers determined that restoring the local street grid and a new bridge across the Milwaukee River would be sufficient to carry traffic. Despite these predictions, opposition to the removal delayed the effort for several years. George Watts, a local businessman who ran unsuccessfully for public office several times, made it

his public mission to stop the removal. Although city, county, and state officials and the public were in favor of removal, Watts spent personal funds running for mayor of Milwaukee, buying radio and newspaper ads opposing the removal. When that was unsuccessful, he filed lawsuits to stop the project. The last of these obstruction attempts failed in March 2002, when the U.S. District Court ruled against Watts. Freeway demolition began in June 2002 (OCL Blog 2008). Contrary to Watts's fear that removing the freeway would kill the city, the removal has spurred growth and a revitalized urban core in Milwaukee.

PORTLAND, OREGON: HARBOR DRIVE

While the Embarcadero and Park East are examples of elevated freeways that choked urban development, Portland's Harbor Drive was an at-grade, four-lane freeway along the west bank of the Willamette River; opened in 1942, it cut off pedestrian access to the river. As in many postwar American cities, freeways were encouraging residents to move out of the city into FHA-financed new construction in the sprawling suburbs, increasing commute traffic on the freeways, and leading to freeway congestion (Siegel 2007). As residents and businesses moved to the car-dominated suburbs, Portland's urban core began to decline. At the same time, additional freeways were built, including Interstate 405, to make room for which the destruction of housing was required. In a sense, the city was demolishing places for people in order to make room for cars.

In 1969, to accommodate increasing automobile traffic, engineers and planners considered widening the freeway from four lanes to six, taking it underground, and covering it with a park (similar

Figure 7.2. The transformation of Harbor Drive in Portland, Oregon, into an urban park has been a catalyst for redevelopment of the adjacent districts. (Courtesy of Mark Gillem)

for Riverfront for People, a group that is leading a fight to remove Interstate 5 from the east side of the Willamette River to create another revitalized walkable neighborhood.

Conclusion

"Reduce, Reuse, Recycle" is the mantra of the American "green" movement, part of the cultural force that is making cities more livable. The nation's most livable cities are finding that they can *reduce* the environmental footprint left behind in abandoned industrial areas, *reuse* and reenvision uses for the existing rail infrastructure that once served industry, and *recycle* these areas into livable, sustainable, urban villages that capitalize on restored waterfront views and the convenience of mixed-use neighborhoods. Enlightened developers have certainly leveraged the marketing potential of sustainable communities built within cities rather than at the edge of cities. But they were not the first to recognize the value of redevelopment. With little fanfare and even less public support, generations of artists were the vanguard. They recognized the value of former industrial sites, abandoned warehouses, and urban living. As artists moved into these areas, property values began to slowly appreciate, and developers and government agencies took notice. Municipalities began to recognize that they had tools to facilitate this process of transformation. These tools include zoning changes, which allow mixed-use development, and appropriate public infrastructure investments, particularly in transit options like streetcar and light rail and in public open spaces to make density more livable. The streetcar effect, for example, can result in sub-

to Boston's Big Dig, three decades later) or splitting the traffic so that a boulevard one block away would carry half the traffic on a one-way street. Oregon's governor, Tom McCall, and the citizens of Portland advocated the removal of the expressway altogether, but state highway engineers insisted that expressway closure was impossible; on the day of the 1969 hearing at which the decision was to be made, the chairman of the Governor's Task Force on the Harbor Drive project was told that closure would "back up traffic all the way to Lake Oswego" (Torrid Joe 2009). Despite this prediction, on May 23, 1974, the state began closing portions of Harbor Drive, and by the end of the year the entire road

was closed, and work began on a waterfront park that would bear Governor McCall's name.

In the 25 years since the closing of Harbor Drive, the area has transitioned from a blighted industrial zone to a thriving urban neighborhood (fig. 7.2) (Buntin 2010). The park now hosts festivals and other public gatherings year-round. The areas adjacent to the park—the Pearl District, RiverPlace, and the Portland South Waterfront—now include both market-based and designated affordable housing, restaurants, shops, hotels, a marina, a swimming beach, and office space. Harbor Drive no longer drives people away from Portland. In fact, the success of its removal has been an on-ramp

Figure 7.3. Photo rendering of Mission Bay development in San Francisco. The dashed line indicates the area of the 300-acre mixed-use project. (Courtesy of Mission Bay Development Corporation)

gested expressways, and the shadowy places created by elevated freeways, the health of urban dwellers is improved, and the city itself becomes a thriving organism: a living and livable city (fig. 7.3).

References

Adams, S. 2008, January. *Portland Streetcar Development Oriented Transit*. http://www.portlandstreetcar.org/pdf/development_200804_report.pdf. Accessed January 30, 2012.

Alvarado, F. 2009, January 8. "Midtown Slowdown." *Miami New Times*. www.miaminewtimes.com/content/printVersion/1309524. Accessed January 30, 2012.

Brown, P. L. 2003, January 23. "A Waterfront Palace of Produce." *New York Times*.

Buntin, S. B. 2010. "UnSprawl Case Study: Portland's RiverPlace." *Terrain.org: A Journal of the Built & Natural Environment*. www.terrain.org/unsprawl/7/. Accessed January 30, 2012.

Carroll, J. 2009, October. Information on Private Development from an Interview with John Carroll, a Prominent Portland Developer Who Has Built Several Mixed-Use Buildings along the Portland Streetcar Line.

Chalkley, T. 2006, January 25. "Harbor Next: The Homely Middle Branch Is Set to Become an Urban Ecotopia (But Don't Talk to Speculators and Don't Touch the Water)." *Baltimore City Paper*. www.citypaper.com/news/story.asp?id=11385. Accessed January 30, 2012.

City of Miami. 2010. "Buena Vista Yards/Midtown Miami Project." In *Economic Initiatives, City of Miami*. www.miamigov.com/economicdevelopment/pages/ProjectsInitiatives/BuenaVista.asp. Accessed January 30, 2012.

stantial development adjacent to the line, which increases property values and reduces environmental impacts associated with fewer automobile trips. The rezoned, mixed-use neighborhoods that are built around efficient public transit and contain a mix of market-rate and affordable housing offer a diverse population of residents opportunities to leave behind long commutes and car-dominated lifestyles. However, as properties are rezoned, the impact on existing residences must be carefully balanced with a city's desire to evolve. Gentrification and affordability, for instance, are two sides of the same coin. As properties are upgraded they may become less affordable, the process of neighborhood

demographic change for better or worse can be the unintended (or intended) consequence, and the sociocultural and economic diversity that adds value to urban life may suffer. Cities should get something in return in addition to a greater tax base that results through increased property values if they invest in brownfield remediation, rezone private parcels, or enter into public-private partnerships through Tax Increment Financing of bond funding. A commitment to providing affordable housing could be one requirement placed on developers who benefit from public policy. In the end, when sunlit public parks and walkable city blocks replace contaminated sites, abandoned warehouses, con-

Department of Civil and Environmental Engineering. 2010. "Midtown Miami." Virginia Tech Land Development Design Initiative. www.lddi.cee .vt.edu/index.php?item=project&func=5&do =view&id=11. Accessed January 30, 2012.

Environmental Protection Agency (EPA). 2009. "EPA's Brownfields and Land Revitalization Programs: Changing American Land and Lives." EPA report no. 560-F-09-519. October 2009. Accessed January 30, 2012.

Florida, R. 2002. *The Rise of the Creative Class: And How It's Transforming Work, Leisure, Community and Everyday Life*. New York: Perseus.

Galef, J. 2010, May 17. "Baltimore Blues." *Architect's Newspaper*. www.archpaper.com/e-board_rev. asp?News_ID=4531. Accessed January 30, 2012.

Gottdiener, M. 1994. *The Social Production of Urban Space*. Austin: University of Texas Press.

HSP. 2010. "Railroad Days." Available at the website of Hoyt Street Properties, www.hoytstreetyards .com/railroad_days.html. Accessed January 30, 2012.

Jacob, A. 2009, February 23. "Next for Trendy Pearl: A Public School Program." *Oregonlive*. www .oregonlive.com/news/index.ssf/2009/02/next_for _trendy_pearl_public_s.html. Accessed January 30, 2012.

Kaplan, S. 2008. "Miami from Afar: Buena Vista 2008." In *Steven Kaplan: What Goes Around*. Available at http://post.thing.net/node/2419. Accessed January 30, 2012.

King, J. 2004, October 17. "15 Seconds That Changed San Francisco." *San Francisco Chronicle*. http://articles.sfgate.com/2004-10-17/news /17450353_1_loma-prieta-central-freeway -embarcadero-freeway. Accessed January 30, 2012.

———. 2000, October 23. "Groundbreaking Today for Big Chunk of Mission Bay." *San Francisco Chronicle*. http://www.sfgate.com/cgi-bin/article .cgi?f=/c/a/2000/10/23/MN101064.DTL. Accessed January 30, 2012.

Korn, P. 2007a, March 13. "The Other Pearl District." *Portland Tribune*. www.portlandtribune.com/news /story_2nd.php?story_id=117373388024001500. Accessed January 30, 2012.

———. 2007b, March 13. "The Pearl District Is as White as Its Name." *Portland Tribune*. www. portlandtribune.com/news/story_2nd.php?story _id=117373384528409100. Accessed January 30, 2012.

Link-Wills, K. 2007, Summer. "Atlantic Station: Model City." *Georgia Tech Alumni Magazine,* 36–40. http://www.nxtbook.com/nxtbooks/gatech /alumni-summer07/index.php. Accessed January 30, 2012.

Norquist, J. 2000. "Tear It Down." In *Removing Freeways — Restoring Cities*. Available at the website of the Preservation Institute, http://www .preservenet.com/freeways/FreewaysTear.html. Accessed January 30, 2012. (Originally published in slightly different form in *Blueprint* [published by Democratic Leadership Council], September 1, 2000.)

OCL Blog. 2008, August 13. "Re-thinking I-81." In *Onondaga Citizens League Study Blog*. Available at the website of WordPress, www.oclblog.wordpress. com/2008/08/13/. Accessed January 30, 2012.

Olmstead, N. 2007, November 26. "Walking on Water — A History of Mission Bay." *UCSF Today*. http://today.ucsf.edu/stories/walking-on-water -a-history-of-mission-bay2/. Accessed January 30, 2012.

Pfaeffle, C. 2010. "Westport Waterfront: Green Harbor." Available at the website of Turner Development, www.turnerdevelopment.com/press /waterfrontgreen.php. Accessed January 30, 2012.

Preservation Institute. 2010a. "Removing Freeways — Restoring Cities: Milwaukee, Wisconsin Park East Freeway." Available at the website of the Preservation Institute, http://www.preservenet .com/freeways/FreewaysParkEast.html. Accessed January 30, 2012.

———. 2010b. "Removing Freeways — Restoring Cities: San Francisco, CA Embarcadero Freeway." Available at the website of the Preservation Institute, http://www.preservenet.com/freeways /FreewaysEmbarcadero.html. Accessed January 30, 2012.

Redmond, T., and M. Hirsch. 2007, August 8. "The Fate of the Eastern Neighborhoods." *San Francisco Bay Guardian News*. http://www.sfbg.com/40/03 /news_fate.html. Accessed January 30, 2012.

Ruggiero, B. 2010, April 14. "Baltimore Begins Ambitious Waterfront Plan." *Construction Equipment Guide*. Northeast ed. www .constructionequipmentguide.com/Baltimore -Begins-Ambitious-Waterfront-Plan/14259/. Accessed January 30, 2012.

San Francisco Redevelopment Agency. 2010. "Mission Bay." Available at the website of City and County of San Francisco Redevelopment Agency, www.sfredevelopment.org/index.aspx?page=61. Accessed January 30, 2012.

Schmidt, S. 2010, June. Phone interview with the author.

Siegel, C. 2007. "From Induced Demand to Reduced Demand." Available at the website of the Preservation Institute, http://www.preservenet .com/freeways/FreewaysInducedReduced.html. Accessed January 30, 2012.

Wang, A. 2010, January 28. "One-Bed Condo in the City's Greenest High-Rise." Available at the website of Curbed San Francisco, http://sf.curbed.com /archives/categories/mission_bay.php. Accessed January 30, 2012.

CHAPTER EIGHT

Rethinking Storm Water

A MODEL FOR SYNERGICITY

JAMES H. WASLEY

In farm country, the plover has only two real enemies: the gully and the drainage ditch. Perhaps we shall one day find that these are our enemies too.

Aldo Leopold, A Sand County Almanac

Zero-Discharge Masterplan for the University of Wisconsin–Milwaukee

In the fall of 2004, the Milwaukee Metropolitan Sewerage District (MMSD) partnered with the University of Wisconsin–Milwaukee (UWM) to undertake two projects; "UWM as a Zero-Discharge Zone," a speculative storm water masterplan for the campus, and "the Pavilion Gateway," an ecological "best management practice" (BMP) demonstration project managing the runoff from a 4-acre portion of the campus (Wasley 2006a, 2006b). The first was the result of an unsolicited proposal by me. The second was in response to a call for proposals that came out before the masterplanning had begun but

could not be executed within the time frame of the funding, leading to the fortuitous agreement that the university would use the demonstration funds to plan in detail a more ambitious project and put off the question of construction funding. The two projects essentially became one, with the detailed design study informing the masterplanning process, and vice verse.

The Zero-Discharge Zone (ZDZ) Masterplan that resulted from this intensive investigation provides a road map for transforming UWM's 90-acre urban campus into a bioregional center for design research into ecological urban storm water management or "green infrastructure." It provides lessons for the transformation of many postindustrial midwestern cities into SynergiCities in their relationship with the region's uniquely abundant freshwater.

Storm Water in the Postindustrial City

Postindustrial midwestern cities, such as Milwaukee, are both blessed and burdened by their relation to water. They are blessed because they have abundant supplies of fresh, potable water — a resource that is becoming more precious throughout the world. Many of these cities owe their existence to the transportation corridors and industrial potentials provided by lakes and rivers. The recent ratification of the Great Lakes Compact is further evidence that freshwater is tied to the economic future of the region as well as its past. These cities are at the same time burdened in that their water-management infrastructures are at the limits of their capacities and life spans. The question of how urban environments should relate to their hydrological contexts is one of the most fundamental ecological issues shaping their futures as postindustrial SynergiCities.

Significant political, educational, and economic resources have been applied to postindustrial cities such as Milwaukee to turn a public face toward the rivers and lakefronts that were once seen solely as the domain of industry. However, less attention has been given to ecological urban storm water management, which recapitulates all of the issues associated with the reweaving of rivers and lakefronts into ecological corridors and public parklands that has already commenced in many cities. Postindustrial cities, we believe, are uniquely positioned to solve their storm water problems ecologically. The same logic that applies at the larger scale of river restoration and greenway development — that is, the need to redevelop urban land and to reduce the crushing costs of maintaining traditional infrastructure — opens the door to opportunities to create new amenities that use water as a critical resource and give it new meaning in postindustrial environments.

VISUALIZING STORM WATER SYSTEMS

Nature is resplendent with fractal branching patterns, from the human nervous system to the structure of trees to the landscape's figuration into drainage basins, streams, and rivers. Within this fractal landscape there is no "smallest branch," but only branching patterns that diminish in scale. Therefore, virtually every surface of the earth receives water and directs it downstream through branches and tributaries of natural and human-made watercourses.

Throughout their history, cities have been en- gineered to channel rainwater away from human settlement through vast networks of underground channels or pipes. This is done to wash away waste, to prevent flooding, to liberate land for human uses, and to reduce the spread of waterborne diseases, among other reasons. Milwaukee, a progressive industrial nineteenth-century midwestern city, was engineered to do all of these things. The construction of a flushing tunnel that pumped water from Lake Michigan to dilute the raw sewerage collecting in the slow-moving Milwaukee River made the city a progressive beacon at the end of the nineteenth century. In fact, public infrastructure was such a high priority for Milwaukee's socialist leaders during the early twentieth century that they were sometimes derisively called "sewer socialists." A typhoid scare in 1909 led to the creation of one of the nation's first sewerage treatment plants at Jones Island in 1925, which innovatively used microorganisms to digest the organic waste (Milwaukee Metropolitan Sewage District 2010).

A century later, the limitations as well as the benefits of this heavily engineered hydrological landscape are now apparent. Like many other aspects of the postindustrial city, the apparent success of infrastructure technology is understood today to have both conceptual flaws and physical limits. This chapter shows that ecological urban storm water management can ameliorate some of the problems introduced by engineered storm water management systems by acknowledging its limitations and implementing new strategies that address storm water before it is collected and redirected to water treatment facilities.

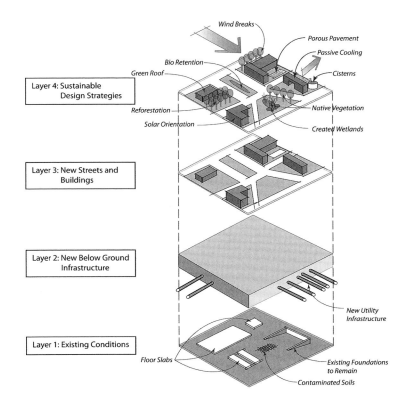

FIGURE 8.1. Conceptual drawing illustrating environmental design strategies for developing sustainable urban infrastructures. (Illustration by Paul J. Armstrong. Courtesy of U.S. Pipe/Wheland Foundry and LA Quatra Bonci Associates/Edward Dumont)

In thinking about how storm water relates to the land on which it falls, there is often a disconnection between the "natural" world aboveground and the subterranean and unseen world of the sewers (fig. 8.1). No matter how urbanized the landscape, it is still quite possible to trace the natural flow of water aboveground. As it is pulled by gravity, water flows downhill and runs across every conceivable surface until it is either evaporated, claimed by plants or porous ground, gathered into a body of water, or collected by subterranean sewers. The sewer system is both unseen (out of public sight) and labyrinthine. While its engineering is often complicated by codes, the patterns of streets and buildings, and the subsurface routes of other public utilities, a sewerage system is conceptually quite simple: it is an extension of the flow patterns of the ground surface. A sewer system, therefore, can be compared to the branching structure of a tree in which small branch structures are collected into larger branches and trunks. In many cases the structure underground is actually a transposition of the aboveground patterns, where natural drainage channels and streams have been buried in pipes to free up the urban land surface for other functions. It is not uncommon for an ancient stream or other watercourse to be contained in pipes below the roadways of a modern city.

Like other industrial cities, Milwaukee is served by a combined sewer system (CSS), which means that sanitary waste is carried in the same network of pipes that collect storm water. The branching pattern of a combined sewer system collects storm water and effluent and directs it to trunk lines that lead to sewerage treatment plants, where the treated water can be then safely discharged back into the system itself or into lakes or rivers. The

elevation of the city of Milwaukee is slightly above that of Lake Michigan. Therefore, rainfall collects on impervious surfaces, such as rooftops, streets, and parking lots, where it is diverted to rivulets, streams, and rivers that all flow eventually into Lake Michigan. The storm sewer system traces a similar path below ground to the same harbor mouth as surface water. It is here where Jones Island serves as the site for the combined sewerage treatment facility.

In newer or historically less densely developed areas, such as Milwaukee's postwar suburbs, sewerage and storm water are carried in separate infrastructure pipelines, which are less self-contained and more closely tied to patterns in the landscape. The branching pattern of the natural landscape is in this case augmented with prosthetic limbs — branches of sewer pipes intertwined with surface flows, providing engineered shortcuts from some specific patch of ground to a once "natural" collecting stream or river.

Though viewed today as economically unfeasible, combined sewer systems arguably are beneficial in that they cleanse *both* human waste effluent *and* contaminated urban storm water before returning it to the environment. However, in certain cases, such as a heavy rainfall, the capacity of a storm sewer system can be overwhelmed, and storm water combined with raw sewerage can be released directly into the environment as a "combined sewer overflow" (CSO). In a separated sewerage/storm water system, the capacity of the sewerage system is not intentionally compromised by storm water, yet the ecologically damaging effects of concentrating urban runoff remain. "Best management practice" literature often glosses over the differences between these two systems and their potential impacts for

ecological design. The ZDZ masterplan presented in this chapter illustrates the significance of both systems as a key to opening up unexpected design opportunities.

CONCEPTUAL PROBLEMS WITH CONVENTIONAL "HARD-PIPE" STORM WATER MANAGEMENT

From an engineering perspective, storm water management in any form must account for three basic variables: *water quality*, *water quantity*, and *rate of flow*. Each of these variables can assume varying degrees of importance in a given situation, which makes storm water management a design challenge, where specific conditions often trump general principles and counterintuitive solutions are often contained within the problem itself.

Modern urban environments have replaced pervious and vegetated surfaces with impervious surfaces, such as concrete and asphalt, which increases both the quantity of water and its flow rate as it moves downhill. A pervious natural surface, by contrast, often acts as a large sponge by absorbing water into the soil or collecting it into wetlands. Only when these natural systems become overburdened, as during a heavy rainfall, does flooding occur. Excess concentrations of water can degrade local water quality by making water bodies "flashy," meaning that their water level fluctuates dramatically during a rain event. Concentrated water runoff that is suddenly discharged into a stream not only raises the water level, which can cause erosion and flooding, but also carries with it all of the contaminants that have been collected on impervious surfaces. Contaminants from streets and parking lots, such as oil and chemicals, can no longer be degraded by the slow dispersed workings of sunlight and microbial activity but are swept away by the rushing water in potentially damaging concentrations. This unregulated process also raises the turbidity and temperature of the surface water in ways that can be detrimental to aquatic habitat as well.

In a css, the surge of rainwater in a storm event collides with the waterborne human waste stream, which stresses the capacity of the system and sets up the potential for a cso. When combined sewer overflows were first regulated in the 1970s by the Clean Water Act, the city of Milwaukee responded with the Deep Tunnel Project. The mmsd created 19.4 miles of tunnels that serve as underground storage vaults that follow the natural geography of the three river valleys and expand the trunk capacity of the combined sewer system's concrete tree (Milwaukee Metropolitan Sewage District 2010). Though Milwaukee's deep tunnels have greatly reduced the number of csos to an average of three per year (half of the federally mandated limit of six per year (Environmental Protection Agency 2009), they are prone to the same water surcharges as any engineered "hard-pipe" network. Further expanding the network's capacity to capture these statistically less and less frequent storms at some point becomes prohibitively expensive because it takes pipes increasingly larger in diameter to divert proportionately smaller quantities of water. In order to eliminate such overflows, the premise of this study is that it is more cost effective to keep storm water out of the sewer system altogether through ecological management practices than it is to add any more additional storage and/or treatment capacity to already overtaxed systems.

In working with a combined sewer system, the problem to be solved through ecological management often thus centers on the system's total capacity, where controlling the volume of water entering the system is the primary concern. At other times, the design may be determined not by the total capacity of the system but by the rate of flow that individual branches of the system can accept without backing up. Interestingly, the design of these ecological features doesn't necessarily turn on issues of water quality, that is, not unless the ecological goal is to discharge water directly into rivers, lakes, or aquifers rather than sending it first to a water treatment facility.

The primary dilemma with any "hard-pipe" engineered system is its ability to meet the changing needs of growing populations in urban areas. As human development covers greater areas of land and surfaces it with impervious materials, more water is channeled into the sewerage system. Since the system is limited and inflexible, because every branch has a fixed capacity, when the system is overcharged, as in a storm-related event, flooding can occur. A second dilemma is that legally prescribed standards for water quality have become more stringent as the science of water quality has evolved. The standards that applied to the nineteenth-century industrial city are not those of the postindustrial city of today. Another concern is that rainfall patterns are changing, due primarily to human practices, such as burning fossil fuels, which have micro- and macro-environmental effects. Global climate change is predicted to increase rainfall in most of the Midwest by 0.6–1.0 inches every 10 years and potentially over 1.5 inches every 10 years in parts of Minnesota, which has thousands of glacial freshwater lakes. These data cast doubt on the efficacies of contemporary municipal ordinances that regulate storm water engineering and the infrastructure of piping and treatment systems that are currently in place to manage both human waste and water.

Finally, both the environmental and economic costs of the treatment process itself are an issue. Conventional sewerage treatment is an energy- and chemical-intensive activity. As we redevelop our postindustrial cities, we also need to consider the ecological relationship between water and energy conservation. Conventional water treatment facilities depend on fossil fuels for energy, which adds carbon-based pollutants to the atmosphere and further affects the climate. The goal of ecological storm water management, therefore, is to reduce the overall negative impacts of water management by employing biological systems and processes to absorb and filter storm water.

THE GOAL OF ECOLOGICAL STORM WATER MANAGEMENT

The practical goal of ecological urban storm water management, especially in a combined sewer system city such as in Milwaukee, is to keep as much storm water *out* of the sewer system as possible. The stresses on capacity created by expanding urbanization, changing weather patterns, increasingly stringent regulation, and the economic and ecological costs of maintaining the status quo are overwhelming. The holistic goal of an ecologically managed water system, therefore, is to employ natural water treatment processes to their greatest potential while maintaining and enhancing the human environment for livability. The goal, then, is to weave natural water treatment processes organically into the city by applying the same principles that have transformed postindustrial brownfield sites along rivers and lakes into parks, sustainable wetlands, and natural biomes.

To do this, it is necessary to understand the properties of water and its behavior as an interdependent organic system. When water management and treatment is perceived as a holistic, natural system, then we can restore the natural hydrology of a place and design our urban environments to perform as an ecologically balanced system of interrelated parts. When planners and engineers use ecological methods to regulate and treat water, it will result in an environment that is more attuned to the natural world.

This is the philosophical underpinning of the ecological storm water research at the UWM campus. This approach does not place the needs of nature against the needs of human settlement but rather enhances a built-up urban environment with rain gardens of various shapes and sizes that treat water as an amenity to be enjoyed rather than an adversary to be controlled. As such, it intensifies the urban qualities of place and exploits the specific attributes of ecological design.

UWM as a Zero-Discharge Zone

The stated goal of UWM as a ZDZ study is to recreate a runoff rate and volume comparable to what would have existed before settlement and development of its 90-acre urban campus. The goal of the Pavilion Gateway Project is to capture as much runoff water as possible within a 4-acre drainage area of the parking lot of the campus power plant, and to transform this service area into a pedestrian storm water interpretive path. This area, in turn,

will become a focal point for a recently constructed gymnasium and the Pavilion underground parking structure.

The first project realized from the masterplan in 2008 (fig. 8.2) was the construction of the Sandberg Green Roof, a 32,000-square-foot vegetated roof on the commons building sitting between the four towers of the campus's high-rise dormitory complex. In 2009, the Sandburg Green Roof was followed by the construction of the first phase of the Pavilion Gateway Project, with a series of demonstration rain gardens known collectively as the Spiral Garden, which collect water from approximately 2 acres of parking and building roofs (fig. 8.3). An observation deck in the center of the Spiral Garden and other sculptural additions and interpretive signage for the project are also being developed. A proposal for an innovative 55,000-square-foot green roof retrofit project on the Golda Meir Library has received over $1 million in MMSD support and will be installed in 2011. And perhaps most significant, the ZDZ Masterplan, a speculative exercise in design research and green campus movement activism, has been adopted as a sustainable prototype model and incorporated into the official UWM campus masterplan.

THE UWM CONTEXT

Although the ZDZ proposal was unsolicited, there was a clear and compelling case for its implementation. In addition, the MMSD had both a vested interest and specific agenda in funding it. So while our agenda was to promote UWM as a bioregional center for urban ecological storm water research and education, the drivers of the project are found in the specific conditions of the surrounding neigh-

borhood as much as in the needs and desires of the university.

To the north of the Milwaukee harbor, the Lake Michigan bluff is separated from the western extent of the city by the Milwaukee River, which flows southward parallel to the lake's glacial rim for much of its length before finally entering Lake Michigan. The neighborhood between the river and the lake, known as the East Side, is built on a narrow strip of poorly drained clay that also forms the subsoil of the UWM campus. An examination of the local topography points out the subtle but important fact that the Milwaukee Teachers' College, the original institution on the UWM site, was built on a slight knoll, which in the late nineteenth century was located on the outskirts of the city. While this topography is subtle, it directs the movement of water across the campus, both above grade and in the sewers below. Historical plat maps show that both the southern edge of the campus, now Kenwood Boulevard, and the northern edge, now Edgewood Avenue, were defined by small watercourses that drained into the Milwaukee River. Neither of these original watercourses remains evident above grade, but the northern drainage area is clearly perceptible today as a low point in the terrain.

This dip, marked by Edgewood Avenue, also happens to be the political boundary between the city of Milwaukee and the village of Shorewood. The Edgewood Avenue neighborhood has a long history of basement sewerage backups and local flooding, which is compounded by an undersized sewer infrastructure system that is regulated by two different municipal jurisdictions. In funding the ZDZ Masterplan, it was the MMSD's intention that an ecological way to contain and filter storm water on the 62-acre UWM campus could be an alterna-

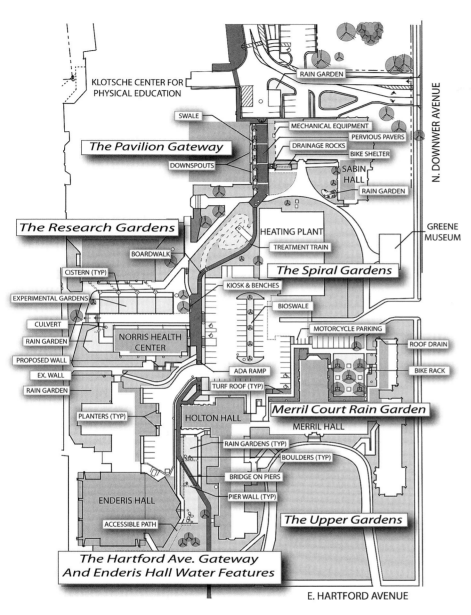

KLOTSCHE CENTER FOR PHYSICAL EDUCATION

RAIN GARDEN

N. DOWNWER AVENUE

SWALE

The Pavilion Gateway

MECHANICAL EQUIPMENT

PERVIOUS PAVERS

DRAINAGE ROCKS

BIKE SHELTER

DOWNSPOUTS

SABIN HALL

RAIN GARDEN

GREENE MUSEUM

The Research Gardens

HEATING PLANT

TREATMENT TRAIN

BOARDWALK

The Spiral Gardens

CISTERN (TYP)

KIOSK & BENCHES

EXPERIMENTAL GARDENS

BIOSWALE

CULVERT

MOTORCYCLE PARKING

RAIN GARDEN

NORRIS HEALTH CENTER

ROOF DRAIN

PROPOSED WALL

EX. WALL

ADA RAMP

BIKE RACK

RAIN GARDEN

TURF ROOF (TYP)

PLANTERS (TYP)

Merril Court Rain Garden

HOLTON HALL

MERRIL HALL

RAIN GARDENS (TYP)

BOULDERS (TYP)

BRIDGE ON PIERS

PIER WALL (TYP)

ENDERIS HALL

The Upper Gardens

ACCESSIBLE PATH

The Hartford Ave. Gateway And Enderis Hall Water Features

E. HARTFORD AVENUE

FIGURE 8.2. Site plan of the Pavillion Gateway–Upper Garden on the University of Wisconsin–Milwaukee campus. (Courtesy of James Wasley, University of Wisconsin–Milwaukee, School of Architecture and Urban Planning)

FIGURE 8.3. Rendering of the proposed Pavilion Gateway and Upper Gardens on the University of Wisconsin–Milwaukee campus. (Courtesy of Celia Liu)

tive to a much more expensive process of reconstructing the existing sewer system. Furthermore, an environmentally driven solution would be an example at a prominent public institution for the community at large to follow.

Based on modeling projections, the goal was to contain a sudden "spike" of water runoff lasting less than 30 minutes at the north end of the campus. This goal also served as the premise for future proposals. The MMSD's regulations stipulate that the rate of flow requires that any temporary storm water storage be fully drained and ready for recharge within 24 hours of a rain event. Thus, *the ability to detain northward-draining storm water for less than a day is the critical metric for success.* Whereas the design study conceptually addresses the entire campus, only the northern half of the campus was modeled in terms of its hydrology. Whereas the MMSD's literature emphasizes "keeping water out of the deep tunnel," this was not the central issue for the UWM campus. In other words, while keeping storm water out of the system altogether is good, simply slowing it down solves the critical problem of control. We were aware that storm water from the entire campus flows eventually into the same combined sewer system as the Edgewood neighborhood, and that demonstration projects on the north side of campus would have a local impact very different from those located on the south side.

On the basis of analyses conducted by the ZDZ, it was determined that averting the Edgewood Avenue combined sewer expansion was not feasible, since the total catchment area for the north draining area of the UWM campus is not physically large enough to retain enough storm water to prevent it from backing up. This realization did not impact the immediate goals of reducing the spike of water rushing to Edgewood Avenue, and

the opportunity for UWM to take a leadership role in demonstrating ecological urban storm water management practices as a whole.

Another site-specific condition that we considered was the layered urban environment in which the UWM campus is embedded. The 90-acre study area includes a public grade school and an adjacent hospital, which will eventually be acquired by the university. Excluding the local streets and the Downer Woods, a small state-protected area of woodland adjacent to the Sandburg residence hall complex, 53% of the campus is comprised of impervious surfaces. In addition, because existing underground fuel storage tanks for the campus power plant were located in the demonstration area for the Pavilion Gateway, ZDZ was required to provide a fuel spill containment strategy. Further complicating our efforts were the underground remnants of the original power plant that serviced the old Downer Teachers' College. Thus, the site chosen for the Spiral Garden was in reality a subterranean maze of active and abandoned steam tunnels and utilities.

The realization that the site was not ideal only enhanced its potential as a demonstration project. It offered a unique institutional setting that could serve as a laboratory of urban conditions and solutions that could be applied to other drainage areas in the city of Milwaukee and many other prospective postindustrial sites as well.

THE ZDZ MASTERPLAN'S QUANTITATIVE FRAMEWORK

While encompassing many related activities, at its core the ZDZ Masterplan is comprised of a design study of the UWM campus as a site for demonstration projects catalogued by type, and a civil engi-

neering study quantifying the potential impacts of BMP strategies. With the goal of capturing storm water at every opportunity, the approach of the design study was to identify BMPs for all surface types. Each surface type was catalogued into one of three categories: priority, secondary, and not suited for capture. *Priority* applications were those that had multiple benefits in terms of storm water management, ecological enhancement, scheduling of campus maintenance projects, aesthetic impact, and symbolic value. Together, priority and secondary equal *full implementation*, which in our analysis represents the maximum feasible extent that capture is possible. Through an iterative process of goal-setting and field evaluation, the masterplan strategy proposed a series of target values for each type of impervious surface. For example, internally and externally drained roofs have a priority implementation target of 40% capture amount of water drained from all roof surfaces, and a full implementation target of 80%. Pedestrian and vehicular hardscapes have priority implementation targets of 20% and full implementation targets of 80%.

On the civil engineering side, a Storm Water Management Model (SWMM) was developed as a graduate thesis project in civil engineering by Elizabeth Locke, under the guidance of her advisor, Professor Hector Bravo. Given the limitations of funding and time, Locke's SWMM model represents only the critical northern drainage area. Calibrated against actual measurements taken at the Edgewood Avenue interceptor, the SWMM model predicts the impact of transforming the surface-flow characteristics of the campus by the application of the priority and full implementation of the design study's categories of BMPs.

The goals of the ZDZ Masterplan were twofold: (1) to create a model of the campus that approximates the hydrological and ecological functions of the landscape as it once existed before settlement, and (2) to apply implementation strategies that will retain storm water in an ecological manner comparable to historic natural drainage and retention patterns while maintaining the urban characteristics of the UWM campus. From a regulatory perspective, the MMSD's targeted release rate for new development is 0.5 cubic feet per second per acre drained (cfs/acre) for a 100-year storm event. By chance or design, this standard also describes quite accurately the peak discharge rate of the northern drainage of the UWM campus as modeled by Locke according to the hypothetical presettlement conditions of the campus, that is, when the campus area was an oak grove. As a result of this convergence, 0.5 cubic feet per second per acre per 100 years emerged as the technical definition of the "zero-discharge" goal.

SOLUTIONS FROM THE TOP OF THE MOUNTAIN DOWN

In describing what could be considered the dawning of his ecological enlightenment, Aldo Leopold writes in *A Sand County Almanac* of learning to "think like a mountain." Leopold realized that the human micromanagement of natural processes is often misplaced unless it is subservient to a larger ecological vision.

The UWM campus may be relatively flat, but "thinking like a mountain" in this context means literally following every rivulet of water as it flows from high ground to low elevations as it seeks ecological equilibrium. The basic strategy of the ZDZ study was to analyze the hydrological cycle beginning with the rain cloud overhead, and to measure and evaluate each horizontal surface of the campus for its potential to capture storm water. The goal

was to collect and disperse the water throughout as much of the campus area as possible. Where hard-pipe engineering seeks an efficient solution by gathering and concentrating water through a network of pipes and directing it to treatment facilities, our "soft engineering" or ecologically informed design approach seeks to mimic the distributed, fractal behavior of the natural landscape. Tracing the downward flow of water, we catalogued water surfaces into the following domains.

INTERNALLY DRAINED ROOFS

Internally drained roofs are flat or low-slope roofs with drains running within the building directly into the storm system. Approximately 23 acres or 20% of the total area of the UWM campus is covered by the barren surfaces of these roofs. These are evaluated for their suitability to be retrofitted with "green roofs" or engineered vegetated roof systems. We have assumed lightweight "extensive" green roof systems 4 inches deep and planted with low-maintenance sedum. A priority design target was established retrofitting 40% of the campus's low-slope roofs with a full-coverage target of 80%. The ensuing analysis justified actual coverage values of 37% and 73%, respectively, based on accessibility, visibility, structural adequacy, and similar constraints.

Quantifying the impact of the study, the now completed Sandburg Commons Green Roof accounts for 32,000 square feet of the entire 423,000 square feet of the northern drainage area. When the 55,000 square feet Golda Meir Library vegetated mat retrofit is complete in 2011 we will have installed green roofs on 20% of the Northern Drainage Demonstration Area's internally drained roofs.

EXTERNALLY DRAINED ROOFS

Externally drained roofs are roofs drained to gutters and downspouts, which are often accessible for diversion into rain gardens and other engineered landscape features. Approximately 7 acres or 6% of the campus area is represented by pitched roofs. The ZDZ catalogues the potential disconnection of 40% and 86%, respectively, captured by rain gardens all located to avoid the removal of existing trees.

The first rain garden demonstration project captured water from the 1,000-square-foot surface of the Sabin Hall roof and was undertaken by the Ecotone student group during the masterplanning process. As a part of the Spiral Garden Project, my graduate studio will be disconnecting downspouts constituting another 16,000 square feet of roof surface drainage at Holton and Merrill Halls and the Norris Health Center, which is approximately 15% of the campus total. To dramatize the water runoff and integrate it into the landscape of the campus, the Norris Health Center downspout disconnections will feed two rivulets that will tumble downward from garden to garden along a newly constructed stairway from the main entry of the building to the Spiral Garden below.

PEDESTRIAN HARDSCAPE

Approximately 20 acres or 17% of the total campus area is dedicated to pedestrian hardscape, though the ZDZ analysis identifies and excludes the quarter of that total that drains to the landscape and not directly to the storm sewer system. Here the variety of recommended BMPs multiplies in response to a myriad of local conditions. Every local topographical relationship that could be used to drain water by gravity and absorbing it into the landscape has been exploited. For example, the Hartford Avenue School Planter Bench addresses the largest single pedestrian hardscape area to date and best demonstrates the principle of "following the flow." The Hartford Avenue public grade school is embedded within the UWM campus and is surrounded by a traditional asphalt playground. The playground is elevated 5 feet above the grade of an adjacent sidewalk, which is wide enough to allow children to queue for school buses. A planter bench will provide gravity-fed storage for water collected from the playground, as well as a place for the students to sit. Together with a proposed dry well at the far end of the playground, this project alone will capture 62,500 square feet or 11% of the total sewer-serviced pedestrian hardscape.

Pervious paving is considered as part of the mix of strategies appropriate for the campus, but only where the option of having the storm water remain above grade and interact with plants is not available. This choice reflects our belief that storm water management should have an aesthetic and ecological benefit as well as an engineering benefit wherever possible. On the other hand, pervious paving BMPs create underground storage capacity that generally cannot be matched by aboveground features. This inherent storage capacity accentuates the impact of these BMPs in relation to all others, especially when modeled for the extremes of a 100-year storm event, making them a potential buffer component in any comprehensive solution.

VEHICULAR HARDSCAPE

Vehicular areas, such as streets, parking lots, and building service areas, are evaluated first with respect to the capacity of the surrounding landscape and second as candidates for pervious paving. First we must ask: are there adjacent down-slope areas where runoff can be diverted to rain gardens? Can these lots be redesigned to incorporate bioretention within their given footprints? With only 9 acres of total vehicular hardscape on the campus, nearly 5 acres is required for loading dock access, disabled parking, and other critical uses that cannot be displaced. Using a bioretention area design standard of 5% of the area to be served, the ZDZ established priority and full implementation target values of 20% and 80%, and verified the design potential to accommodate 19% and 71%.

The construction in 2009 of the Spiral Garden Project represents the first implementation of a parking lot disconnection from the storm sewer, which captured surface runoff from an acre of asphalt, or approximately 18% of the vehicular hardscape at the northern drainage area of campus.

Eliminating the Dunce Cap: Storm-Pipe Daylighting

According to the analysis provided by Locke's SWMM model, the volume of storm water draining into Edgewood Avenue in a 100-year storm is approximately 5.6 acre-feet. The peak flow rate, which is the critical variable in terms of the interceptor's capacity, would be 120 cubic feet per second in that situation. Full implementation of all of these surface strategies throughout the northern drainage would reduce this total by 54% to 2.6 acre-feet, with a peak flow reduction of 44% to 67.5 cubic feet per second. These are sizable reductions but do not meet the 100-year zero-discharge standard of 0.5 cubic feet per second per acre, which translates to 30 cubic

feet per second across the 60 acres of the Northern Drainage Area. Graphically, this results in a "dunce cap," a small red spike in the volume/time graph representing water leaving the Northern Drainage Area into the Edgewood Avenue interceptor at a rate greater than 0.5 cubic feet per second per acre. With every horizontal surface accounted for, the ZDZ Masterplan has failed thus far to achieve its stated objective.

In response to this shortfall, the final strategy explored will be "daylighting" water that has already entered the drainage system. Here we are seeking to coin a new usage for the term "daylighting," extrapolating from the concept of "stream daylighting." Whereas stream daylighting refers to restoring large urban waterways that have been encased in underground pipes to the surface, storm-pipe daylighting implies capturing stormwater that has already entered the smallest branches of the same underground system and retaining it in rain gardens, filter strips, and other biomes. The goal in both instances is once again to bring water as a visible feature into the human-experienced environment, where it can serve both ecological and aesthetic functions (fig. 8.4).

Here a final specificity of the UWM campus becomes critical — while the campus is situated within the combined sewer district of the city, the piping infrastructure on campus is designed to keep storm water and sewerage separated. It is only when the campus storm sewers tie into the adjacent streets that they are combined.

Taking the concept of daylighting water that is already within the storm drainage tree as the starting point, the masterplan goes on to analyze several distinct categories of storm-pipe capture. *Liberating* storm water from internally drained roofs, *capturing* water running through accessible plumbing in underground parking structures, and *directing* storm water from existing detention pipes into engineered wetlands were all explored. Furthermore, the campus's storm drains remain separated until they join the streets that define the perimeter of the campus and its lowest elevation. This realization led to the idea of creating a "moat" of rain gardens comprised of water-loving flowers and pervious sidewalks that will ring the entire campus. Water in the moat will be replenished by sump pumps located just upstream of each of the connection points between UWM's subterranean concrete storm water trees to those of the combined sewer system.

Capturing water that has already entered the labyrinth turns out to be the only viable way to meet the 100-year ZDZ goal. However, once this possibility has been realized, there are many other locations on campus that will allow us to combine easy access to captured water with landscape features to manage water runoff and enhance human interaction. The essential idea of the Pavilion Gateway, for instance, is to create an interpretive path starting at the newly constructed Pavilion parking structure on Edgewood Avenue and progressing uphill to the top of the knoll at the center of campus. This interpretive path is metaphorically seen as a stream, gathering storm water from every possible surface in its discrete drainage basin. As we sought to capture water from an internally drained roof, which represented the highest point on campus, this led us to the realization that even after this water was underground there was enough topographical change along the path that the campus storm sewer could actually be daylit as the headwaters of the Pavilion Gateway's storm water garden

system, similar to an Italian Renaissance grotto. Likewise, a lower internally drained roof on the same building could have its plumbing rerouted to daylight high on an exterior wall, where a sculptural scupper could be installed to mark the presence of the hidden grotto and the start of the garden path below.

Until funding is available and this proposed upper garden can be realized, we have fabricated a prototype for a sculptural scupper that will direct the entire 13,000 square feet of water from the internally drained roof of the UWM power plant into the largest garden in the Spiral Garden chain. It will mark the downstream gateway into the project. Incidentally, this last gesture was completely overlooked until the Spiral Garden was constructed and it became clear that the final garden was not being used to its capacity. If evidence of good design is in the details, then the evidence of good ecological design is in the exploitation of every niche, the interconnection of every node, and the elaboration of every system. While the ecological management of storm water may seem exotic, the Pavilion Gateway demonstration project has shown that it is a strategy that has both practical and aesthetic potential.

Conclusions

Several insights emerge from this research that might guide postindustrial cities everywhere seeking to sustainably and ecologically reweave storm water management systems back into their urban fabrics. The first insight is to find creative solutions in the complex mesh of existing urban landscapes by analyzing and understanding the intertwining

Figure 8.4. Spiral Garden project at the University of Wisconsin–Milwaukee campus. Storm water is directed in a spiral path toward a retention area with aquatic native plants and natural features (as shown in the photograph). (Courtesy of James Wasley)

worlds of free-flowing water in natural habitats and that of the engineered sewerage system, and to be specific about the problems to be solved at each juncture. The flow of storm water in cities is a tangle of site-specific conditions, but when they are untangled they reveal unexpected opportunities. The liberation of water from the campus storm water system through storm-pipe daylighting is possible only because this small catchment area has been separated from the combined sewer system into which it flows. The fact that the combined sewer system at Edgewood Avenue creates a local bottleneck that promotes flooding is due not to the amount of stormwater runoff but to the timing of its arrival, which means that we can use surface containment methods to solve the immediate runoff problem. Our research shows that rain gardens and filter strips work, even though the campus is situated on impervious clay and water may never reliably infiltrate into the ground and be absorbed into the water table below.

A second insight rooted in this view of sustainable storm water management is the realization that the same limits that apply to hard-pipe solutions in terms of the law of diminishing returns also apply to ecological storm water BMPs. Designing a single rain garden to have the capacity to hold water from a 100-year storm means that much of that capacity is going unused most of the time. All storm water systems are designed to have reservoir capacities, and the best way to think of them working efficiently is to think of the combined system working together in a truly distributed fashion — the greater the distribution in an area, the more likely that there are situation-specific ways that each individual system can support the other. Our research has shown that the best solutions of storm water management for the postindustrial city are truly ecological ones, in which an organic network of biological water channels and nodes are artfully woven into urban landscapes. This is also the lesson that can be extrapolated from site-specific research and applied to the postindustrial city. When stormwater is managed in an enlightened and sustainable manner, it creates synergy that enhances our experiences of both the natural and humanmade environments. It provides a new form of infrastructure for the development of economic, social, and environmental opportunities that will allow postindustrial cities to prosper and evolve into global SynergiCities.

References

Environmental Protection Agency. 2007. Report to Congress on Combined Sewer Overflows in the Lake Michigan Basin. Executive Summary. Available at the website of the Environmental Protection Agency, www.epa.gov/npdes/pubs /cso_reporttocongress_lakemichigan.pdf.

Leopold, Aldo. 1966. *A Sand County Almanac with Essays on Conservation from Round River*. New York: Ballantine Books.

Milwaukee Metropolitan Sewerage District. 2010. History. May 2009. Available at the website of the Milwaukee Metropolitan Sewerage District, http://v3.mmsd.com/history.aspx. Retrieved January 2, 2012.

Milwaukee Sewer Socialism. 2010. Available at the website of the Wisconsin Historical Society, www.wisconsinhistory.org/turningpoints/tp-043/?action=more_essay. Retrieved January 2, 2012.

National Weather Service. 2010, May. National Weather Service Climate Prediction Center: U.S. Temperature and Precipitation Trends. Available at the website of the National Weather Service Climate Prediction Center, www.cpc.ncep.noaa.gov /anltrend.gif.

Wasley, James. 2006a, May 5. The Pavilion Gateway Demonstration Project. Available at the University of Wisconsin at Milwaukee PantherFile website, https://pantherfile.uwm.edu/xythoswfs/webui /_xy-39703776_1-t_cuPZank6.

———. 2006b. UWM as a Zero-Discharge Zone: A Stormwater Masterplan for the UWM Campus. Available at the University of Wisconsin at Milwaukee PantherFile website, https://pantherfile .uwm.edu/xythoswfs/webui/_xy-39703775_1-t _cuPZank6.

CHAPTER NINE

Ecological Urbanism in the Postindustrial City

CHRISTINE SCOTT THOMSON

GLOBAL ECONOMIC RESTRUCTURING HAS SPARKED urban crisis and long-term economic decline in many industrial and manufacturing centers since the 1950s, but today Ecological Urbanism is an important urban design theory, providing communities with tools to renew local economies by restoring ecologically and urbanistically compromised landscapes. This chapter explores how an understanding of urban dynamics grounded in the framework of Ecological Urbanism can be used to address the negative effects of the physical and social transformations brought about by globalization and chronicles how a major midwestern city is creating a world-class park and exceptional ecological corridor to secure its future.

Former industrial centers in America's heartland have keenly felt the negative effect of globalization, characterized by expanding flows of ideas, capital, goods, and people throughout the world. These cities have also experienced globalism's tendency to separate economy and materiality, erasing the specificity of place. The result has been a rapid departure from an urban form focused around local-

ized mills, breweries, or factories and toward one based on far-reaching transnational global production networks (Clark 1997).

For the city of Milwaukee, this has meant a pattern of disinvestment and significant economic decline. Over 40 years (1960-2000), the city lost approximately 20% of its population, from a high of 741,324 to a low of 596,974 ("Population of the 20 Largest U.S. Cities, 1900-2005" 2011; "Top 50 Cities in the U.S. by Population and Rank" 2011). In 1970, the 10 largest employers in the city of Milwaukee were based in manufacturing and brewing; by 2004, the 10 largest employers included healthcare, grocery, banking, utility, printing, retail, and insurance, with none of the former leaders. The city's descent was chronicled by the local paper, which noted, "Milwaukee falls to the bottom of nearly every index of social distress" (Boyle 2008).

Decline linked to globalism's increasingly dynamic, invisible, and far-reaching relationships has left former industrial cities struggling to find ways to rebound in the face of physical and social disruption. How can these cities benefit from the forces

of change, and what strategies can they employ to harness the potential of globalism's universality, while simultaneously capturing the value of the single and the local? How will they be able to create design agency in the context of distress?

A Context for Ecological Urbanism

Ecological Urbanism incorporates contemporary thinking about city development and combines it with landscape ecology considerations to integrate functional goals for human use, ideology, and aesthetic style, as well as ecological processes and demands. This contextual framework, when applied to the restoration of a riparian landscape within a former industrial center, creates the conditions to consider new forms of space-making guided by dynamic ecological processes (habitat restoration, biological diversity, etc.) and restrained forms of traditional spatial definition guided by known relationships (low-impact trails, green building, etc).

The inclusive nature of this ideology, a logical companion to theories of globalization, acknowledges the broad economic structure that binds the entire world together and focuses on knowable limits, requiring a rigorous framework for value identification, goal setting, and measured performance.

Today, urban space-making in the context of globalization is dominated by two important areas of urban design theory that, by themselves, are inadequate to address the spatial transformation brought about by new patterns of finance linked to increasingly rapid transportation, communication, and organizational technology. The first area of urban design theory, New Urbanism, focuses on recapturing the spatial definition typical in nineteenth-century cities and advocates for design response that seeks a coherent, pedestrian-scale constructed environment using built form (Duany 2000; Solomon 2003). This thinking views globalism pessimistically and rallies for design that resists the tendency of global capital to disperse homes, stores, and community institutions across the landscape. New Urbanism uses design to channel the forces of global capital toward compact communities that rely on traditional urban form and resist sprawl. The second area of urban design theory, Landscape Urbanism, focuses on new forms of urban space-making and advocates for a design response that utilizes alternative elements, such as landscape, to create a coherent urban condition (Sassen 2006; Waldheim 2006). This theory is generally optimistic about globalism and its potential as a generative force. Landscape Urbanism concedes that constructing new meaningful urban form through traditional built means may be impossible, given the strength of speculative capital and the popularity of the private automobile, and instead uses design to create an urban condition though nontraditional urban elements such as social networking, interstitial spaces, and landscape.

Ecological Urbanism is distinct from, and dependent on, the ideas expressed by these two theoretical positions because it does not ally itself with one or the other but incorporates tenets of both. Ecological urbanism is neither fully resistive, advocating for a design response that seeks a coherent pedestrian scaled constructed environment using built form typical of the nineteenth century's spatial definition, nor fully embracing, seeking unbridled form-making without familiar urban elements that contain a heritage of sociocultural priorities. Instead, Ecological Urbanism is both resistive, with an awareness of the earth as a closed system of limited resources, and embracing, with an understanding of dynamic and recombinant processes that have the potential to convey urban qualities through all spatial elements within the physical world (buildings, landscape, surface, location, etc.). For postindustrial cities, this theory demands restoration of generative physical elements (water quality improvement, soil toxin removal) and seeks civic and economic prosperity within the context of a budget bound by the ecology of place.

The development of Ecological Urbanism as a theoretical position informing design not only mirrors the evolution of the principal stages in urban development beginning in 1950 but also tracks changes to ecological theory since the 1960s. Ecologists have refined thinking about change over time in ecological patterns and processes and redoubled efforts to understand the significance and dynamics of biodiversity (Hill 2000). A greater emphasis on dynamic equilibrium than on steady-state balance within nature has become more prevalent as a focus of research. Ecological Urbanism adopts a similar vantage point, understanding the urban as a dynamic network of multiscaled systems. This view has strengthened an emphasis on process and renewed the importance of collaborative and dynamic community planning and design.

Ecologists are also identifying patterns and predictable relationships occurring over time, even with the acknowledged complexity of multivariable dynamic processes. These patterns and processes are tied to known limits and metrics within the physical world. Whether it is the size of a crow population that limits songbird reproduction (Hill 2000: 93) or the dimensional systems that identify a socioculturally determined concept of ideal beauty, physical limitations and dependencies are a critical part of our understanding of the material world. Ecological Urbanism acknowledges that physical patterns and relationships that govern spatial development have real and knowable limits. These limits, whether tied to biologic or cultural drivers, are all part of a closed system that we understand as a logical outcome of having awareness and connectivity that is global in scope. Ecological Urbanism embraces new forms of the urban made possible by interweaving natural, social, and infrastructural layers but prioritizes economy based on knowing the globe as a finite entity.

Milwaukee River Greenway

In an effort to bolster adaptive capacity and flourish, former industrial cities are searching for ways to combine their unique place-based heritage and to productively harness contemporary urban development forces. With global networks decentralizing manufacturing activities locally or removing them altogether, an economic engine is lost, but landscapes once dedicated to the service of processing and finishing materials can now be recovered and reimagined. As the city develops an identity for itself, these landscapes can play a pivotal role in creating a variety of cultural and leisure venues that enhance the physical landscape for existing residents and invite the creative classes back to the city. In this way, these places become one of the many "short lines" that communities are creating as they find themselves "almost constantly engaged in adjusting to changing conditions" (Van Boom and Mommaas 2009).

The Milwaukee River Greenway Master Plan (the Plan) focuses on one such landscape and has embarked on comprehensive strategy for the river's (and the city's) renaissance. The Plan sets forth a vision for a unique urban wilderness containing restored natural communities and shared recreational opportunities. With a conceptual framework grounded in Ecological Urbanism, the project seeks to create a place with robust ecological integrity and high-quality spaces for urban recreational use. The Plan aims to create a territory within the city that alters the traditional relationship between society and nature from that of naturalized landscapes domesticated for human use to that of ecologically robust landscapes that both provide human use and contribute to the regenerative capabilities of the postindustrial city. The Plan's strength emanates from its ability to establish a greenway-focused governance structure; set forth key principals and goals around habitat improvement and recreational use; and clearly articulate tasks, responsible parties, funding needed, and timelines for action.

The study area is a 7-mile section of the Milwaukee River that cuts through the northeast side of the city, forming a wide and expansive landscape at its northern end and a steep-walled valley at its southern end to create a unique natural setting surrounded by compact urban neighborhoods. The Milwaukee River Watershed is a 448,000-acre area that contributes to the Great Lakes Basin and lies within portions of seven counties. In total, the river system covers a region that is home to about 1.3 million people (fig. 9.1).

Prior to the arrival of Europeans, Native American settlements of the Ho-Chunk, Menominee, and Potawatomi (Wisconsin Cartographers' Guild 1998) could be found near area rivers. The river ecosystem provided a rich biotic community that contained wetlands and forested bluffs abundant with waterfowl, wild rice, fish, and game. The downstream end of the Milwaukee River became a bustling port that attracted German, Scandinavian, and central European immigrants (fig. 9.2); the upstream stretch of the river became the country playground of city residents. Estates, swimming schools, and parks with a country carnival atmosphere attracted great numbers of urban dwellers, providing relief from daily work.

As industrialization blossomed, so did the need for water power, drinking water, and waste disposal associated with thriving factories, breweries, and rail transport in a growing industrial city. The

North Avenue Bridge

Locust Street Bridge

Milwaukee River Ecological Center

Humbold Street Bridge

FIGURE 9.1. Aerial view of the Milwaukee River corridor ecological study area and its relationship to urban neighborhoods in the city of Milwaukee. (Courtesy of Kimberly Gleffe)

working river began to decline as water quality deteriorated (1887-1925), the beer gardens and amusement parks closed (1920-1930s), the swimming schools closed (1940s), and a riverside disposal area was established (1954). The city turned its back on the river, and what was once a playground became a dumping ground. Today the citizens of Milwaukee are rediscovering the river corridor as a vital natural link for both natural and human communities. Through hard work, the water quality has been steadily improving, natural communities are being restored, and river access, trails, and parks are being rediscovered.

The Greenway has the potential to be a key piece of a cultural and leisure program that generates tourism, attracts investments, and supplies a competitive advantage over other cities. Already it has drawn $9-10 million from various state agencies and environmental organizations in direct investments, and it anticipates unlocking another $16.5 million to restore a shared open space system con-

Figure 9.2. Swimmers at Gordon Park on the Milwaukee River in 1921. (Courtesy of Journal Sentinel Historic Milwaukee Photos Archive)

taining a major waterway, numerous parks, and areas of urban wilderness in the heart of the city (Milwaukee River Work Group 2010). In addition to direct investments, a restored greenway will raise local property values as commercial and residential property is valued for its adjacency to a unique "central park" (rather than a polluted abandoned waterway). In addition, several identified "strategic sites" on the perimeter of the greenway are likely to be redeveloped as housing, a wellness campus, mixed-use commercial, or soccer and baseball fields, following public investment in the corridor. Finally, the greenway will generate associated tourism dollars and draw a new urban middle or "creative class" who possess both the economic and creative capital required to generate a restructuring of the city (Florida 2002).

Overview of the Plan

The Plan was developed over eight months and sets forth a structure to advance improvements along a stretch of the river between Silver Spring Drive and the former North Avenue Dam on the northeast side of Milwaukee. With the conceptual framework of Ecological Urbanism, the Plan prioritized a robust community planning process and made central to its focus essential natural patterns and ecological relationships. The result was the beginning of a sustainable design agenda, one that associates social, economic, and environmental elements with an inspiring and mobilizing program capable of restoring collaborative relationships and contributing to a new economic base for this postindustrial city.

The community participation process included

a series of public information meetings held to gather public comments and to provide a forum for discussion about this focused effort. In addition, stakeholder interviews were conducted with a series of representatives from neighborhood groups, public agencies, and river-focused institutions, as well as private land owners. A half-day design workshop that included over 75 people was held where participants assisted in creating a corridor-focused vision that would capture the aspiration for an exceptional greenway and a robust environmental corridor. The design workshop was tailored to utilize the substantial collection of existing conditions information, honor previous community participation, and set forth a coherent road map toward implementation.

The design workshop divided participants into six groups focused on the three topics (two groups per topic), allowing more detailed discussion of the existing conditions mapping, which showed existing connectivity, habitat, and recreation along the entire length of the corridor. The topical "vision maps" created by each group demonstrated significant agreement about priority recreation elements, trail links, and access points, as well as critical areas of habitat. When the community mapping was synthesized, a common approach emerged, emphasizing trail-based recreation, educational and sanctuary areas in the southern half, and park-based recreation and ecosystem restoration in the northern half (fig. 9.3). Much of this consensus on accommodating both recreation and ecology was an outgrowth of active conservation organizations, strong community groups, community design workshops, and draft documents generated over the previous four years. This workshop served to further develop the corridor-wide view, confirm

FIGURE 9.3. Proposed ecological redevelopment along the Milwaukee River, Milwaukee, a joint project of Plunkett Raysich Architects, RA Smith National, and the University of Wisconsin-Milwaukee. (Courtesy of Milwaukee River Greenway Coalition)

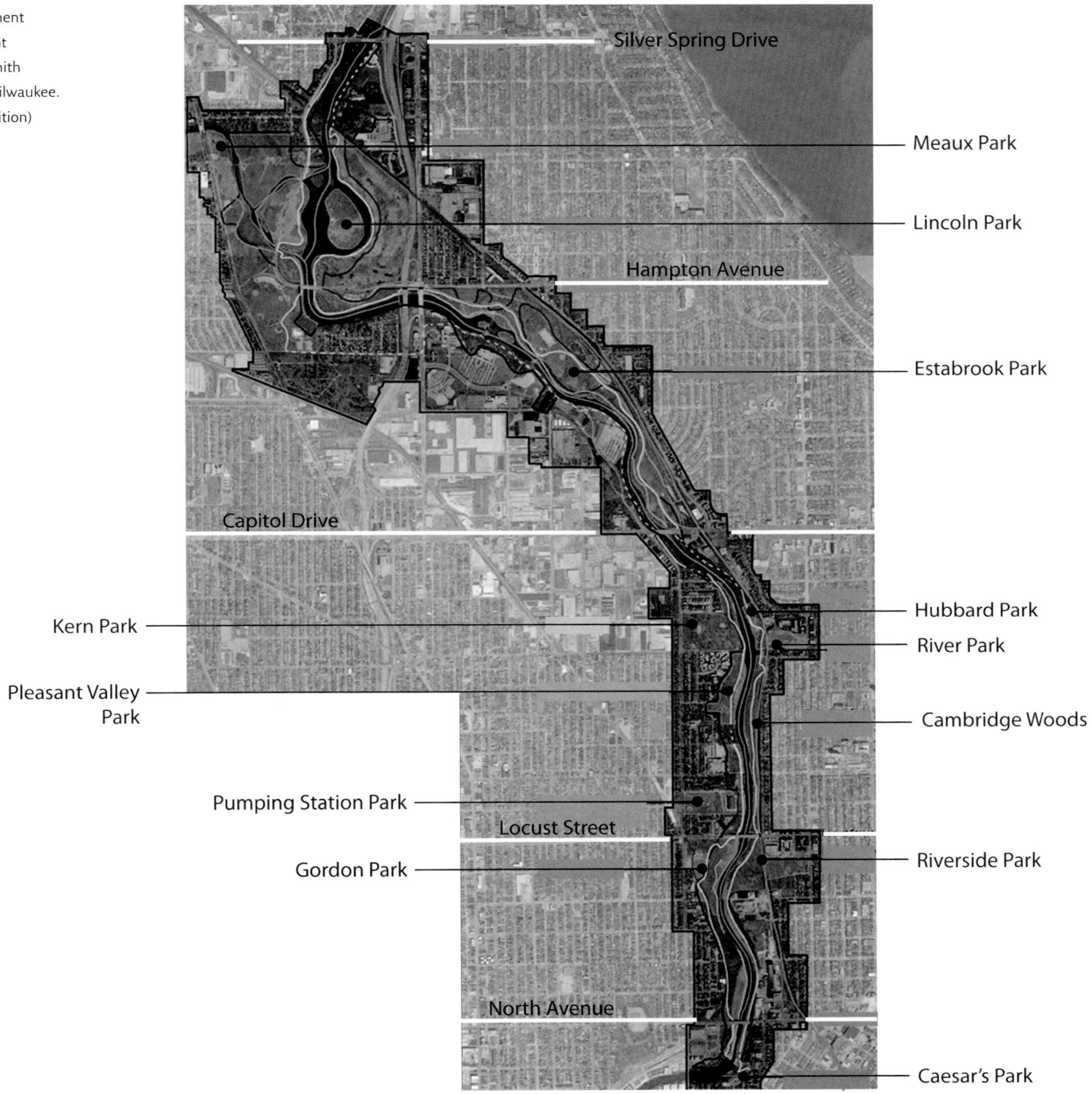

Silver Spring Drive

Meaux Park

Lincoln Park

Hampton Avenue

Estabrook Park

Capitol Drive

Hubbard Park

Kern Park

River Park

Pleasant Valley Park

Cambridge Woods

Pumping Station Park

Locust Street

Gordon Park

Riverside Park

North Avenue

Caesar's Park

priority elements, and provide a forum for public discussion.

An advisory committee of technical experts and community leaders was another important part of the planning process that improved the quality of the Plan. Members of the committee assisted with both general oversight and development of the plan, as well as specialized subcommittees concerned with easements, governance, habitat, and trails. Representatives from national, state, and local environmental organizations (the National Park Service, Wisconsin Department of Natural Resources, Urban Ecology Center, River Revitalization Foundation, Milwaukee RiverKeepers, etc.) were at the table with representatives of all major municipal entities (Milwaukee County, the city of Milwaukee, city of Glendale, village of Shorewood, Redevelopment Authority of Milwaukee, etc.) and specialists in law, landscape architecture, journalism, architecture, and so on. One of the challenges of the Plan was working with multiple municipalities that have interlocking areas of jurisdiction and a complex web of plans, ordinances, and regulations. However, with the stakeholders at the table, individuals were able to identify and resolve potential areas of conflict early in the process. The technical oversight in combination with the local planning process resulted in a plan that was informed by current ecological and community priorities, as well as providing a venue to restore collective trust for residents who have felt powerless over past spatial transformations of their urban environment.

The Plan includes a "vision" that captures diverse sets of information and presents a unified strategy to realize a greenway that meets community goals and aspirations. The project sets the groundwork to guide future efforts toward a river corridor that is a restored system of intertwined natural and humanmade communities. Rather than a typical "park plan" focusing only on creating a set of pastoral landscape areas or identifying key play structures or recreation facilities, the vision describes the corridor as connected systems of water, wetlands, forested wetland, urban forest, open parkland, and urban neighborhoods. The vision shows the extent of the riparian corridor surrounded by green spaces and embedded in the urban neighborhoods, indicates wetlands, identifies slopes and canopy type, marks special habitat or sanctuary areas, shows the routes of the new and existing trails, indicates new and existing access points, highlights corridor-focused institutions, points out exceptional views, and locates landings and piers that provide water access. The vision describes local environmental quality and unique habitat areas and will be informed by a future biotic inventory and map, identification of target species, and metrics for guiding improvements to ecological integrity. The vision also includes a trail route and park spaces that will be informed by future detailed design of trail segments, trailheads, and water access points.

The Plan includes chapters on principles, existing conditions, vision, focus areas, habitat, recreation, and implementation that set forth a strategy to create an outstanding local resource and a world-class destination that enables natural and urban communities to thrive. The Plan describes a corridor-wide identity focused on a forested river valley and surrounding green landscape that will draw not only people who want to hike, paddle, fish, play field sports, and so on but also those who want to learn, wonder, contemplate, appreciate, and so on. The document sets forth a program that anticipates greater stewardship as an outcome of thoughtful development of a trail network and limited but inviting access points integrated with restoration efforts to revive and highlight unique natural communities. Finally, the Plan creates the Milwaukee River Greenway Coalition to lead implementation and develop a fundraising plan, and describes tasks and responsible groups for work over the next 15 years in the categories of governance, remediation, trail development, habitat restoration, and signage/branding.

Existing Conditions

The study area contains a total of 878 acres and includes the Milwaukee River and adjacent land on the city's northeast side, including the Riverwest, Cambridge Woods, and Riverside neighborhoods. The study area contains a Primary Environmental Corridor (PEC), as well as portions of neighborhoods that surround streets and entry points leading to the green corridor (fig. 9.4). (See SWRPC [2010], defining "environmental corridors" as "linear areas . . . containing concentrations of significant natural resources and resource-related features"; for a map of Wisconsin's PECs, see SWRPC [2006]: 40, map 10.)

Like many urban rivers, the Milwaukee River suffered decades of neglect and abuse. A capped landfill containing municipal and industrial wastes is adjacent to the waterway, and PCB-laden sediments exist in the river channel in the northern half of the corridor. Recently exposed mudflats, visible and reachable after the removal of the North Avenue Dam, also contain contaminated sediments, and degrading shoreline stabilization matting coats the

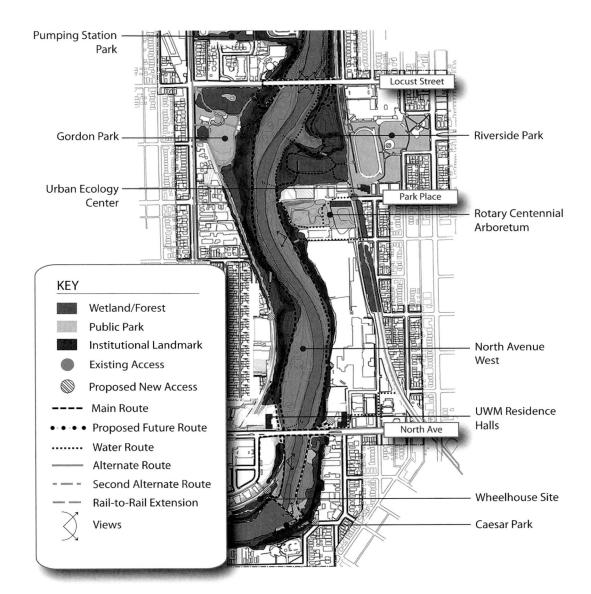

Pumping Station
Park

Locust Street

Gordon Park

Riverside Park

Urban Ecology
Center

Park Place

Rotary Centennial
Arboretum

KEY

- ■ Wetland/Forest
- ▨ Public Park
- ■ Institutional Landmark
- ● Existing Access
- ◍ Proposed New Access
- ---- Main Route
- •-•-• Proposed Future Route
- .... Water Route
- —— Alternate Route
- -- -- Second Alternate Route
- — — Rail-to-Rail Extension
- ⋈ Views

North Avenue
West

UWM Residence
Halls

North Ave

Wheelhouse Site

Caesar Park

FIGURE 9.4. Milwaukee River Greenway Masterplan, Milwaukee, a joint project of Plunkett Raysich Architects, RA Smith National, and the University of Wisconsin-Milwaukee. (Courtesy of Milwaukee River Greenway Coalition)

river channel in the southern half of the corridor. Throughout the study area, brush, leaves, clippings, and snow laden with road salt are disposed of, and both sanitary sewer outfalls and combined sewer outfalls regularly overflow to pollute the water, which means that it is not meeting public health standards mandated by the Federal Clean Water Act.

Despite the legacy of dumping and polluting, this segment of the river also contains 515 acres of the land deemed as a concentration of natural resources and features (the PEC), 148 acres of which is covered by the river channel itself. The corridor contains 12 parks and more than 28 miles of hiking, biking, and water trails. The corridor crosses four jurisdictions, all with a vested interest in the area's health and productivity. Milwaukee County is the primary land holder in the area (70%), and the city of Milwaukee, the city of Glendale, and the village of Shorewood oversee portions of riverbank as well as associated commercial areas and neighborhoods.

The corridor has five primary east-west and one north-south crossing that divide the length of the study area into five segments envisioned as loops or "links" within the larger corridor or "chain" of connected recreational trails and associated park spaces. The plant communities are organized along the length of the river channel in sinuous bands forming wildlife corridors with different mixes of flora and fauna based on water and soil conditions, as well as slope and level of disturbance.

The Plan grouped existing conditions information into three sets of data with similar characteristics and illustrated systems of dependent elements. Connections were depicted as a set of pedestrian access points, conditions of land ownership, and crossings that illustrated important area qualities, thresholds, and adjacencies. Habitat was shown as a field of forested canopy, green areas, and wetlands with distinctive habitat qualities. Recreation was portrayed as a system of interlocking paths and nodes of natural landscapes (five trails and 12 parks) showing a network of places to gather and enjoy the outdoors. The exercise of collecting relevant information, grouping data, and visualizing these as a set of layers was critical for identifying a common baseline of information to build a collective understanding about the entire length of the corridor.

In addition, the layered analysis began the process of understanding the quantitative and spatial information relevant to framing a strategy for revitalization. It simultaneously clarified elements for consideration through grouping and provided opportunity for unforeseen juxtapositions by layering. The process also tested the collective understanding of each group of information around connections, habitat, and recreation. Through this process connections and recreation information was easily collected from official and recently updated sources — trail maps, assessor's data, aerial photographs, park maps — but habitat information was noticeably more elusive and contested. Although ecological information was available from more than five detailed reports, these reports were completed over a time span of more than one and a half decades, and each concerned itself with a limited area or were narrowly focused on specific topics such as urban forestry, water quality, wildlife, and so on.

The Plan addressed this condition by using the regional spatial data for wetlands and tree canopy and adding nonspatial information on plant and animal species. Key native vegetation, mammals, fish, birds, reptiles/amphibians, and invertebrate species were indicated, as well as any species with threatened, endangered, or protected status. An overall base number of species that reports indicated were observed within the corridor was noted to demonstrate the relative presence and potential importance of specific plants and animals. In addition, nonnative species that were known to be the focus of eradication efforts or observed to be crowding out other desirable species were identified.

Collecting existing conditions information demonstrated how the legacy of understanding economic prosperity in opposition to environmental quality is particularly problematic for communities searching for comeback strategies in an era of globalization. Whether habitat and natural community information is difficult to gather because it was never studied (the Milwaukee River has no direct economic value, so why bother) or because it is willfully withheld due to fears of misuse (the Milwaukee River is kept safe by locking it up and keeping people away), both attitudes are a byproduct of conceiving of the natural and urban worlds as separate and independent, if not contradictory. The urban design theory of Ecological Urbanism breaks from this view and seeks to establish performance characteristics for natural systems and criteria for human use, understanding that both are needed for long-term success. It will be more difficult for postindustrial cities to reinvent themselves if they are not prepared to access the potential of new relationships between nature and society.

Design Principles

A community-based process was used to advance the discussion about next steps to improve the ecological quality and recreational experience within the study area. The design principles were an outgrowth of the design workshop and demonstrate community interest in a dynamic and ongoing process of urban place-making through both restoration of the ecological quality and improvement of recreation spaces for people. The principles also indicate an awareness of the patterns and predictable relationships between easily disrupted ecological performance and sets of constructed elements. The principles call for a responsiveness to maintain a natural value in addition to more typical social and economical values.

The community recognized that the environmental quality of the river and the surrounding green spaces is strong and growing. The steep slopes, the wet conditions, and the public ownership that has maintained a connected corridor of nonurbanized land mean that it has the potential to be restored into a healthy ecosystem. Industry and settlement have often overwhelmed natural systems and reduced ecological robustness. However, today residents are stewards of these green areas. The first principle is to use *ecological integrity* (defined by common scientific indicators, such as water quality at fishable/swimmable/drinkable levels, target species with a strong or unique role in an ecosystem, presettlement vegetation comprised of native plant species, plant and animal distribution representing favorable ecosystems, settlement pattern limitations that signal lack of competition, etc.) to focus and form ideas about the quality and quantity of recreation throughout the study area.

Users also observed that the isolation of the corridor created by its natural terrain and riparian features has had the beneficial effect of limiting disruptive human activity and the deleterious effect of encouraging dumping of trash and unintended uses (vagrancy, gay cruising). In addition, barriers that prevent the community from experiencing the corridor as a diverse set of connected spaces were noted. Although community members were concerned about the possibility of "loving it to death," the Plan seeks to increase stewardship for further ecological restoration by setting forth clear rules of engagement governed by a shared-use philosophy and overseen by a greenway advisory committee. The second principle is to create *stronger links* between the community and surrounding neighborhoods and the river. Stronger links will foster the creation of enjoyable, life-affirming places while building a shared responsibility for the study area.

Participants noted that an uncoordinated collection of signs is distributed throughout the corridor marking parks, trails, poor water quality, restricted fishing, combined sewer overflow outlets, and private property. The signs communicate a collection of local issues but fail to create a brand identity that inspires and invites people to use and care for the corridor. The landscape is a connected territory of overlapping systems of natural and human communities that, when considered as isolated patches, fails to engender a coherent approach that balances ecology and recreation along its length. The third principle is to develop an *imaging and signage program* that creates a unified identity, provides a sense of entry and arrival, imparts educational/interpretive information, indicates warnings about sensitive or special places, and marks preferred routes for way finding.

Discussion about parks, boat landings, play fields, pools, golf courses, rails to trails, and hiking trails noted that recreational elements provide opportunities for city residents and visitors, but use of certain areas can be in direct conflict with natural communities containing rare plants and animals. Making visible existing ecological re-

sources and prioritizing a corridor biotic inventory and map to set a baseline for restoration is only part of the solution; integrating design elements that avoid ecosystem disruption is also a critical component of accommodating both natural and human communities. The fourth principle is to use *high-protection recreational elements*. New recreational elements, most notably a riverside trail, would remain primitive in sections, would be designed to stabilize banks, would incorporate boardwalks where needed, and would communicate performance metrics that demonstrate limited ecological impact. Improvement to boat landings, future park shelters, and parking design would all integrate sustainable approaches and best management practices, as well as an educational component to advance knowledge about the best techniques to create low-impact/high-protection recreational elements.

Recreation

Recreation plays a central role in the corridor, since there are 12 public parks and four recognized trails. The Plan identifies a recreation component, but the greenway is not conceived of as a "park" in the traditional sense, nor is it a pristine "nature sanctuary." The Plan envisions recreation and habitat interwoven, based on a balance between recreational and ecological needs. Recreation is intended specifically to increase the number of responsible users who enjoy and look after the corridor. Recreation is limited in the areas identified in the Habitat component where conflicts are known and natural communities take precedence.

Beyond the formal park spaces and trails, an almost continuous informal (social) riverside trail has

been cut by people walking alongside the waterway. Many of the recreational spaces have suffered due to the legacy of dumping and polluting or have been abandoned due to the lack of maintenance and budget cuts characteristic of former industrial cities with shrinking revenues. The Plan focuses on providing safe, environmentally sensitive, and interesting river access while expanding the passive and active recreational activities, such as hiking, bird watching, nature education, golf, biking, paddling, Frisbee, and so on.

The central recreation initiative is to improve and maintain a new 13-mile loop and link trail that serves a wide variety of recreational activities without harm to wildlife habitat. Recreational activities that are, for the most part, accommodated by the trail and river include such nonmotorized uses as hiking, bird-watching, fishing, biking, dog walking, cross-country skiing, snowshoeing, and so on. The Plan envisions the trail system as using a mix of mostly moderate- and low-intensity trail treatment and uses photo examples to suggest a variety of materials, media, and characters possible for both trail types.

The Plan includes a shared-use philosophy for this new trail that sets forth principles of community use to balance both recreational and ecological principles. The shared-use philosophy is intended to foster people's connection and sense of responsibility to the river ecosystem. It provides guidance on managing conflicts through design of trails and communication of the goals. The philosophy includes directives to provide "quiet" areas for nature appreciation and fostering respect for the corridor as an "urban wildlife ecosystem and a place for recreation." It also insists on building and managing trails to minimize impact on the natural habitat.

Additional minor recreation initiatives focus

on improvements to the existing Milwaukee River Urban Water Trail, a mapped series of boat landings, portages, and water hazards for paddlers. Eight specific areas along the Water Trail will be enhanced as part of building a greater constituency within the corridor that includes boaters and paddlers. By reuniting people with the river corridors, the water trail is intended to promote stewardship and community engagement. To support recreational use (and meet habitat objectives) the Plan calls for the development of a graphically unified signage program that asserts the corridor's identity as a single place containing ecological and recreational resources. Four key sign types with two themes were developed to facilitate communication and graphically characterize each function.

The recreation program identified by the Plan takes the first steps toward reuniting people in multiple ways with a river that is recovering from industrial use. The recreational elements primarily address the most significant missing experience along the river corridor today — enjoying a forested and flowing world at the water's edge — and set forth a structure with flexibility to accept additional arrangements of urban activities and biologically productive fields. The Plan establishes a priority route and shows sensitive landscapes but resists further development of phasing, animal habitats, succession planting, and hydrological systems, favoring instead the mobilization of community by suggesting the potential of the multifaceted, multiscalar corridor and creating a culture of stewardship.

Habitat

This segment of the Milwaukee River is also known for its character as a remarkable valley that opens into a broad plain at the confluence of the main stem of the Milwaukee River and Lincoln Creek further upstream. From a canoe or along a riverside trail, it is easy to forget that you are in the heart of a major metropolis. The steep, forested banks shelter wildlife and visitors from the noise and views of the city's hardscape. Further upstream the waterway is surrounded by sculpted islands and wetland marshes surrounded by golf courses and play fields providing uninterrupted views of natural and naturalized landscapes.

For the most part, this land was set aside from urban development to serve as a desirable environment that contained natural landscapes undefiled by industrialization. In 1907, a newly formed Milwaukee County Parks Commission was created to acquire land to provide places for recreation, education, and "inspirational advantages" for a fast-growing community. Charles B. Whitnall, widely considered the father of the Milwaukee County Park System, noted at the time, "we are badly in need of social adjustment in which land use appears to be a most vital factor" (Allison 2005: 86-87). Although the insight that it was important to preserve natural landscapes for the future was ahead of its time, the way landscapes were viewed as a social safety valve in opposition to the industrial city is distinctly different from contemporary views that observe urban and natural landscapes as similar fields with different biological patterns and processes at work.

The Plan describes the "life cycle" of the riparian landscape that has transitioned through presettle-

ment, settlement, industrial, and postindustrial phases and imagines this local asset as a source of vitality and New Urbanity, defined by a dynamic balance between ecological potentials and human use. The Plan's habitat element recognizes that the groundwork of documenting and understanding the ecology of the corridor as a whole had not been completed and prioritizes immediate completion of biotic inventory and map of existing plant and animal communities. In addition, the habitat element identifies seven known unique locations for habitat where sanctuaries either exist or will be realized, as well as providing information on the state of birds, fish, bats, and reptiles/amphibians. Finally, the Plan recommends that redevelopment of several specific urban sites adjacent to the corridor be coordinated with greenway objectives seeking to extend an understanding of how built places can integrate human needs and ecological performance requirements.

A critical component of the Plan was to focus the work of the newly created coalition on the immediate task of completing the biotic inventory and map. To use landscape as a suitable medium through which to order programmatic and social change over time, the coalition will create an ecological baseline and a set of metrics for temporal change, transformation, adaptation, and succession to ensure measurable improvements to ecological integrity.

The Plan sets out a structure that builds momentum at the community and organizational (nonprofits, regulatory agencies, municipalities) level to enable broad support for new approaches to urban place making and meaningful habitat improvement. It acknowledges that recreation priorities and traditional landscape approaches are significantly more established and that not only should additional information and analysis to understand habitat considerations be undertaken but also a public process is needed to establish consensus on habitat objectives. The Plan seeks to build local capacity, align initiatives, clarify a conceptual framework, and initiate a fundraising program to support design development. The Plan is the first step toward creating an urban park that will change the relationship between society and nature.

Conclusion

Globalism is making it difficult to address the causes of decline in the fabric and topography of former industrial cities. The ecologically and urbanistically compromised landscapes, a byproduct of spatial transformations resulting from transnational global production, reinforce decline and inhibit revitalization. For these communities to be successful cities, they will have to envision, plan, and implement transformation strategies that work with contemporary economic and sociocultural conditions.

In a post-Fordist economy, characterized by rapid and widespread flows of ideas, capital, goods, and people that divorce economic prosperity from local conditions, the framework of Ecological Urbanism can simultaneously harness productive forces within the new economy and revitalize elements of place. Utilizing this conceptual context, communities can soften the negative effects of waning community development forces and rebound from economic decline. By focusing on a diversity of place-making strategies and utilizing an inclusive framework that aligns environment and economy, communities can avoid the social disruption caused by the collapse of a single, dominant industry. Most important, communities can reorient value creation to restore (rather than degrade) the ecological systems on which the economy and community depend.

Postindustrial cities have experienced firsthand the folly of an economic model that derives value at the expense of local ecology and must be willing to move towards a model that realizes productivity by aligning economic success and restoration of natural communities. Just as twentieth-century theories of urban design helped to introduce naturalized landscapes (large public parks) into the city as an antidote to the "social adjustment" taking place in fast-growing communities, as described by Charles B. Whitnall, as well as to directly address environmental crises, so too, twenty-first-century theories of urban design are helping to integrate ecologically robust landscapes (environmental corridors, habitat reserves) into the city as an antidote to the social adjustment taking place in fast-shrinking communities, as well as to directly address the carbon crisis of today. Communities must be willing to engage in a collaborative planning and design process that not only activates the general public but also focuses (and catalyzes) efforts of municipal governments, nonprofit organizations, and state and local agencies. Communities must look within and beyond their borders to identify and reimagine landscapes that have the potential to activate a collective imagination and establish a sense of place even in the absence of the traditional urban form.

The Milwaukee River Greenway Master Plan is the first step in a strategy to create a unique culture and leisure venue that provides a positive image and a compelling vision of "thriving recreation wilderness in the heart of the city" inviting reinvestment and rediscovery. The Plan coordinated a public process and created a political entity to mobilize citizens, municipalities, nonprofits, and environmental agencies. It also envisions a new kind of shared space through the framework of Ecological Urbanism, a place that dynamically balances habitat and recreation priorities. The vision will draw new resources and bring the benefits of design agency to the corridor.

The spatial transformation necessitated by globalization may have sparked crisis in midwestern postindustrial cities, but the same forces can be used to forward transformation strategies and renew economic prosperity. The Plan illustrates how this unique local topography and specific industrial heritage can be reimagined and the Milwaukee River's potential can be realized to bring resources and people back to the city.

References

Allison, B. R. 2005. *Every Root an Anchor: Wisconsin's Famous and Historic Trees.* Madison: Wisconsin Historical Society Press.

Boyle, J. 2000. Milwaukee Wisconsin, the Northwest Neighborhood, 2000. In David Erickson et al., *The Enduring Challenge of Concentrated Poverty in America: Case Studies from Communities across the U.S.* [Richmond, VA: Federal Reserve Bank of Richmond.]

Clark, D. 1997. *Interdependent Urbanization in an Urban World: An Historical Overview.* Hoboken, NJ: Wiley-Blackwell.

Duany, A., E. Plater-Zyberk, and J. Speck. 2002. *Suburban Nation: The Rise of Sprawl and the*

Decline of the American Dream. New York: Northpoint Press.

Florida, R. 2002. *The Rise of the Creative Class.* New York: Basic Books.

Hill, K. 2000. "Urban Ecologies: Biodiversity and Urban Design." In *Downsview Park Toronto,* ed. Julia Czerniak. Munich: Prestel Verlag, 90-101.

Milwaukee River Work Group. 2010. *Milwaukee River Greenway Master Plan: A Vision for Recreation and Restoration.* Milwaukee: Plunkett Raysich Architects.

"Population of the 20 Largest U.S. Cities, 1900-2005." 2011, June 10. Infoplease. © 2000–2007 Pearson Education, publishing as Infoplease. http://www .infoplease.com/ipa/A0922422.html.

Rubin, Bruce, and Gerald Emmerich. 2000. "Redefining the Delineation of Environmental Corridors in Southeastern Wisconsin." In *Twenty-Five Years of Regional Planning in Southeastern Wisconsin: 1906-1985.* Technical Record 4.

Waukesha: Southeastern Wisconsin Regional Planning Commission.

Sassen, S. 2003. "Reading the City in a Global Digital Age between Topographic Representation and Spatialized Power Projects." In *Global Cities: Cinema, Architecture and Urbanism in a Digital Age.* Piscataway, NJ: Rutgers University Press, 15-30.

Solomon, D. 2003. *Global City Blues.* Washington, DC: Island Press.

Southeastern Wisconsin Regional Planning Commission. [SWRPC]. 2006, June. "A Regional Land Use Plan for Southeast Wisconsin: 2035." Planning Report no. 48. Waukesha, WI: SWRPC. Available at http://www.sewrpc.org/SEWRPC /LandUse/EnvironmentalCorridors.htm. Accessed February 17, 2012.

———. 2010. Environmental Corridors. Available at http://www.sewrpc.org/SEWRPC/LandUse /EnvironmentalCorridors.htm. Accessed February 17, 2012.

Thomson, C. S. 2010, July 8-11. "Responsive Urbanism: Sustainable Development Strategies for small communities with an Intercultural Focus." Paper presented at Fabos International Planning and Greenway Conference, Budapest.

"Top 50 Cities in the U.S. by Population and Rank." 2011, June 10. Infoplease. © 2000–2007 Pearson Education, publishing as Infoplease. http://www.infoplease.com/ipa/A0763098.html.

Van Boom, N., and H. Hans Mommaas, eds. 2008. *Comeback Cities: Transformation Strategies for Former Industrial Cities.* Rotterdam: NAi.

Waldheim, C., ed. 2006. *The Landscape Urbanism Reader.* New York: Princeton Architectural Press.

Wisconsin Cartographers' Guild. 2000. *Wisconsin's Past and Present: A Historical Atlas.* Madison: University of Wisconsin Press.

PLATE 1. Outdoor restaurants and pedestrian boardwalks along the Milwaukee
River in Milwaukee's Third Ward District enhance urban enjoyment for residents and visitors.
(Courtesy of Paul J. Armstrong)

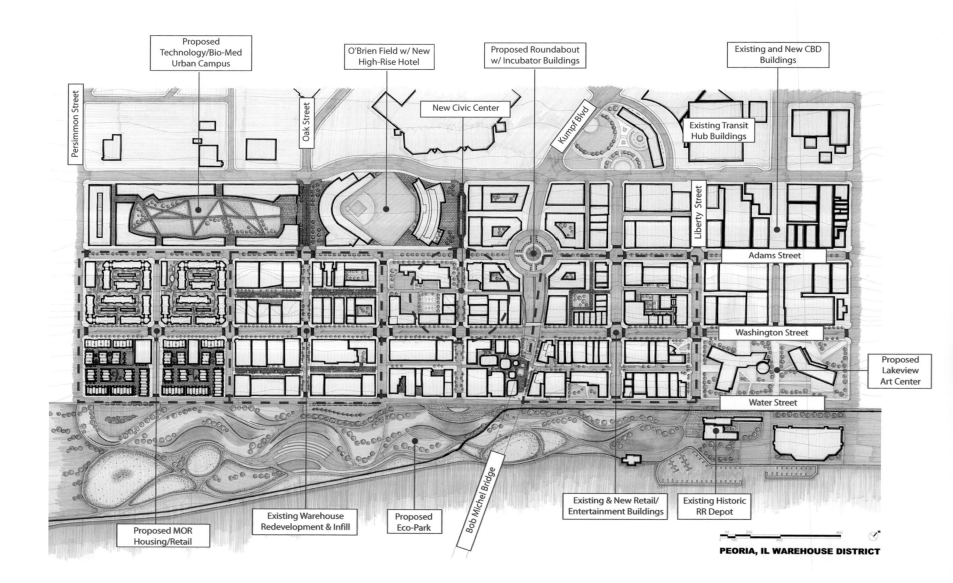

PLATE 2. SynergiCity Masterplan, Warehouse District, Peoria, Illinois.
(Courtesy of School of Architecture, University of Illinois, Urbana-Champaign)

Proposed Technology/Bio-Med Urban Campus

O'Brien Field w/ New High-Rise Hotel

Proposed Roundabout w/ Incubator Buildings

Existing and New CBD Buildings

Persimmon Street

Oak Street

New Civic Center

Kumpf Blvd

Existing Transit Hub Buildings

Liberty Street

Adams Street

Washington Street

Proposed Lakeview Art Center

Water Street

Proposed MOR Housing/Retail

Existing Warehouse Redevelopment & Infill

Proposed Eco-Park

Bob Michel Bridge

Existing & New Retail/ Entertainment Buildings

Existing Historic RR Depot

PEORIA, IL WAREHOUSE DISTRICT

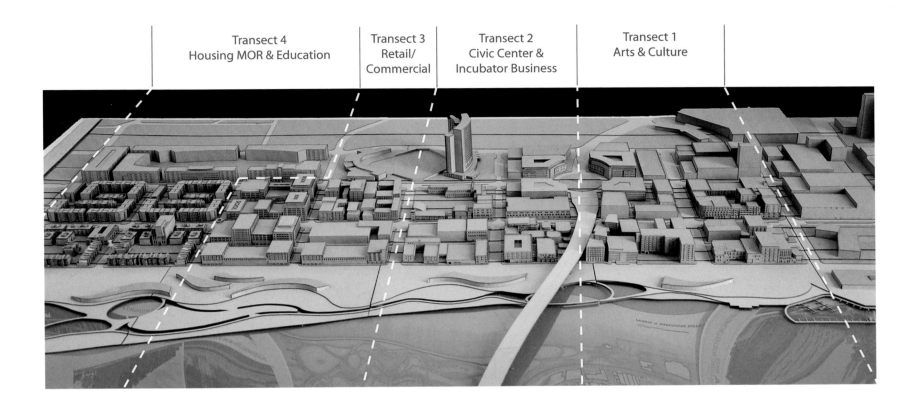

PLATE 3. SynergiCity Masterplan Model with Transects, Warehouse District, Peoria, Illinois.
(Courtesy of School of Architecture, University of Illinois, Urbana-Champaign)

Transect 4
Housing MOR & Education

Transect 3
Retail/
Commercial

Transect 2
Civic Center &
Incubator Business

Transect 1
Arts & Culture

PLATE 5. Rendering of proposed Eco Park sustainable redevelopment, including recreation and a wetlands biome along the Illinois River. SynergiCity: Warehouse District, City of Peoria, Illinois. (Illustration by Meghan Roller. Courtesy of School of Architecture, University of Illinois, Urbana-Champaign)

PLATE 6. Proposed SynergiCenter plaza. In SynergiCity: Warehouse District of Peoria, Illinois (Illustration by Cody Bornsheuer and Michael Logunetz. Courtesy of School of Architecture, University of Illinois, Urbana-Champaign)

PLATE 7. Proposed roundabout at the intersection of Klumpf Boulevard and Adams Street, defined by high-tech incubator business and retail buildings. A pyramidal skylight brings light to subterranean circulation and shopping. SynergiCity: Warehouse District of Peoria, Illinois (Illustration by Ben Lyons. Courtesy of School of Architecture, University of Illinois, Urbana-Champaign)

PLATE 8. Banbury Place, a mixed-use redevelopment of a former UniRoyal Tire Factory in Eau Claire, Wisconsin, offers affordable apartments for students and low-income residents, studios for artists, and commercial lease-space. (Courtesy of Paul J. Armstrong)

PLATE 9. The historic DeWitt-Seitz Building in Canal Park in Duluth, Minnesota, features retail shops and offices and provides a district landmark. (Courtesy of Paul J. Armstrong)

PLATE 10. Atrium of historic Butler Square in Minneapolis. An early example of adaptive reuse in the Midwest during the 1970s. (Courtesy of Paul J. Armstrong)

PLATE 11. The lobby of the Iron Horse Hotel, located at Walker's Point in the Fifth Ward of Milwaukee, combines old and new architecture to create a comfortable yet slightly edgy atmosphere featuring "industrial chic" design. (Courtesy of Paul J. Armstrong)

PLATE 12. Courtyard view of WireWorks features condominiums and retail adaptive reuse in St. Louis, Missouri. The WireWorks complex, a former wire factory, was redeveloped after a catastrophic fire. (Courtesy of Paul J. Armstrong)

PLATE 14. Milwaukee's Third Ward District, developed during the 1980s, provides livable neighborhoods with retail, cultural, and entertainment amenities all located within a compact, walkable district. (Courtesy of Paul J. Armstrong)

PLATE 15. Pedestrian-friendly streets have been created with shops, paving, trees, historic outdoor light fixtures, public sculptures, and outdoor seating in Canal Park in Duluth, Minnesota. (Courtesy of Paul J. Armstrong)

PLATE 16. Aerial view of Silo Point, Baltimore, by Turner Development Group transforms a former brownfield industrial site on the harbor into a vibrant community of mixed-used buildings and activities. (Courtesy of Turner Development Group)

The Sustainable Transportation Agenda for Postindustrial Cities

NORMAN W. GARRICK

AT THE VERY MOMENT THAT THE INDUSTRIAL CITIES of America were beginning to lose their industrial base, they were also faced with the issue of how to cope with the unprecedented increase in motorization sweeping post–World War II America. Most cities chose to meet the challenges of the new era by adopting measures designed to facilitate car travel and to accommodate car storage — highways were built through the center of cities, on-street parking was eliminated for efficient traffic flow, and large numbers of historic buildings were cleared for surface lots and parking garages.

Fortunately, a handful of cities in the country eventually adopted a different approach — they focused less on mobility and more on maintaining or even strengthening their urban fabric. Cities like Cambridge, Massachusetts, and Portland, Oregon, reduced urban space devoted to automobile use with such strategies as removing freeway sections, reclaiming street space for civic and nonmotorized use, and giving priority to public transit over private vehicle travel. One measure of the success of these strategies is that these cities now have fewer people driving than they did in 1960 and are among the most vibrant cities in the country.

Today, a new wave of cities is taking tentative steps toward overcoming the 1950s-era approach to transportation planning and provision. Examples of cities in the Midwest with transportation policy that supports the development of the SynergiCity include Milwaukee, with the trendsetting removal of an urban freeway; Madison, Wisconsin, where biking has been adopted as crucial to a prosperous future not just as a means of transportation but also as one strand in nurturing home-sprung industries; and Chicago, which has embraced sustainable transportation planning as a way of enhancing its status as a global city.

What we are learning is that successful cities all have a similar approach to transportation planning. They treat their transportation system first and foremost as a tool or lever to enhance urban life, prosperity, and vitality. They do this by giving priority to walking, biking, and transit in the design, planning, and funding of transportation. In other words, they have adopted a city-friendly approach to transportation planning.

This approach is city-friendly because the means of travel that are favored — walking, biking, and transit — are much more compatible with city life, and in particular, with the need for cities to effectively use space and to facilitate face-to-face interaction. These modes of travel are also generally much cheaper and, without a doubt, much cleaner, more equitable, and more social — all factors that are essential to well-functioning cities.

These successful cities have rejected the more common approach to transportation provision in which cities all but bend over backward to accommodate car travel. This quest to accommodate cars that we see in so many cities is incredibly inefficient and wasteful of space. The results are cities that are hollowed out to make room for bigger roads and more parking. The ironic outcome is that this drive to accommodate more vehicles not only saps the energy from cities but also creates such a dysfunctional transportation pattern that it does not work — even for cars.

In this chapter we look at specific examples of transportation planning and design strategies that have been shown to work to strengthen the structure and vitality of cities in America and around the world. And we will examine how the lessons from these cities can be more broadly applied to postindustrial cities that are still struggling to develop effective transportation strategies that set the groundwork for a more prosperous future.

The Era of the Automobile and the Decline of Postindustrial Cities

The history of America's mythical love affair with the car is dramatically illustrated by the graph showing the century-long runup in the total of miles driven each year in America (graph 10.1). Although the production of the automobile dates from 1888, the number of miles driven did not start to tick upward sharply until around 1910, in response to the introduction of Henry Ford's Model T in 1909. By 1920, Americans were collectively driving 47 billion miles each year, and the number of vehicles on our streets had increased twentyfold in just 10 short years. Clearly something had to give — cities of the day had not been built to handle cars in any great volumes, and they were unprepared for the assault to come.

Peter Norton, author of *Fighting Traffic*, writes about the process of remaking American cities

into places that were ready to accommodate the car (Norton 2008). According to Norton, before the advent of the automobile, the users of city streets were diverse and included children at play and pedestrians. By 1930, most streets were primarily motor thoroughfares where pedestrians were condemned as "jaywalkers." Norton persuasively makes the case that "to accommodate automobiles, the American city required not only a physical change but also a social one: before the city could be reconstructed for the sake of motorists, its streets had to be socially reconstructed as places where motorists belonged. It was not an evolution, but a bloody and sometimes violent revolution" (p. 1).

By the early 1930s, this battle for the social acceptance of the automobile was essentially over, to the detriment of both the quantity and quality of civic spaces in the cities. Now our cities bore the battle scars of newly widened streets to accommodate

moving vehicles and buildings demolished to accommodate vehicles at rest, leaving huge gaps that frayed the urban fabric and made it less attractive to be on foot.

Although these changes were not inconsequential, in looking back at that period, it is important to remember that cities of the 1930s and 1940s still continued to function largely as they had done 20 and 30 years previously. People still lived, worked, shopped, and went to schools in their neighborhoods; they took the trams to thriving downtowns that bustled with people; and people from the burgeoning suburbs of the day were connected to the city, physically by rail, and psychologically by the sense of a shared destiny. In the 1930s and 1940s, the cities were still the most dominant part of urban America. Suburbs were still just that — places that were subordinate to cities, not their competitors.

The bloody revolution Norton describes had

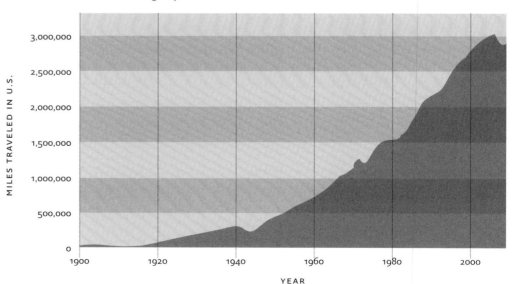

GRAPH 10.1. Total Miles Traveled in U.S., 1900–2000. (*Source*: Federal Highway Administration 2008)

damaged cities but had not dealt them a mortal blow. That was yet to come.

From 1910 to 1940, the amount of driving in America increased at a steady rate and then plummeted during the war years. But the truly fascinating story of cars in America relates to what happened after the war. Fueled in part by the Interstate Highway Act, in the period between 1950 and 1980, the rate of increase in driving more than doubled that in the prewar period.

Now we had moved into a new and largely uncharted territory in terms of the effect of cars on cities. Given the furious pace of this change, it must have seemed at the time that its effects on the cities and the growth of the automobile suburbs were inevitable—the results of natural forces that just swept along everything in their path. However, while these forces may have been furious, they were distinctly manmade.

In *The Long Emergency*, James Howard Kunstler points to two decisions that changed everything for American cities after 1950. The first of these was a decision at all levels of government to continue the project of suburbanization that began in the 1920s but was stillborn due to the Great Depression and the war. The second game changer was the decision in 1955 to build the interstate highway system. According to Kunstler, "the result of these two decisions was technological lock-in. Once the investment was made in the infrastructure and furnishings for suburbia, we were stuck with it, and with the enormous amounts of oil required to run it" (2005, p. 41).

And we were also stuck with cars—millions of cars that demanded accommodations in cities. In 1945, there were 220 cars for every 1,000 Americans; by 1960 that number had almost doubled to 410 per 1,000. It took another 45 years for that number to double again, topping out at 825 cars per 1,000 in 2001 (U.S. Department of Energy 2007). Given the tsunami of cars that was unleashed on the cities in the 1950s, the decision facing our cities at the times was how to react—what was being asked of them now was not simply a matter of widening a few surface streets or creating a few more parking lots. Given the sheer size of this new invasion of cars, it is not surprising that many cities agreed to urban renewal and highway construction. Few stopped to contemplate the scale of these changes and how they would alter the cities and at the same time how these actions would shift the balance of power and prosperity from the cities to their hinterlands.

In the United States the allure of millions of federal dollars for urban renewal and for highway construction did not help. Few politicians could resist the carrot of federal dollars, but in some cities—notably San Francisco, Boston, New York, and Washington, D.C.—residents and activities waged successful battles that stopped the construction of highways they felt would eviscerate their cities. These were among the few American cities that were saved from the full excesses of this period. But all across America, many other cities bore the full brunt of highway construction.

Mark Goldman in *City on the Edge* describes the experience in Buffalo, New York, where officials were out ahead of the rest of the country:

> They began to plan well before [World War II] was over for what everyone fully expected to be the new golden age of the automobile. By war's end the mechanism for bringing it about—a sweeping plan for the construction of a whole new system of city and region-wide highways and arteries—was

in place. . . . The report, which became the bible for transportation planning in Buffalo for the next thirty years, was rooted in the belief that the city's survival required that it take immediate steps to accommodate the projected enormous increase in private vehicle ownership. (2007, p. 143)

According to Goldman, this 1946 plan was used as the rationale for a 1953 proposal to superimpose on the existing pattern of the city (indiscriminately cutting across some of America's finest streets, parks, and neighborhoods) a massive grid of five superhighways to connect Buffalo's declining downtown to the rapidly growing suburbs. He goes on to state that "the price that would be paid for this plan was enormous, and the damage has so far been irreparable. The people of Buffalo watched as the fabric of their city came tumbling down. Falling with it was their history and their heritage and, unbeknownst to them, their future as well" (2007, p. 147).

The effect of this mass destruction of place on the physical and mental health of the people and of the community itself is perhaps still not fully appreciated. But in retrospect a city like Buffalo seems to have been devastated on a psychic level by this loss of place. This in turn led to a loss of identity and self-confidence that has been hard to recover from (few people now remember that Buffalo was once one of America's most celebrated cities).

The social psychiatrist Mindy Fullilove has coined the term "root shock" to describe the loss of place and its effect on the prospects of a community. In her book of the same name she describes root shock as "the traumatic stress reaction to the destruction of all or part of one's emotional ecosystem" (2005, p. 11). By her definition the changes in Buffalo in the 1950s were a classical example of root shock.

But Buffalo was not alone. The journalist Alex Marshall writes in *How Cities Work* that his hometown of Norfolk, Virginia, had the dubious honor of being the first city to make use of federal urban renewal money. This money was used to tear down over 1,000 acres of buildings in a historic downtown that dated from the eighteenth century. Lost in the blink of an eye, Marshall writes, were "the century-old burlesque theaters, the old train station, the fabulous city markets, one built Art-Deco style in the 1930s and the other with medieval turrets in the 1880s. Gone were the often elegant buildings near the water. Most of all, gone was the tiny network of streets, many of them cobblestoned, that invoked the memory of the city's oldest days" (2000, p. 52).

In Norfolk, this destruction was done in part to accommodate the construction of giant freeways downtown. Marshall goes on to report:

> As part of the redevelopment, the old city hall
> and courts, which formed a central square at the
> city's heart, were closed, and a giant, windswept
> plaza with modernist skyscrapers of concrete and
> glass was built as the new municipal center. It sat
> at freeway's edge, with the mayor's and council
> members' parking spaces appropriately placed
> under a freeway off-ramp. The downtown was left
> with only a few churches that the city couldn't quite
> bring itself to wipe out. They sat like lonely monks,
> ornate spires in a sea of concrete, refuges from a
> massacre. (2000, p. 52)

Marshall's evocation of the lonely churches in Norfolk brings to mind my first visit to Buffalo. I remember the drive into the downtown along Broadway, where I was confronted with a landscape the likes of which I had not experienced on that scale before (I had not yet experienced Detroit) — acres upon acres of abandoned land dotted every few blocks with the ruins of once magnificent churches. In Norfolk and Buffalo, urban renewal and highway construction was a massive failure that has plagued these cities for the last 60 years. According to Marshall, the destruction was lamentable not just because these things happened but, more, because they did not work.

Marshall felt that the catastrophic effect of urban renewal and highway construction on cities was due to the fact that the very premise of highways in cities was fatally flawed. He explains it this way:

> What Norfolk and other cities did not foresee was
> that the new transportation system — the limited-
> access, Interstate-style highway — was too radical
> for the city to ever re-form around it. This intended
> savior would destroy its intended beneficiaries.
> What development around highways needed was
> plenty of open land for giant parking lots, vast
> separation of uses, and giant cloverleaves. With
> space demands this extreme, older city centers, built
> on the scale of the human foot, could never compete.
> They killed themselves trying. (2000, p. 53)

In the 1950s and 1960s, the story of Buffalo and Norfolk was replicated thousands of times in cities around the country. In city after city, the focus was on moving cars, which worked to the detriment of the city, its life, and its economy — the legacy in America 60 years later is hollowed-out central cities from sea to shining sea.

And smaller cities tended to fare worst. For example, much of the downtown of the tiny industrial city of Newburgh, New York, was cleared for urban renewal that never happened. (Logan and Doherty [2005] have written that the clearing was really removal of African Americans.) This land on the Hudson River still remains fallow, having been abandoned in anticipation of the modernist city that, luckily, will never be.

Some other cities were less impacted by highway construction and urban renewal. In New England these included cities like Portsmouth, New Hampshire, and Northampton, Massachusetts, which by luck or design found themselves slightly off the path of the approaching highway and are today two of a handful of vibrant small cities in New England.

Cambridge, Massachusetts, was also lucky to avoid removal for highway construction, but in this case the luck was helped by a good dose of community activism. Cities like Cambridge that rejected many of the false promises of conventional transportation and land use planning are becoming increasingly important models as more cities look for answers to developing transportation systems that will put them on a more prosperous and sustainable path.

The Pitfalls of "Predict and Provide" Transportation and Parking

The 1950s era was not just damaging for the physical destruction that befell thousands of American cities; it was also the period in which much of the new autocentric approach to transportation planning was invented, tested, and then eventually codified into zoning and financial regulations, and in engineering design and operating manuals.

Goldman's description of the highway planning process in Buffalo has all the hallmarks of an approach that is now standard practice—and the history of transportation in Buffalo is a classic example of the pitfalls of this approach.

In the 1940s and 1950s, planning in Buffalo was based on the idea that car traffic volume had grown enormously since the war, that it would continue to grow, and that something had to be done about it (Goldman 2007). The feeling at the time was that traffic was like water—there was a certain volume of it, and it had to go some place. There was little understanding or recognition that place mattered and played a huge role in this process. The thinking was that traffic—car traffic, that is—was going to grow regardless of the type of places we created and the type of transportation facilities we provided. This deterministic approach to transportation planning—now sometimes referred to as "predict and provide" planning—has been rejected in places like Cambridge, Massachusetts, where the focus is on creating a transportation system that supports a prosperous and vital city. The "predict and provide" approach is, however, very much the practice that continues to prevail in most parts of the country.

According to Goldman, even as late as 1955, buses in Buffalo still carried 2.5 times more shoppers to downtown than did automobile, yet most of the planners of the day were obsessed with cars and with accommodating cars (Goldman 2007). There was no sense at the time that better accommodation for cars and deteriorating facilities for bus users and pedestrians would eventually lead to even more people resorting to using cars. In other words, the planners did not understand or, perhaps, only vaguely suspected that their actions were creating more car traffic by pushing people away from walking and transit and into cars.

It is perhaps not surprising that planners of the 1950s would fall into this trap, since they were operating in the midst of a massive growth in automobile traffic for which there had been no precedent. They had little experience to draw on, but they were also operating in the belief that by providing some magical amount of road space, the problem would be solved.

What is surprising, and unforgivable, is that 60 years later, with the body of experience we now have, conventional transportation planning still uses the methods of the 1950s that should have been abandoned years ago. All we have done in the interim is to add on layers of fancy models and sophisticated equations that only serve to obscure the underlying flaws in the system. But all that is in the black box is still the old "predict and provide" models that are based on the flawed idea that more activity and more people always mean more cars.

In reality, what we are finding is that the opposite is often true—Cambridge has increased activity while decreasing car use. They have done this by creating an atmosphere where transit, biking, and walking are prioritized. Car use is accommodated, but it is not the controlling and dominant factor it is in other places.

In Buffalo the dominance of cars over the transportation planning process manifested itself in the building of highways . . . and the provision of parking. In the end it was parking that really brought the downtown to its knees. According to Goldman,

With projection indicating fifty thousand cars by 1960, Moot (chair of the City Planning Commission) projected a need for fourteen thousand new spaces. Mayor Joseph Mruk agreed. Not only, he said, would the city build three parking ramps (garages), it would also encourage the private development of parking facilities downtown "by assisting in the condemnation and assembly of necessary sites." The campaign to build parking spaces for twenty-five thousand automobiles began in 1950. The process, which fifty years later is still ongoing, destroyed streets and buildings and left many people to wonder if there might soon be nothing left downtown but an ever-growing sea of parking lots. (2007, p. 147)

In Hartford, Connecticut, the changes came a bit later, but when they did, they occurred swiftly. The aerial images illustrate the extent and swiftness of the changes that occurred in Hartford in the late 1950s and early 1960s (figs. 10.1 and 10.2). As a former resident of Hartford, I was surprised at the extent of the change in the city over such a relatively short time span. What is even more surprising is that the basic structure that was created in the 1950s and early 1960s still persists in its basic configuration to this day, almost 50 years later.

Figures 10.1 and 10.2 show clearly the extent to which the urban fabric of the city was disrupted by both the freeways and the razing of buildings for parking. What was once a coherent place that was easy and pleasurable to negotiate on foot was suddenly a much more difficult and hostile environment for pedestrians. In addition, many small storefront businesses were lost forever—where they were replaced, the replacements were much larger buildings that were occupied by businesses that were of much less interest to pedestrians or had underground parking garages with blank walls

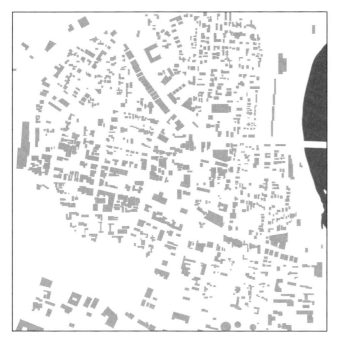

FIGURES 10.1 AND 10.2. Figure-ground diagrams of Hartford in 1957 (above) and in 2000 (below), comparing the impact of public parking on the downtown fabric. Note the portion of buildings removed by the year 2000. (Courtesy of University of Connecticut Libraries Map and Geographic Information Center)

at street level and entrances that disrupted the pedestrian flow.

Connecticut residents often lament the state of Hartford, but what is surprising is not that the city struggles but rather that it is still doing so well, despite having so much of its innards removed. The fact that cities like Hartford did not die completely is a testament to the resiliency of pre-1950s urbanism and hints at the vibrancy that is still possible if we learn how to repair, or even just mitigate, the damages from the 1950s. Postindustrial cities with their dense network of connected streets and charming industrial or mixed-use buildings are extremely versatile and are highly desirable. But they need a transportation system that is compatible with their form and function.

In Buffalo, for instance, Goldman was particularly struck by the degree to which planners and city officials were obsessed with parking. He says that as early as 1949, the chairman of the City Planning Commission wrote, "the downtown parking problem is our most serious and our most urgent problem" (2007, p. 147).

In reality, the focus on the so-called parking problem represented a gross misunderstanding of the situation facing this city. What the City Planning Commission was really saying was that Buffalo was having a hard time competing with the then fast-growing suburbs. In trying to understand the reason why they were losing out to the suburbs, the planners realized that one attraction of those suburbs was free and ample parking. Not surprisingly, the seemingly easy fix became the rallying cry — we need more parking for our cities! The problem was that efforts to provide more parking in cities always results in the loss of some urban fabric. This loss of urban fabric inevitably makes the

city less attractive to people on foot. This in turn leads to more cars and cries for even more parking. The result is the start of a vicious downward cycle that many cities have never been able to escape.

In the 1950s, the Buffalo Planning Commission was simply trying to compete with the suburbs on the basis of parking. We now know that this was an impossible quest — cities that were built up in the nineteenth and early twentieth centuries simply cannot compete with the suburbs on the basis of parking. It is a physical impossibility — parking and autos need space; nineteenth-century cities simply cannot afford that amount of space. In trying to compete with the suburbs, cities degrade the features that gave them their special value — they lose their walkability, their charm, their historic building stock, and their economic base.

In Hartford, even though the discussion about parking was a bit more nuanced than in Buffalo, over the last 60 years parking has been the single most important factor whittling away the fabric of the city that remained after the highway construction and urban renewal of the 1950s.

The small incremental changes each year added up and left us with a hollowed-out shell of a city (fig. 10.2). The numbers are staggering. In 1957 we estimated that there were approximately 15,000 parking spaces in downtown Hartford (only 500 in the one garage that existed at the time) (McCahill and Garrick 2010b). By 2000, there had been a threefold increase in parking spaces to 46,000, with approximately half of those in parking garages built at a cost of more than $20,000 per parking space. Overall a quarter of the land in downtown was devoted exclusively to parking. Concurrently with the city tripling parking spaces and devoting so much land to parking, it was also losing 50%

of its residential population, 10% of its jobs, and almost all of its downtown retail.

These figures support Alex Marshall's contention that older American cities were congenitally unsuited to being rebuilt as automobile-dependent places. But for whatever reasons, cities like Hartford have spent the last 60 years trying to roll the proverbial stone back up the hill. Now with evidence accumulating on the one hand about the futility of trying to make cities over in the image of automobile suburbs and on the other about the success of cities like Portland, Oregon, and Boulder, Colorado, more places are beginning to adopt a more city-friendly approach to transportation.

After 60 years of the automobile era, the idea of a city-friendly transportation is really a rediscovery of a fundamental concept: cities are primarily places for people to come together. Therefore, a city-friendly transportation system is one that is first and foremost about people. Cars are one way of getting people to cities, but they cannot be the dominant mode of travel. For one, the amount of space that is needed when the ratio of cars to people exceeds a reasonable amount is simply too much to allow the city to retain the character and compactness that foster vibrant public life. Therefore, a city-friendly transportation system by necessity must give priority to walking, biking, and public transit, as these are much more efficient means of travel in the compact places that we call cities.

Rediscovering City-Friendly Transportation Planning

Cambridge, Massachusetts, should be on any city planner's list of great case studies for how to get transportation right. One reason that it doesn't get on that list is that many people reflexively reject Cambridge as a model because its recent history is just too different from those of most other cities, especially from the point of view of transportation. On the face of it, this reaction is understandable — Cambridge is different. For one, it has the lowest rate of car commuting in the country of any city except New York. Furthermore, the rate of car commuting in Cambridge is lower than it was in 1990 or even in 1960. Only a handful of other cities in the country have a similar record, including other easily dismissed places like Berkeley, California, and Boulder, Colorado.

In Europe, the story of cities in the automobile era is somewhat similar to that in America. Although the cities and national governments never went quite as far in facilitating car travel, the trend in the 1950s and 1960s was toward street widening, highway construction, and the provision of off-street parking. As in the United States, a handful of European cities realized early on in the process that they were on a path that could prove devastating for their economy and city life. Two cities whose stories are worth noting are Copenhagen and Zurich. Efforts at city-friendly transportation planning in both cities date back to the late 1960s, predating any such concerted effort by an American city. Like Cambridge, Berkeley, and Boulder, these two European cities are often dismissed as not being realistic models of transportation for the typical American city. They are often considered to be too different and irrelevant to our experience.

But there are good reasons for not dismissing any of these cities so easily. What is important to recognize is that these places are different not just because of what they are but also for what they did in the planning process. They have developed an approach to transportation planning that has enhanced their sense of place; they have taken advantage of their character, thus in fact setting the table for their current success. Most cities could learn from what they did. Their experience provides the playbook for what should be done to start to put cities in a position to capitalize on their inherent advantages over the suburbs.

What might be more difficult to replicate is the how — the steps they took to reach where they are today. The issue is that the success of these cities was in part due to their having an informed population who were willing to question conventional wisdom about transportation planning. But with the problems of conventional wisdom becoming more evident by the day, and with more people beginning to appreciate city living, the potential for creating a city-friendly transportation planning approach is much greater these days.

CAMBRIDGE, MASSACHUSETTS

In 1960, Cambridge had a very different status from the one it has now. It was a well-off but struggling industrial city not unlike Hartford at the same time. But Cambridge underwent a very different fate regarding urban renewal and highway construction from Hartford and Buffalo. This can be seen in figure 10.2, which shows for Hartford the highways planned in the 1950s and the highways that were eventually built. In Hartford, the state and the city were very successful (so to speak) in building many of the highways that were planned. Cambridge was much less successful; the number of miles of highways built was exactly zero.

Community activists in Cambridge were able

to prevent the permanent taking of any land in Cambridge for highway construction. They seem to have been very prescient in understanding that highway construction would have stifled rather than promote the future of Cambridge. It is not easy to attribute an economic outcome to something that was not built — we cannot "prove" that a Cambridge with the proposed highways would be any less prosperous. However, it is easier to imagine what Cambridge would have looked and felt like today with a highway in a 170-foot-wide trench in the vicinity of Harvard Square. For most people who know Cambridge today, this vision is nightmarish, but it is important to understand that it could easily have happened, as it did all over America. What is indisputable is that a Cambridge crisscrossed by highways of this type would have been a much different place than it is now.

The highways battles left much of the urban fabric in Cambridge intact, unlike most other small New England cities, including Hartford. But Cambridge officials were also much less aggressive about providing parking. While Hartford was increasing the amount of land covered with parking from 0.54 to 1.45 square miles (in a city of a mere 17.3 square miles), in Cambridge the area for parking went from 0.25 to 0.50 square miles (McCahill and Garrick 2010b).

In interpreting these numbers it is also important to remember that as Hartford was madly building parking, it was being drained of vitality, which resulted in declines of population, employment, and retail activities. Cambridge also saw some small erosion in its population base but impressively added 70% more jobs, and in the process bypassed the once powerful Hartford as an important employment center in New England.

Aside from the highway battles, the history of

transportation planning in Cambridge during the early automobile era was not that different from that in most other cities in the country. For example, in this era the city took action to facilitate car movement by banning on-street parking, as was the practice around the country. And as we discussed earlier, the city did work to provide off-street parking even though this was at a lower rate than in other cities such as Hartford. As a result, in the 1960s through the 1980s, car use drifted upward and walking, biking, and public transit use all drifted downward in Cambridge. Although these changes were in the same direction as in the rest of the country, Cambridge never saw the same level of increase in car use as did much of the rest of the country.

Nonetheless, the increased motorization of the city did have a noticeable effect — the major streets took on more of the character of highways, some neighborhood streets were overrun with cars, and the squares were converted into spaces more for car use and less for civic use. It was not until the 1980s that activists in Cambridge, and then the city government, woke up to the realization that conventional transportation was having a deleterious effect on the character of city, its quality of life, and the local and global environment.

One of the first actions the city took to turn the situation around was to adopt a parking plan in 1981. This plan signaled a 180-degree turn in the city's attitude toward parking and transportation. Up until that time the city had specified that developers provide a minimum amount of parking for any development project. The specification of a *minimum* parking standard is the ultimate in the "predict and provide" approach to transportation planning. It is based on the idea that each square foot of development that was added in the past is

associated with a certain number of parking spaces, so we need to provide that amount of parking space for each new square foot of development.

Cambridge turned this approach on its head by implementing a parking *maximum*, not a parking *minimum*. In other words, developers are restricted in the amount of parking they are allowed to build — so much and no more. In other cities, developers are compelled to provide a certain minimum number of parking spaces. This represented a minor revolution, as it signaled that the city was shaping the transportation system to the needs of the city and not the other way around. Residents and visitors were being asked to adjust their transportation needs according to the physical limitations of a city — the city would no longer be reconfigured (or dismantled) to adjust to the needs of a specific transportation system.

This was a major breakthrough for Cambridge and led to a series of incremental changes in the municipal codes that focused on building a transportation system that was consistent with this new paradigm. In 1992 a vehicle trip reduction ordinance was adopted that focused on alternative modes of travel and instituted restrictions and higher fees to discourage the use of parking spaces for long-term commuter parking. The city's growth management document, "Toward a Sustainable Future," first released in 1993 by the Cambridge Planning Board and the Department of Community Development, acknowledges that the city had nearly reached its vehicular capacity and identified "non auto forms of transportation" as the "best hope for improving mobility."

The city's parking and transportation demand management (PTDM) plan was introduced in 1998. This program requires businesses that build or expand parking facilities to register all nonresidential parking spaces with a designated PTDM planning officer and file a PTDM plan meant to reduce single-occupancy-vehicle trips below a specified share based on travel patterns and transportation options in the surrounding area (Cambridge Community Development 1998).

Most important, Cambridge officials acknowledged that modes other than driving are crucial to the city's functioning and that the city could thrive without ever-increasing supplies of parking. Recommendations from the city's Pedestrian Advisory Committee, established in 1995, and Bicycle Committee, established in 1991, have led to significant measures for improving nonautomobile facilities and networks (McCahill and Garrick 2008). The city's "super-crosswalk" project was developed with the goal of helping pedestrians regain access to the streets in the busy Harvard Square business district. Since the city first began retrofitting its streets for bicycles in 1995, more than 35 miles (56.3 km) of two-way bicycle facilities have been constructed, which cover more than 20% of the city's streets. This includes innovative solutions such as contraflow bicycle lanes on otherwise one-way streets and blue bike lanes to indicate a yield maneuver.

Our review suggests that parking policy in Cambridge has evolved from a relatively conventional approach in the 1960s and 1970s to one in which parking is explicitly linked to transportation demand management. It is a policy approach that is based on acknowledging the role of transportation and parking in meeting broader societal goals such as climate change. This is a link that officials in Hartford, as in many U.S. cities, have not yet made.

The results of this approach to planning have been astounding. Between 1990 and 2008, the rate of biking in Cambridge doubled, walking stayed constant, and public transit use increased more than 30% (McCahill and Garrick 2010). Conversely, automobile use for commuting plummeted from 47% to 37% in fewer than 20 years. The 37% automobile-commuting rate was five percentage points *less* than it was in 1960. With fewer cars on the roads, the city has continued to aggressively restore civic space to public use, but it has also been pushing an aggressive program of commercial development that allows it to convert once underutilized land (that was often in surface parking) to productive use.

COPENHAGEN

Cambridge's experience in moving toward a transportation agenda that is directed at urban vitality, and not traffic movement, mirrors those of two cities in Europe, Copenhagen and Zurich, that are now celebrated for the success of their transportation planning process. Like Cambridge, these two cities avoided the worst excesses of highway construction in the 1950s and 1960s. However, they realized much earlier than Cambridge that they needed to change their transportation paradigm.

Both cities are worth studying because they have such a long experience with developing transportation policies and systems that have served as framework for rejuvenating city life. The process of creating a city-friendly transportation system in each of these cities is similar in many ways, but the specific details show some interesting twists that are unique to each community.

The story of city-friendly transportation planning in Copenhagen dates back to the early 1960s. The renowned urban planner Jan Gehl and his colleague Lars Gemzoe have chronicled the transformation of Copenhagen in *Public Life — Public Spaces*, pub-lished in 1996. In Copenhagen, the early focus was on taking back land in the center from car use and using this land to create high-quality urban spaces. As Gehl and Gemzoe (1996) explain, until 1962 all the streets in the city center of Copenhagen were filled with car traffic and the squares were used as car parks. In other words, in the early period of the automobile era, Copenhagen was not very different from most other cities in the developed world, where a sudden flood of cars was degrading public spaces and quality of life.

However, in November 1962, the city began an innovative experiment. They decided to convert Copenhagen's main street, the Stroget, to a pedestrian street. This change was not uniformly welcomed, and a hot debate raged about its appropriateness. According to Gehl and Gemzoe, "It was argued that a pedestrian street in Denmark would never work. Newspapers made sweeping statements like 'We are Danes, not Italians,' and 'Using public space is contrary to Nordic mentality.' Although skepticism was rampant, the new car-free environment proved extremely popular with Copenhageners from the very first day" (1996, p. 11).

The irony, of course, is that today many people consider a pedestrian-oriented city center to be quintessentially Danish. In fact, the word "Copenhagenization" has been coined among some planners to describe the act of creating a city center with few cars and high volumes of pedestrians and bicyclists. But before Copenhagen would lend its name to an urban planning phenomenon, it had to overcome substantial internal doubt about the wisdom of putting a brake on the growth of car traffic.

Gehl and Gemzoe point out that what was done in Copenhagen was not simply a pedestrinization scheme but really a plan to tame and control city traffic, and to reclaim streets and create quality spaces for popular use. They sum up the overall scheme in 1996 thus: "For more than 30 years, Copenhagen has followed a policy targeted to reduce the impact of traffic on the city center, and to improve conditions for users. A once car-oriented city-center has become more beautiful, less polluted, and less noisy in the process. This new friendlier city center has been given a fine reception, and the city is now used by more people and in new ways" (1996, p. 7). They go on to contrast Copenhagen with other cities: "Whereas city centers in many other places in the world have deteriorated over the years — becoming noisy and heavily trafficked places that are rather unpleasant and at times frightening to be in — Copenhagen has followed a different path. The city center has improved every year, becoming more and more used and appreciated" (p. 7).

From a transportation point of view the changes in the city were dramatic: Between 1970 and 1995, car traffic entering the city *decreased* by 50,000, while bicycle traffic increased by 65,000 (Gehl and Gemzoe 1996). Parking policy was a major factor contributing to this change. Interestingly, the main goal of Copenhagen's parking policy was not to reduce parking per se but was aimed at reclaiming "the city's fine squares for people activities, rather than for parking" (p. 41). Prior to this policy all the squares in the city had been appropriated for car parking.

As with other policies in Copenhagen, the changes in parking were enacted slowly over time to allow people to get used to the changes. Parking was steadily reduced by 2–3% each year. By 1996, 600 spaces had been eliminated, and Copenhagen had only 3,100 parking spaces in its downtown (Gehl and Gemzoe 1996). To put that number in perspective, in that year downtown Stockholm had 8,000 spaces and Hartford had an astounding 45,000 spaces in a downtown about the same size as Copenhagen's. Gehl and Gemzoe also observed: "Amazingly enough, Copenhagen city center goes on working well despite the gradual reduction in parking spaces. The Copenhagen policy seriously puts in question the widely held belief that many parking places are needed to ensure that a city center functions well" (p. 41).

When Gehl and Gemzoe wrote their book in 1996, the story of Copenhagen was still largely a story about pedestrianization of the streets, the reduction of city traffic, and the reclamation of the squares for people. But these changes really were setting the stage for a travel revolution. Today Copenhagen is known more for the army of bikers who throng its streets than for its pedestrian-oriented streets. But without the gradual changes in the character of the streets that was accomplished over 40 years, biking in Copenhagen would probably not be as prevalent, or as celebrated, as it is today.

Biking is the dominant mode of travel to Copenhagen, with over 40% of commuters traveling to the downtown area by bike. But the city is not done pushing the envelope; it has set its sights on increasing the proportion of bike commuters to over 50% by 2020. It is able to do this because city-friendly transportation planning measures that were once controversial now have broad support in Copenhagen.

The physical transformation of Copenhagen over the last 40 years has been truly remarkable, with motor traffic volumes decreasing and parking lots being reborn as elegant squares. This is an important story, but as Gehl and Gemzoe (1996) point out, the transformation in how the city is seen, and how it is being used, has been equally as spectacular. The number of strollers on the streets shot up and, in general, people increasingly see the city as a place to linger, meet, and people-watch. Ultimately this is the bottom line: Copenhagen used the transportation system to craft a highly desirable and productive city for its people.

ZURICH

Like Copenhagen, Zurich is now also celebrated as a vibrant and graceful city that at the same time is relatively free of traffic noise and stress. The Zurich story is also like Copenhagen's in that it is the result of a process of steady transformation over the last 45 years. Unlike Copenhagen, the spark that started the transformation in Zurich was not the pedestrianization of the streets but rather a modest "People's Plan" to strengthen transit in the city.

The city's modest sky-blue tram is perhaps one of the most enduring symbols of modern Zurich and lies at the heart of the story of its transformation (fig. 10.3). In the early 1960s, Zurich, like most of its contemporaries in Europe and America, was straining under the rapid rate of motorization, and policy-makers recognized the need for action. One of the solutions that was developed at the time was a plan for the construction of a system of subways designed to remove the existing trams from the surface streets and give them their own dedicated underground right-of-way, but before major construction could go forward the Swiss system of governance required that the plans be put to a public referendum (Nash and Sylvia 2001).

In 1962, to the surprise of the government, vot-

FIGURE 10.3. Light rail public transportation in Minneapolis. (Courtesy of Paul J. Armstrong)

ers in both the city and the wider canton of Zurich rejected plans for the subway system by a margin of 61% to 39% (Nash and Sylvia 2001). Concurrent with the rejection of the subway, there was also a great deal of public criticism about the general direction of transportation planning in the city. At the time, these plans included the proposals for three major expressways that were designed to intersect in the form of a giant Y in the center of the city. These highway plans were highly unpopular and were subsequently defeated in a later referendum.

One faction opposing the subway's construction was in favor of the government redirecting its attention toward improving the existing transit. This position was very influential and laid the foundation for the future of transportation planning in the Zurich region. One important change made in Zurich that followed the rejection of the subway plan in 1962 was the formation of the city's first ever planning department. Interestingly, this department was headed up by Hans Marti, a strong critic of the then prevailing approach to transportation planning (Nash and Sylvia 2001).

Marti believed that "transportation should serve the greater interest of the city and not the other way around." This was revolutionary thinking for its time — almost all places were still focused on the imperative of making sure that traffic was accommodated. He also believed that the attempt to adopt cities to the automobile was doomed to fail because of the financial cost and the space required.

In the late 1960s and early 1970s, the city government took tentative steps to improve the operations and efficiency of the surface transit system. Despite this promising start, by 1973 the city was once again back before the voters with a new plan — this time for a joint subway (U-Bahn) and commuter rail (S-Bahn) system. Once again this system was designed as a plan to partly replace the city's system of surface trams. And once again the voters shocked the politicians by voting down the plan — this time by a margin of 57% to 43%.

One reason given for this defeat was the fear among voters that Zurich was developing too fast. In the language of the era, Zurich was being "Manhattanized." Many felt that a subway system would just be in service of facilitating excessive growth of their city. There was also a second, more nuanced reason for the defeat. Some voters felt that a subway system would improve longer distance travel (especially for people coming from the suburban towns) and would at the same time disadvantage people traveling shorter distances in the city.

The third reason for the defeat was perhaps the most telling. Environmentally oriented voters were afraid that replacing the surface trams with a subterranean system would serve to free up road space for cars and thus attract even more cars to the center city. This was deemed highly undesirable because of the noise and pollution that additional cars would bring. People were also very concerned that increasing car traffic would mean more demand for parking in the historic downtown.

The most fascinating outcome from the campaign against the U-Bahn/S-Bahn plan was that it actually encouraged the antisubway activists to develop their own transportation proposal in opposition to the government's plan. This "People's Initiative for the Promotion of Public Transit" represented an important shift in strategy by the activists and was based on the realization that it is harder to argue against something with nothing. The People's Initiative was important in getting people to understand that these opponents of the subway plan were not against transit but just against the specific type of transit proposed, and the consequential intensification of the city, that the subway plan represented.

The People's Initiative was largely based on the idea of giving public transit priority over automobile traffic. The Initiative drew on the experience of the Swiss cities Bern and Basel, which had already implemented their own transit priority programs in the early 1970s. The Zurich plan, according to Nash and Sylvia (2001), was based on six points: (1) give absolute priority to buses and trams by making changes in traffic regulations, (2) create exclusive transit lanes and traffic signal priority, (3) increase the frequency of transit service, (4) expand the transit system, (5) improve interchanges between lines, and (6) improve the stop areas.

Some of these steps were already being implemented by the government, but the People's Initiative called for a much more aggressive implementation program that would affect the whole system. The People's Initiative was also much bolder in asserting that the plan should be implemented regardless of its effect on the automobile network. The People's Initiative called for the spending of 15-25 million Swiss francs over a period of 10 years, for an overall budget of about 160 million Swiss francs — one-eighth of what the government subway plan would have cost (Nash and Sylvia 2001).

The plan was presented to the government in June 1973, one month after the defeat of the U-bahn/S-bahn scheme. But the government took another three years to study the plan. In March 1977, the People's Plan was put before the public and squeaked by to approval on a vote of 51% to 49%. Ironically, one of the objections some people had to the plan was that it was too costly, even though it was only one-eighth of the cost of the 1973 government subway scheme (Nash and Sylvia 2001).

However, the plan was popular with some because it was consistent with the "Small Is Beautiful" philosophy that was pervasive in Zurich at that time. It was a plan that many saw as a way to invigorate city life, rather than one that would simply facilitate growth. Although the plan passed, the government was seen at the time as being reluctant in adopting it. Today this approach to planning is considered to be widely popular in the city of Zurich (less so in the canton, where the cantonal government is still perceived as reluctant in some ways). The plan is considered to be an extremely successful example of the "Small Is Beautiful" concept. An astounding 63% of trips by city residents in this very wealthy city are by public transit ("European Urban Audit" 2004). The Zurich transit system is considered to be a worldwide model, one that is extremely efficient and effective in moving people in a way that does not have great social or economic cost.

The Lessons of City-Friendly Transportation Planning for Postindustrial Cities

The starting point for developing a city-friendly approach to transportation is the recognition that a reliance on automobiles as the predominant mode of travel in a city is very disruptive to the city fabric, and to city life in general, largely because the space required for the operation and storage of motor vehicles is so vast, and space is not normally available in a traditional city without massive disruptions. The evidence is overwhelming.

On the one hand, we have as evidence the thousands of cities in America, Europe, and the rest of the world that have done their best to accommodate cars as much as possible. After 60 years of trying, most of these cities limp along in a highly compromised manner, having lost a sizeable fraction of their urban fabric, character, and vitality. Cities like Buffalo and Hartford do continue to function, but as little more than glorified office parks at their core. In this chapter we have focused on these two cities because their physical decay has been well documented. The changes in other cities are not as well documented, but the patterns described for Buffalo and Hartford should resonate with anyone familiar with most postindustrial cities in the country.

On the other hand, we can point to a handful of cities in the United States, and a larger number in Europe and other places in the world, that have been leaders in developing a city-friendly approach to transportation (fig. 10.4). All of these communities are prosperous, vibrant places with great public spaces and, also notably, less car traffic and less space devoted to car traffic than other comparable cities in the United States or in Europe. These cities also, perhaps more significantly, are more vibrant and have less traffic than in their pre-city-friendly planning stage. They have become progressively more vital over the last several decades.

The details of transportation strategy in each place vary. For example, Cambridge and Zurich are mostly public transit cities, while the linchpin of transportation in Copenhagen is biking. What

FIGURE 10.4. Light rail public transportation and pedestrian activity in the central business district of Zurich. (Courtesy of Norman Garrick)

they do have in common is an approach to planning that is based on the idea that transportation is primarily about the health, wealth, and happiness of the city and not primarily about the movement of vehicles. In practice, this means that walking, biking, and transit are the favored modes of travel in these cities. This prioritization is achieved by ensuring that these cities are walkable, that is, all streets are of modest dimensions, there are lots of destinations in close proximity, and the street environment is attractive and interesting for people

on foot. In these cities walkability also goes hand in hand with first-class transit service and, generally, with high bike use.

Conversely, places with non-city-friendly transportation policies typically degrade walkability over time through small but persistent measures such as the widening of streets and the removal of on-street parking to facilitate more efficient traffic flow, or by massive measures, such as the construction of freeways or other major highways that destroy buildings and fragment the city. In these cities there is usually also little hesitation about taking other steps that are disruptive of the urban fabric, including the replacement of (often historic) buildings with parking lots or parking garages and the construction of new buildings with blank facades surrounded by parking lots.

The issue of parking provision deserves particular attention in this discussion. Parking not only degrades walkability, thus creating and attracting more car traffic, but it also decreases the economic potential of the city by reducing the amount of land available for productive use. In cities like Buffalo and Hartford with non-city-friendly transportation policies, the provision of parking has been the unrelenting obsession of government for at least the past 60 years. The result is that in Hartford, for example, parking spaces tripled while the city was losing 50% of its population, 10% of its jobs, and almost all of its retail. Yet even as the level of activity in the city plummeted, the amount of land taken up by parking lots and parking garages in Hartford tripled to 25% of the total land in the downtown. The sad irony is that the provision of parking, which was done in the name of increasing the economic viability of the downtown, was actually having the opposite effect of causing the economic lifeblood of the city to seep away.

In Cambridge, Copenhagen, and Zurich we saw a very different approach to parking provision — on the basis of their city-friendly transportation policies, these cities have made a concerted and sustained effort over decades to reduce downtown parking. The policy adopted in Cambridge is particularly relevant to postindustrial cities in America. Cambridge used a policy device of setting maximum parking standards by placing a cap on the amount of parking that can be provided to accompany any new development. Most places in the United States mandate a minimum amount of parking for any development. In many cases, they even require that any reuse of an existing property is accompanied by the addition of new parking to bring the parking numbers up to some prescribed level. This is a policy that has proven to be very detrimental for downtowns. It results in the destruction of historic buildings and prevents adaptive reuse of existing buildings because space often cannot be found for the additional parking. The Cambridge policy, on the other hand, works to increase economic activities in the city without the harmful side effect of a concurrent increase in space devoted to parking.

Parking is a specific illustration of a general principle that is essential in developing a city-friendly transportation system. The fundamental rule is that vehicle traffic volume is never preordained in urban places. Cities get the level of car traffic that they plan for. Most cities planned for a high percentage of car traffic in the fear that they would lose out if this traffic volume was not accommodated. This is a mindset that reveals a fundamental misunderstanding about the true nature of cities. It is the belief that car traffic is proportional to the amount of activity in the city. This is a belief that is so basic to conventional planning that it is deeply embedded in zoning regulations and traffic generation models. In city-friendly transportation planning, no such connection is assumed, and the goal is to maximize traffic — people traffic that is — while minimizing car traffic. The thinking under this approach is that people go to cities to be with other people, not to be around cars.

The bottom-line lesson from studying cities such as Cambridge, Copenhagen, and Zurich is that city-friendly transportation planning works to create vibrant places. Forty years or so ago, these cities willingly made themselves into test cases by adopting an approach to transportation planning that was largely untested for the burgeoning automobile era. The gamble paid off, and the instinct these cities had toward fiercely protecting their urban character was the right one. Today, the success of these places is encouraging a new wave of cities around the world to rethink their approach to transportation planning. In the United States, the new wave that has adopted city-friendly transportation planning in the last decade or so include Seattle; Portland, Oregon; Washington, D.C.; New York; San Francisco; and Chicago. Other American cities, including the postindustrial cities of the Midwest, are in the fortunate position of being able to learn the lessons of these pioneering places without feeling that they are taking a plunge into the unknown.

References

Cambridge Community Development. 1993. *Towards a Sustainable Future: Cambridge Growth Policy Document.* Cambridge, MA: City of Cambridge.

———. 1998. *Parking and Transportation Demand Management.* Cambridge, MA: City of Cambridge.

European Urban Audit. 2004. www.urbanaudit.org/.

Federal Highway Administration. 2008. *Highway Statistics 2008.* Washington, DC: U.S. Department of Transportation. Available at www.fhwa.dot.gov /policyinformation/statistics/2008/vmt421.cfm. Accessed January 14, 2012.

Fullilove, M. T. 2004. *Root Shock: How Tearing Up City Neighborhoods Hurts America, and What We Can Do about It.* New York: Ballantine.

Gehl, J., and L. Gemzoe. 1996. *Public Spaces — Public Life. Copenhagen.* Copenhagen: Danish Architectural Press and the Royal Danish Academy of Fine Arts School of Architecture.

Goldman, M. 2007. *City on the Edge: Buffalo, New York*. Amherst, NY: Prometheus Books.

Kunstler, J. H. 2006. *The Long Emergency: Surviving the Converging Catastrophes of the Twenty-First Century*. New York: Atlantic Monthly Press.

Logan, T., and J. Doherty. 2005, Summer. "The Promised Land: Thirty Years Later, Can Newburg Find Its Way Back Home?" Special Report. *Middleton (NY) Times Herald-Record*.

Marshall, A. 2000. *How Cities Work: Suburb, Sprawl and the Road Not Taken*. Austin: University of Texas Press.

McCahill, C., and N. W. Garrick. 2008. "The Impact of Transportation and Urban Planning on Carbon Emissions: A Case Study of Cambridge, MA." Paper presented to Congress for the New Urbanism, Austin, TX.

———. 2010a. "The Influence of Parking Policy on the Built Environment and Travel Behavior in Two New England Cities over the Period 1960 to 2007." *Transportation Research Record* 2187: 123-130.

———. 2010b. "Losing Hartford: Transportation Policy and the Decline of an American City." Paper presented to Congress for the New Urbanism, Atlanta.

Nash, A. B., and R. Sylvia. 2001, January 13. *Implementation of Zurich's Transit Priority Program*. MTI Report. Zurich, Switzerland: Mineta Transportation Institute.

Norton, Peter D. 2008. *Fighting Traffic: The Dawn of the Motor Age in the American City*. New York: MIT Press.

U.S. Department of Energy. Energy Efficiency and Renewable Energy. Vehicle Technologies Program. 2007. Fact of the Week. Fact no. 474. Available at the website of the U.S. Department of Energy, www1.eere.energy.gov/vehiclesandfuels/facts/2007 _fcvt_fotw474.html. Accessed January 18, 2012.

PART III

Making
SynergiCity
a Reality

CHAPTER ELEVEN

Creating a Town-Gown Partnership

THE MILWAUKEE MODEL

ROBERT GREENSTREET

MANY FACTORS MUST CONVERGE TO SUCCESSFULLY stimulate the growth and reinvention of cities, and as many agents of creative change as possible need to be harnessed toward the positive regeneration of the urban environment. One such agent, which can often be overlooked in the municipal decision-making process, is that of education, specifically higher education, for universities and colleges can provide a continuous stream of fresh, new ideas and alternatives that can enrich the debate on future development. Faculty and students, particularly in design-related disciplines, can focus their intellectual exploration on city issues and help to inform and influence physical change. However, their efforts can only be effective if their work reaches the appropriate level of political decision-making and, as important, if they can do this on a regular basis. Without this consistent engagement good ideas, whether potentially useful or not, will remain untested in the realm of theory. In order to promote a more effective engagement between academic exploration and practical development, a formal, structural relationship can promote the chances of new ideas being introduced at the appropriate political level and increase their capacity for contributing toward positive regeneration.

In Milwaukee, an innovative partnership between city government and a major public university has been developed to explore the role education can play in "real-world" urban development. Now in its sixth year, the "town-gown" initiative structurally links the vision, energy, and diverse abilities of the faculty and students of the University of Wisconsin–Milwaukee (UWM) School of Architecture and Urban Planning (SARUP) with the ongoing infrastructure needs and interests of the city of Milwaukee. Through the direct engagement of the school in city development on a *daily* basis, faculty and student perspectives are introduced into the routine activities and awareness of the city. In addition, regular coordination of semester courses, studios, and theses in both academic departments with prevailing governmental interests and initiatives enables the exploration of a continuous stream of focused ideas and to their ultimately being shared with city personnel, enhancing the potential for positive change.

This chapter will articulate the nature of the partnership that has been forged between the city of Milwaukee and SARUP. The mutually established agenda will be examined to assess its impact after six years, and lessons learned from the experience will be outlined as a potential blueprint for other communities where a relationship between city government and local universities could be similarly beneficial. This includes enriching the academic experience for students with real-world projects, engaging faculty in applied research opportunities, and injecting fresh, innovative ideas into governmental departments responsible for urban redevelopment.

FIGURE 11.1. Aerial view of the now demolished Park East Freeway in Milwaukee. The combined efforts of the city of Milwaukee working in partnership with the School of Architecture and Urban Planning at the University of Wisconsin–Milwaukee convinced planning officials that the freeway should be removed and the Park East corridor should be redeveloped instead with mixed-use buildings. (Courtesy of the City of Milwaukee Department of City Development)

The School of Architecture and Urban Planning: The Urban Focus

Since its inception 40 years ago, SARUP has always been mindful of its urban context and has tried to be a relevant agent for change and influence within the city of Milwaukee. Certainly, there has been a long history of involvement that has led to significant redevelopment. Projects that were initially explored in the 1980s and 1990s in design studios or as special projects and that ultimately came to fruition include O'Donnell Plaza (a public plaza built on a parking garage at the lakefront), the Public Market, East Pointe Commons, and the removal of the Park East Freeway (fig. 11.1).

During the tenure of Mayor John Norquist, the city raised urban design in Milwaukee to greater significance, and the relationship between SARUP and the city began to formalize. Both the mayor and his director of planning taught as adjunct faculty at UWM, and the dean of SARUP chaired the City Plan Commission during the 1990s at the mayor's request. A number of faculty members also served on related city committees and task forces (for example, the Historic Preservation Commission). At the same time, as the program matured, SARUP evolved into a significant influence in Milwaukee architecture and planning. For example, the skyline of the city has been effectively shaped by the many alumni (and faculty) who work in local practices, while the architect selection process for major projects invariably involves SARUP influence, most notably in the cases of Discovery World, the Public Market (fig. 11.2), the Bradley Technical School, the Milwaukee Theatre, and the extension to the Milwaukee Art Museum. However, the relationship between town and gown, while often useful, was predicated on a project-by-project basis, so interaction was not always as consistent or information sharing as effective as some believed it could be.

With the election of Tom Barrett as the new mayor of Milwaukee in 2004, a new opportunity arose to create a more formalized relationship between academia and government. After considerable discussion, the city appointed the dean of SARUP concurrently to the position of director of planning and design for the city of Milwaukee, thereby creating a new structural link that brought the ideas and viewpoints of the SARUP directly into the Department of City Development (DCD) and the mayor's office on a regular basis. These partnerships have resulted in an increase in student and faculty involvement in city planning and design, an intensified coordination of city interests and needs with student course and studio direction, and the exposure of governmental decision-makers to a wider variety of design-related ideas. As faculty and students have engaged directly in city projects, city staff have become more regularly involved in teaching classes and attending design juries at the university, thus simultaneously enriching the academic process.

Formulating the Agenda

While creating a structural link through a formalized, contractual relationship was at the heart of the initiative, the intent was not to transform the university into a quasi-governmental unit performing routine duties. Initial discussions led to the development of an overarching strategy that has directed the work completed over the past six years. Influenced by the thinking of Allison and Peterson Smithson, English visionary architects of the mid-twentieth century, early presentations of the initiative likened the arrangement of streets and buildings within the city to the intricate weaving of fabric, most specifically the fabric contained within a single valuable entity like a tapestry or carpet. While this did perhaps on occasion engender some bafflement and amusement among city personnel, it was effective in highlighting two maxims derived from the metaphor that have driven efforts ever since:

Everything is Important.
The Whole must exceed the sum of the Parts.

The notion of conceiving all 99 acres of the city as a single entity has helped to articulate the position that *all* areas of the city are important, from the downtown to the furthest southern neighborhoods, and that all parts of the urban fabric — buildings, streets, alleys, parking lots, parks — have to work in harmony to enhance urban quality. Furthermore, it is important to convey that *all* buildings matter, regardless of size and function. While big, prominent iconic structures are important, the less glamorous building stock — big box retail, parking garages, signage, strip malls, and so on — still have a powerful and sometimes deleterious impact on urban quality and are deserving of equal attention from the city. (Of course, these principles were not entirely new to city planning, as evidenced by the success of the Riverwalk development along the Milwaukee River under Mayor John Norquist and in recent area planning efforts, such as the Third Ward Plan, adopted in 2005.)

From this early strategic thinking, a three-part agenda was developed, as follows.

FINISH THE PLAN

Since its incorporation in 1846, Milwaukee has never undertaken comprehensive citywide planning. It certainly undertook some excellent planning that has been very effective — for example, the Menomonee Valley Plan and the 1999 Downtown Plan — but the plans tended to be localized, discrete, unrelated to each other, and predominantly clustered around the downtown.

Based on the success of several Area Plan exercises that engaged local organizations, businesses, and individuals in the planning process, the DCD Planning Department launched an ambitious initiative to complete all planning for the city of Milwaukee within five years, including a Comprehensive (Smart Growth) Plan and 12 Area Plans (two of which were updates of existing plans) that collectively covered every part of the municipality. Given the considerable expense to the taxpayer of this extensive venture, the department pledged to reduce the anticipated cost of each plan by bringing work normally contracted out to consultants in-house. (The initial plan costs were estimated at $200,000–$250,000. The DCD Planning Department calculated that they could work efficiently with consultants and reduce the cost per plan to $150,000.) In each case, only half of the plan cost was requested from the city and ultimately the taxpayer. The DCD Planning Department agreed, in an unprecedented move, to privately raise the other half of the funding from grants and private donations between 2005 and 2009 — despite the challenge of adopting the new role of fundraiser. (The Department personnel successfully raised the matching funds necessary to complete all the plans and even extended their work by agreeing to update the 1999 Downtown Plan.)

At the time of writing, all Area Plans and the Comprehensive Plan have been fully funded, completed, and approved. The original 1990 Downtown Plan has also been updated and awaits imminent approval from the city, and work has also been completed on the Mayor's Green Team report, which entailed considerable contributions from UWM faculty and students and has led to the establishment of the Office of Sustainability within the mayor's office. The overall exercise has engaged countless organizations, businesses, community groups, and

FIGURE 11.2. The Milwaukee Public Market in the Third Ward. (Courtesy of Paul J. Armstrong)

FIGURE 11.3. Addition to Eero Saarinen's Milwaukee Art Museum by Santiago Calatrava. The sculptural *brise-soleil* opens and closes like the wings of a bird to regulate light entering the interior atrium. (Courtesy of Paul J. Armstrong)

individuals from across the city, empowering them to participate in the visualization of their future. The power of the planning process and the engagement of so many citizens have already led to actions both predictable and unforeseen, such as the successful securing of development grants, the creation of new business organizations, including the Airport Gateway Association, and the creation of neighborhood amenities such as parks.

RAISE THE BAR

In 2001, the extension of the Milwaukee Art Museum, by Spanish architect Santiago Calatrava, was completed (fig. 11.3). This proved to be a catalytic event in Milwaukee, helping to raise public awareness and expectations for future development. This phenomenon, coupled with mayoral support from two administrations, a regular, persuasive voice of architectural review in the local newspaper, and the growing influence of SARUP, led to the formation of the Design Review Team within the DCD. The stated purpose of the Design Review Team has always been to consistently raise the bar on Milwaukee architecture by working collaboratively with architects and developers. Members of the team, who are comprised almost entirely of architecturally trained UWM alumni and interns who work in the DCD, review all projects that require any form of city subsidy or approval. Commentary to applicants is confidential and, wherever possible, constructive, in an attempt to, at a minimum, make every project, however modest, a little better than it might have been. Major successes include the Intermodal Station, certain big box developments (a seven-part set of guidelines has been developed), bridges, parking lots, garages, and even signage: the maxim "Everything is Important" underlies all activities.

THINK OUTSIDE THE BOX

While the strength of the academic role lies primarily in the development of new ideas that inform the decision-making process in the physical environment, faculty and students play an expanded role in neighborhood development, many of them through Community Design Solutions (the out-

reach arm of SARUP, which completes over 20 projects a year), and work directly with city agencies and numerous community groups and businesses (see appendix A).

However, an added strength of the academic world lies in its role as "idea factory"—the promulgation of alternative futures that require out-of-the-box thinking initially freed from political and financial constraints. The SARUP has had significant success in this role. For example, under the direction of former planning director Peter Park, SARUP successfully explored the demolition of an infrequently used and aging freeway, creating plans for redevelopment as a reweaving of the urban fabric that was displaced by its original construction. The plans were met with interest, the ideas were adopted by the city, and the freeway has now been razed. The area awaits development; many plans created within the redevelopment area have been temporarily deferred due to prevailing economic conditions. Looking at politically charged projects such as knocking down a freeway (the demolition was completed by April 2003) from an academic perspective effectively insulates government from attack, as the work remains within the academic arena and at a theoretical level. Should the ideas find favor in the public realm, however, they can be speedily adopted and adapted for municipal use.

Another such project that the current mayor requested students and faculty to address concerned the future of MacArthur Square, a sprawling, ill-used park disconnected from the grid of the city, sitting atop a 2,000-space underground parking garage exhibiting significant signs of wear and water damage.

It was estimated that over $20 million worth of reconstruction would be necessary solely to fix the leaks, while the parking garage would remain as isolated and underutilized as ever. What could be done, if anything, to address this problem that had been ignored or overlooked for many years?

Under the visionary guidance of SARUP professor Larry Witzling and with strong support from DCD commissioner Richard "Rocky" Marcoux, a scheme was developed that effectively reconnected the raised park to the city grid, thereby allowing vehicle access, by bringing two ramps up onto the surface of the park. This then opened up hitherto unrecognized development opportunities, which were visualized by local architectural practices in a two-day *charrette*, funded by a local philanthropic group, the Herzfeld Foundation (fig. 11.4).

While economic uncertainty has stalled plans for repair and therefore major redevelopment of the square, the radical thinking in the plans will provide a provocative perspective on redevelopment that will shape planning decisions at the appropriate time.

Summary

The structure of city government differs considerably from that of an academic department, and while their objectives may differ, it is possible to link them in a way that benefits both agendas. The structural linking of SARUP with DCD ensures continuous dialogue between the two entities, primarily hinged around the joint appointment of the dean/ director of planning and design (now the chair of DCD). This has led to greater coordination of class and studio projects with city interests, the results of which are collectively presented to government officials each year in an archival publication, *SARUP in the City* (see appendix B). In addition to the approximately 25 projects and 15 theses that are focused on Milwaukee each year, Community Design Solutions often undertakes as many as a further 20 projects that are directed toward neighborhood redevelopment. The structural link also ensures a two-way transfer of personnel between the institutions. There are a number of interns working in the city, and DCD planning personnel, as noted, often teach or participate in classes and studios.

As an urban institution, SARUP has a responsibility to respond to its immediate environment and do whatever it can to be a force for positive change. The creation of a formal relationship with an enlightened city government ensures ongoing dialogue and the flow of new ideas and perspectives directly to the decision-making levels of government. This enables the city to be enriched and informed by its academic partners and the students and faculty to become a relevant force for renewal in their environment, thus enriching their professional development. While this model may not be appropriate to all schools or cities, the benefits of a win-win partnership are worthy of exploration by the academy and government alike in all cities that could benefit from similar partnerships.

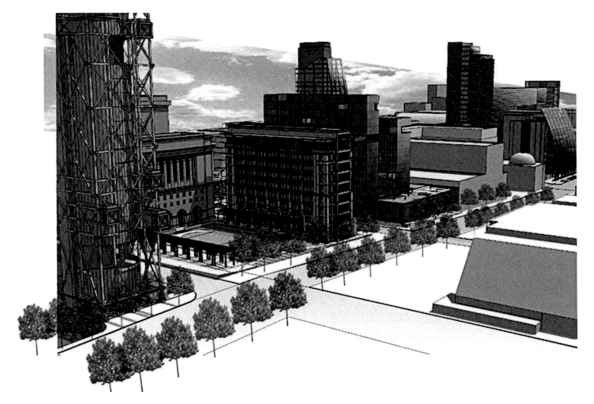

FIGURE 11.4. Artist's rendering of proposed redevelopment of Kilbourn Avenue and MacArthur Square around the County Courthouse in Milwaukee. Town-gown partnerships can yield powerful and innovative solutions when civic leaders, city planners, and academic partners share a unified vision. (Courtesy of the City of Milwaukee Department of City Development)

Appendix A

COMMUNITY DESIGN SOLUTIONS PROJECT LIST, SUMMER 2008–SUMMER 2010

Planning and design

PROJECT	DESCRIPTION
Oconomowoc Design Guidelines for Southwest Summit Avenue Land Use Development Plan	Establish architectural design guidelines; develop landscape theme; suggest streetscape elements; develop gateway features
Waterford Design Guidelines	Work with Plan Commission Ad Hoc committee; educate; create guidelines document; include implementation and administration
Milwaukee River Greenway Master Plan	Provide design and mapping assistance to Milwaukee River Greenway committee for a master plan of the publicly accessible areas along the Greenway between Commerce Street and Silver Spring Drive

Residential

Layton Boulevard West Neighbors Target Investment Neighborhood (TIN) Workshop	Conduct a workshop with residents to inform them about the TIN home improvement program and assist them in developing renovation ideas
Housing Re-design 76th and Bender	Facade, landscape, streetscape renovation to make a safer, more attractive block
Johnson's Park Fill-In Building Model	Parcel at 19th & Walnut, want mixed-use building that will fit in well with neighborhood, residential on top
Capitol West Neighborhood Association—Improving Residential Quality	Develop, update models for four middle-income housing types in neighborhood Created "Housing Resources" guide, member focus on energy pilot program committee

Institutional

New Facility for Wildlife in Need—Waukesha	Create a design for an expansion of the existing building at the University of Wisconsin–Waukesha Field Station to accommodate labs, treatment facilities, and exhibit space
Maryland Avenue Montessori School Landscape Design	Develop concepts for the open space around the school; work with parent organization
Bradford Beach House: Three-Year Renovation Plan	Develop renovation ideas for beach house and concession, for business that received long-term County lease to run concession
Cardinal Stritch Library Partial Modernization	Develop preliminary ideas for renovation of the SW portion of library first floor to meet technological and operational needs of today's students
Red Cross Phase 1: Exterior Building Modifications	Develop green facade options for existing Wisconsin Avenue building
Vision of a New Mt. Moriah Baptist Missionary Church	Visioning for new church building; preliminary design of new church
Improving University of Wisconsin–Milwaukee Film Department Facilities	Suggest how best to locate film department, estimate space needs, program changes, look at Mitchell and Kenilworth
Plankinton Building 5th Floor Renovation	Renovate for use by University of Wisconsin–Milwaukee extension for computer classes/other
Mary Ryan Boys and Girls Club Renovation	Renovate first floor of building at 3000 Sherman Blvd to better meet student, programmatic, and efficiency needs
Marshfield Public Library	Create design concept for an addition that connects library and next-door Senior Center

Continuing partnerships

CLIENT SUPERVISION — CITY OF MILWAUKEE,
DEPARTMENT OF CITY DEVELOPMENT

PROJECT	DESCRIPTION
Facade Grant/Main Street Contract with City of Milwaukee, Department of City Development	Fill positions of Main Street Facade grant program specialist and Facade grant specialist with Community Design Solutions team Holton Street streetscape project
27th Street Corridor Main Street	
Fond du Lac & North	
Processing facade grants	
Planning scholar intern for the City of Milwaukee	Works under supervision of City Planner and assists with master planning, historic preservation, and other areas, as needed

CDS SUPERVISION — CLIENT: RIVERWORKS DEVELOPMENT CORPORATION AND RIVERWORKS BIDS

Signage and Guidelines Riverworks	Help decide what exactly they want in boulevard and develop a long-range maintenance plan for design elements in the boulevard
Buffum Street Riverworks	Design mixed-use (commercial/residential) building in empty lot as model of type of buildings that could fill lots in area
Other Properties Facade Recommendations	Number of properties along Keefe, Holton that were determined in earlier study to need work or that are being promoted by Riverworks Development Corporation for sale/lease
Riverworks Center Design Guidelines	Develop a master plan for Riverworks Center
Capitol and Humboldt	Develop improved gateway image, especially on southwest corner

Source: Compiled by Susan Weistrop, Community Design Solutions coordinator

Appendix B

MILWAUKEE-FOCUSED COURSEWORK, STUDIO WORK, AND THESES PUBLISHED IN *SARUP IN THE CITY*, ACADEMIC YEAR 2009-2010

Coursework, Department of Urban Planning

Riverworks Neighborhood Indicators

The Zilber Institute

The Solar Initiative

The Hoan Bridge

University of Wisconsin–Milwaukee Campus Plan

WIRED R

The Milwaukee Foreclosure Crisis

Riverwest Neighborhood Plan

Village of Wauwatosa Business Improvement District

Transit in Milwaukee

Brown Deer Road Corridor Redevelopment

Kinnickinnic River Parkway

Public Participation Plan

M. Arch. Theses, Department of Architecture

The Residential Alley

Popular Houses of West Allis

University of Wisconsin–Milwaukee Catholic Student Center

St. Francis Cousins Center

University of Wisconsin–Milwaukee Residence Hall

The Loyalty Building

Interconnectivity — Space in the City

Urban Energy Center

Milwaukee Intermodal System

Sofi Urban Spiritual Retreat

The Urban Dance Center

Oak Leaf Trail Center

Family Co-housing in Downtown Milwaukee

Milwaukee Industrial Museum

Reed Street Yards

University of Wisconsin–Milwaukee Daylight Institute

CHAPTER TWELVE

Peoria's Warehouse District

CHALLENGES FOR DEVELOPMENT

RAY LEES AND CRAIG HARLAN HULLINGER

MOST PEOPLE ARE NOT AWARE THAT PEORIA WAS a bustling, prosperous regional center for territorial trade, transportation, and commerce long before Chicago (Fort Dearborn) was much of a settlement on the banks of Lake Michigan. Peoria's location on the Illinois River and within the fertile central Illinois prairie has been a positive factor in its development and growth throughout its history (fig. 12.1). Its natural resources of freshwater for drinking and transportation and rich, productive soils for agriculture have attracted resident entrepreneurs and many others who have capitalized on these and other resources offered by the region.

Like Peoria, many communities have experienced the economic transitions from an agrarian base to manufacturing and, now, to the information age. The ebb and flow of these transformations have certainly been evident in Peoria, from its earliest history, when the riverboat packet companies hauled freight up and down the Illinois River, to the nineteenth and early twentieth centuries and the distilleries that formed the Warehouse District and, more recently, as the world headquarters of Caterpillar, the world's largest manufacturer of earth-moving equipment.

The economic legacies of these historic enterprises are evident today — not the least of which is the built environment of substantial warehouses and commercial structures located in the community's former rivercentric warehouse district. This chapter will explore the issues, challenges, and opportunities involved in the reinvigoration of this important area within Peoria.

The "Rest" of Illinois: Beyond Metropolitan Chicago

"Just outside Chicago, there's a place called Illinois." The state of Illinois developed this catchy slogan for its tourism marketing program to encourage Chicago-area residents to visit Illinois south and west of Chicago, instead of visiting Wisconsin and Michigan. The strategy is aimed to keep tourism and the dollars it generates in Illinois.

The strategy need not stop at tourism, though. Communities in downstate Illinois, like Peoria, should employ a similar strategy when attracting businesses and economic development. Attractive "assets" abound. Outside of the Chicago metropolitan area, the cost of home ownership and renting, as well as, generally, the cost of doing business, is much lower. Congestion, often cited as a quality-of-life issue, is virtually nonexistent; "rush hour" in smaller communities is often the "rush minute."

Demographic trends indicate that the challenges are only going to increase for northeastern Illinois. By 2030, the state is projected to grow over 15%, but of the 2 million more people who will live there, most will be living in or near metro Chicago. While growth is encouraging, it comes with associated costs. Both Chicago and Illinois would be better off if some of the projected growth occurred in other Illinois communities.

Illinois communities outside the greater Chicago metropolitan area, and Peoria in particular, could accommodate and welcome much of this projected new growth. Many communities are at best experiencing moderate growth, while many more are losing population. These smaller communities often have housing stock, roads, schools, and other infrastructure that have greater capacity than they need to meet their present and future needs.

This potential is illustrated by comparing two large metropolitan areas in Illinois. The moderately growing Peoria metropolitan area is the second largest metro area in Illinois. However, as a quality-of-life comparison between Peoria and Chicago illustrates, there are significant advantages to locating or relocating "downstate" in Illinois (table 12.1).

Relocating Businesses and Employees Downstate

Before the Great Recession of 2008–2009, more people were able to determine where they would work in the United States. Today, the internet permits people to work remotely. Telecommuting allows mobile professionals to flee large, congested metro areas and work and live in less congested cities or even rural environments. Freelance writers, advertising executives, entrepreneurs, artists, computer experts, and salespeople are typical employees and entrepreneurs who often have control of their work location. Jack Manahan is a government computer consultant who left the Chicago suburbs for Peoria. When he needs to visit a client, he simply drives 10 minutes to the airport. "I saved half the cost of my auto insurance and got a much nicer home in Peoria when I left Chicago," says Manahan. "And the rush hour is much less than in Chicago. Peoria is a pleasant place to live and work, without the hassle of a really big city."

Manufacturers, agencies, sales forces, and consulting companies no longer need to be located in a large metropolitan area to conduct business, with modern communications technologies and globally connected transportation hubs conveniently located to regional business areas. The same connectivity that permits telecommuting allows business leaders the flexibility to move their entire companies to smaller, more attractive communities where both the quality of life and the cost of doing business can be better. This trend is accelerating and will likely continue to be popular, especially as big city congestion increases.

Peoria's Warehouse District Strategy circa 2006

Peoria is the city center for the second largest metropolitan area in Illinois and boasts the second most intensely developed downtown. The downtown is a vibrant and successful commercial district with an attractively redeveloped riverfront, beautiful buildings, and, until recently, a strong and growing employment base. Like many older cities, however,

Figure 12.1. Peoria in the early twentieth century. Peoria's growth throughout its history was due to its access to the Illinois River. (Courtesy of Peoria County Historical Society)

TABLE 12.1 *Chicago and Peoria: Quality-of-Life Comparisons*

	CHICAGO	PEORIA
Median home price 2006-2010[1]	$269,000	$119,000
Average commute time (2006-10)[2]	34 minutes	17 minutes
"Cost of doing business" rank[3]	90th	47th
Cost-of-living index composite[4]	103.9	96.9
Student/teacher ratio[5]	16.4	14.4

Source: Courtesy of Chris Setti, Ray Lees and Craig Hullinger.

[1] "U.S. Census Bureau 2006-2010." http://quickfacts.census.gov/qfd/states/17/1714000.html

[2] "U.S. Census Bureau 2006-2010." http://quickfacts.census.gov/qfd/states/17/1714000.html

[3] "Best Places for Business and Careers," *Forbes*, May 5, 2005.

[4] Cost of Living Index, 2nd Quarter 2005, Council for Community and Economic Research, http://www.coli.org/store.asp. Accessed January 6, 2012.

[5] "Best Places to Live 2005," CNN Money, http://money.cnn.com/magazines/moneymag/bplive/2005/index.html. Accessed January 6, 2012.

FIGURE 12.2. The fitness room in the Murray Building in the Warehouse District of Peoria allows tenants to stay in shape. With over 80,000 gross square feet of space, the Murray Building illustrates the potential of adapting warehouses for almost any use. (Courtesy of Paul J. Armstrong)

it is in need of new housing and retail in and near the downtown core. The city has many historic industrial buildings that could be adaptively reused as housing and retail space. Some vacant tracts could welcome new construction of single-family homes and townhouses.

The formally designated Warehouse District, located immediately south of downtown Peoria on the Illinois River, has great redevelopment potential. Many well-constructed and structurally sound masonry buildings constructed in the late 1800s and early 1900s are located in the district, as are one-story industrial buildings of more recent vintage, along with many vacant land parcels. While many of these buildings are in good condition and some have been adapted to new uses today, the economic value of many of the historic multi-

story buildings located in the district had greatly diminished by 1980. During the 1960s and 1970s many industrial and warehousing operations were relocated to modern one-story buildings in other areas of the city or suburbs, which left many of the buildings to be mothballed or barely maintained, while others were abandoned and, regrettably, allowed to deteriorate to the point that demolition was required.

As the proposals for a SynergiCity approach to this area have already shown, it could once again become a vibrant urban neighborhood with a mix of residential and commercial uses. Examples of the adaptive reuse of the old industrial lofts already exist on Water Street between State and Liberty streets. Street-level space makes prime commercial and retail uses, and upper floors can be occupied

by offices and residences. Artists and artisans have already relocated to the district, leasing studios primarily in former warehouse buildings such as the Murray Building (fig. 12.2).

Recognizing the economic value of this historic building stock and the proximity of the Warehouse District to the city center and Central Business District, the city of Peoria has formulated a Redevelopment Strategy to promote the revitalization of this area into a new urban community.

To more effectively assess and plan for the Warehouse District's revitalization, the city has supported a wide variety of initiatives and studies, including developing a Comprehensive Plan and conducting a Detailed Building Inventory. This was followed by the planning guidelines and recommendations published in *Heart of Peoria*, the result of a

FIGURE 12.3. The adaptive reuse of 401 Water Street for prime office space illustrates the potential of historic warehouses to meet modern living and working requirements. Renovation of existing buildings is often cost effective; the average purchase price may be less than $11 per square foot, and retrofit can cost as little as $40 per square foot. (Courtesy of Paul J. Armstrong)

community *charrette* led by Andres Duany of DPZ Architects in 2003. The city of Peoria then commissioned the Warehouse District Redevelopment Plan and TIF Study, which recommended creating Tax Increment Financing (TIF) zones throughout the city to encourage development. *Heart of Peoria* had recommended using a form-based code to promote a mix of uses based on market research conducted by the focus group Ferrill Madden and Tracy Cross.

Public-Private Collaboration: A Key to Success

Each of the community stakeholders knows that the long-term success of redevelopment is dependent on both the city and the private sector coming together and working collaboratively to achieve common goals and objectives. A few of the "action" items expected to be accomplished by developers and the city include Developer Actions and City Actions.

Developer Actions include (1) acquiring or optioning for developable real estate for new buildings in the district, (2) renovating existing buildings for mixed uses, (3) implementing the Heart of Peoria Plan using Smart Growth planning, (4) market redeveloped buildings to a wide range of buyers or leases, and (5) creating and promoting new livable urban neighborhoods.

City Actions would be done jointly or concurrently with development and include (1) implement the Heart of Peoria Plan with Smart Growth principles; (2) add parking and an enhanced streetscape on Washington Street; (3) reconstruct the historic character of existing streets around the Railroad

Depot and Artist Alley with brick pavers; (4) optimize on-street parking with diagonal and parallel configurations; (5) create economic incentives such as TIF and Enterprise Zones to finance streetscape improvements and building renovations (6) lobby the state of Illinois to create a State Historic Tax Credit program for the District and facilitate the Federal Historic Tax Credit program; and (7) facilitate market research and area planning to promote the Warehouse District and the city as a livable community for business, culture, and living.

Some of these actions are already under way. The redevelopment of the Kellerher's Block and the former Sealtest Ice Cream Factory are just two examples that are helping to revitalize the district. Another has been the adaptive reuse of 401 Water Street into prime office space (fig. 12.3). Dewberry Architects, Inc., which handled the design of exterior improvements and interior public spaces, occupies the seventh and eighth floors in upscale offices that provide dramatic views of the Illinois River. According to James Kemper, associate principal and design director at Dewberry, retrofitting an old warehouse building for modern offices is challenging. Wiring for modern data systems had to be routed under existing floors, and exposed ductwork for heating and air conditioning is suspended from structural beams. Sprinkler systems also had to be installed to meet stringent fire codes. Historical features, such as the water tower and an exterior materials chute, were retained and have become part of the aesthetic. The result combines modern materials and finishes with the historic warmth and character of traditional materials such as masonry and wood.

Community Profile: Changing Demographics

Peoria, over the past several decades, has successfully shifted from a manufacturing-based economy to one centered on professional and technical jobs. While Peoria is still its headquarters, Caterpillar Corporation's local presence is dominated as much by its "white-collar" engineers, researchers, managers, and executives as by its "blue-collar" factory workers. As a result, Peoria has seen a dramatic increase in its "creative class" due to expansion of the economic sectors of health services, research, and development, higher education, finance, and law. The city has become a major medical center for most of central and downstate Illinois and a referral center for specialty disciplines beyond Illinois. To respond to this market growth, the three hospitals in the city are working together to invest over $500 million in capital expansion projects. Research and development activities valued at over $1 billion annually are being conducted by Caterpillar, Bradley University, the University of Illinois College of Medicine, and the National Center for Agricultural Utilization and Research, as well as up-and-coming companies like zuChem and IPICO Sports. In addition, Peoria is home to a number of regional banking institutions, as well as serving as central Illinois's legal center as the county seat and having a federal courthouse.

Downtown Peoria employs nearly 20,000 people. This rise in the creative economy has changed the demographics of the city. Every day newly recruited engineers, doctors, lawyers, professors, and other professionals move to Peoria, often from large urban areas. While many of these transplanted individuals and families desire urban living, they find that opportunities to live close to where they work, in and around downtown, are limited.

In 2006, the city of Peoria retained the urban planning and design firm Ferrell Madden and Associates to assess and evaluate development patterns in the older sections of the city. That effort involved the study of the city's demographic, employment, and housing patterns and determined that urban Peoria could support 3,600 new dwelling units between now and 2025.

Ferrell Madden found that between 1996 and 2005 the Peoria employment picture had shifted dramatically. The sectors that declined significantly were durable goods manufacturing, nondurable goods manufacturing, and retail trades.[1] The areas with the most job growth in the same time period were education, health services, and professional business services. Given these patterns, the consultants projected that through 2010, the greatest growth would be in health and education, followed by professional and business services and durable goods manufacturing.

While Peoria has been growing outward in terms of land area, its population has remained relatively flat. The 2,100 homes added in the last decade have mostly occurred along the suburban north and northwestern edges of the city, not in the urban core. Throughout the metropolitan area an average of 1,200 housing units are built each year. Given the job trends, however, we believe there is a great opportunity for a denser, more urban housing product. As part of their study, the Ferrell Madden team looked at demographics from a study done by the Environmental Systems Research Institute (ESRI) to project the lifestyle patterns of Peoria residents.

Of note in what the ESRI study termed "Tapestry Segments" is the significant number of people who are projected to be members of "Metropolitan,"

"Midlife Junction," or "In Style" segments. These three segments comprise approximately 30% of Peoria's population (about 13,000 households). More important, demographers believe that individuals in these segments are more likely to be drawn to vibrant, urban environments. The Metropolitan segment, especially, is more likely to live in higher density areas with nearby big-city amenities.

Ferrell Madden also documented that Peoria is becoming a wealthier city. They projected that by 2010, the jobs added to the economy would result in a substantial gain in individuals earning more than $75,000 a year. Ferrell Madden also indicated that this gain is seen across all age categories, with significant gains in the population aged 55-64. This population segment represents a tremendous opportunity for upscale loft condominiums targeting "empty nest" professionals.

Peoria is an exciting market with an excellent potential for return on investments in its urban areas. Along with the demand for 3,600 new urban housing units over the next two decades, the same market will need over 220,000 square feet of retail space. The reinvestment in areas such as the Warehouse District will also drive demand for additional office space. Given the policies being implemented by the city — form-based codes and TIF — Peoria is a prime location for quality urban development.

Cost Base in the Warehouse District: Attractive Opportunities

By any reasonable measure of real estate value, the cost base of properties in the district is attractive. Many of the buildings have sold for as little as $5 per square foot during the past five years. Over 400,000

square feet was listed for sale in 2006 for an average asking price of $11.87 per square foot, which was still a bargain. By 2008, costs had dropped further, reflecting the softer economy, with over 500,000 square feet listed for sale at an average asking price of $10.61 per square foot. Admittedly, many of the buildings have environmental, structural, and/or building envelope issues that need to be addressed.

Table 12.2 shows the average asking price for buildings in the Warehouse District in 2006. The average price was very low — a little over $10 per square foot. Thus, the land and building shell of a 1,000-square-foot condominium was only $10,000.

Economic Incentives: Tools to Motivate the Market

City governments today have a number of financial incentive tools that can be used to direct investment into underdeveloped urban areas. Public funding for urban redevelopment can come in the form of state- and federally-supported grants or loans, as well as partnerships with lending institutions, such as banks and mortgage lenders, the real estate divisions of insurance companies, and not-for-profit developers.

TAX INCREMENT FINANCING

The Warehouse District redevelopment area requires a TIF. However, without government incentives, the area cannot be redeveloped. For decades, this area has existed in its present condition and will probably continue as is without government support and leadership. The area qualifies for a TIF

TABLE 12.2 *Asking Price for Properties in Warehouse District, Peoria, Illinois, 2006*

PROPERTY	DESCRIPTION	SQ FEET	ASKING PRICE	PRICE PER SQ FT
404 & 408 SW Adams	Brick 2-story	22,400	$600,000	$26.73
1000 Adams	Brick 2-story	8,500	$119,000	$14.00
1001 SW Adams	Brick 2-story	43,000	$350,000	$8.14
316 SW Washington	Office unfinished	9,516	$532,896	$56.00
711/725 Washington	2-story Warehouse	35,000	$370,000	$10.57
800 SW Washington	Brick 6-story	88,000	$975,000	$11.08
927 SW Washington	Brick 1-story	9,800	$100,000	$10.20
933 SW Washington	Brick 1-story	8,640	$100,000	$11.57
1003-1309 SW Washington	Warehouse/office	89,442	$1,162,746	$13.00
1301-1309 Washington	Brick 5-story	81,484	$350,000	$4.30
114 SW Washington	Warehouse/office	11,325	$795,000	$7.14
414 Water-Edgewater	Warehouse/office	20,000	$140,000	$7.00
Totals/Average		*527,151*	*$5,594,642*	*$10.61*

Source: Courtesy of Ray Lees and Craig Hullinger.

for a number of reasons, including the presence of vacant buildings, vacant land, deteriorated buildings, and poor infrastructure. Some of the buildings are obsolete for current uses, suffer from declining or stagnant assessed evaluation, have environmental problems, are located in the floodplain, or just suffer due to lack of insightful planning. The TIF would be a normal 23-year TIF, but the incremental incentive would be provided only for projects constructed within five years from the creation of the TIF. Development created after five years would pay normal taxes to all the taxing bodies.

HISTORIC PRESERVATION TAX CREDIT ACT

Federal historic tax credits are a major incentive to help cities renew older declining neighborhoods.

The tax credit makes the preservation and renewal of dilapidated historic buildings much more likely and is an important factor in revitalizing older communities. The credit can be 20% of the investment in rebuilding historic buildings. A number of states have similar programs. The city of Peoria has proposed that the state of Illinois develop such a program, and the state legislature recently approved the proposal. The area now benefits from a 25% state historic tax credit.

Urban Living: Market and Demand

The city of Peoria in 2008 commissioned Tracy Cross & Associates to provide a market analysis regarding the potential for residential development in the city's downtown, with particular interest in the feasibility of redevelopment within its Warehouse District. The city updated the study in 2009 at the request of developers, to determine if the market remained strong as the national housing recession deepened. Tracy Cross confirmed that the market remained strong and encouraged the city to continue to pursue its urban redevelopment goals.

The analysis demonstrates that the downtown of Peoria has the capacity to absorb 194 residential units annually, including higher density attached housing types. In fact, for the products/prices outlined below, the downtown/Warehouse District has the capacity to absorb 102 loft-style apartments converted from existing structures, 66 new construction rental apartments, 16 new garden condominiums, and 10 new construction townhomes/row homes.

Tracy Cross's conclusions of aggregate potentials assume that a strategic approach to the introduction of new housing is taken with respect to both geography and the order in which the various housing forms are brought to market. This is to say, maximum absorption will most likely be achieved only with a concerted effort to introduce new housing in a way that extends the sphere of residential desirability and does so on an order that does not concurrently pit competitive housing forms against each other.

Much like other urban centers undergoing gentrification and redevelopment, the potential for Peoria's downtown is very strong. The Warehouse District has already demonstrated its promise and feasibility as a place for new housing through several recent successful residential programs. In the meantime, the city of Peoria has supported additional redevelopment through the adoption of its innovative form-based zoning code and has approved generous incentives packages for developers and entrepreneurs. What is needed to continue Peoria's downtown and Warehouse District revival is the application of a sensible and strategic plan of development that builds on existing strengths and maximizes the potential for future sites. (See plates 2 and 3 for the masterplan proposals for the Warehouse District.)

"If You Build It They Will Come"

A focus group comprised of young Caterpillar engineers and developers indicated a great interest among young people in living in a vibrant downtown neighborhood. "If you build it, they say they'll come."

Real estate developers who were contacted about building in the Warehouse District wanted to see market data demonstrating the interest level among people who were likely to live in new or renovated housing and commercial development around downtown Peoria. In conjunction with a number of city stakeholders, Peoria's Department of Economic Development created a brief paper survey that gauged people's interest in three distinct areas: (1) downtown Peoria, (2) the Warehouse District directly south of downtown, and (3) "Renaissance Park," an area of older, single-family homes just outside downtown. The survey also gathered some demographic information about age, marital status, and other factors.

Initially, the survey was hand-distributed to a limited audience in order to refine the questions and get initial feedback. The interest level of those respondents was so positive that the city decided to release the survey more widely. Contracting with

iceCentric, a Peoria-based technology company, the city made the survey available online from January 10 to February 10, 2006. Using the resources of the Chamber of Commerce and other local entities, employers were requested to ask their employees via email to complete the survey.

In one month, the survey generated 1,545 responses. According to iceCentric, the response rate exceeded the industry standard by 10%. Even better, the results themselves validated the city's desire to have increased focus on these areas. Among respondents, 31.2% were interested in downtown, 30.2% were interested in Renaissance Park, and 29.6% were interested in the Warehouse District. Some respondents indicated an interest in one area but not others; in total, 42.8% of respondents expressed interest in at least one of the three areas in the survey.

The survey also yielded useful data about what types of people were most interested in these areas. Generally speaking, interested individuals were more likely to be single and have fewer dependent children living at home than those not interested. (In fact, 68% of all those expressing interest had no children living with them at the time of the survey.) There seemed to be an equal distribution among education levels and income, with interested individuals trending toward a slightly younger demographic than their counterparts. These demographics are important when talking to developers about what to build and to whom to market their developments.

An important feature of the survey was to determine what an ideal price range would be for those surveyed. The survey indicated the housing price range of people interested in these areas, as well as the types of property they are looking to buy.

Another important aspect of the survey was that

people who were interested in living in one of the target areas were able to leave their email addresses on the site. The city now has 250 email addresses that will be provided to developers as they consider various development scenarios and potential clients. Under this scenario, the developer could get an option on a building, email all those interested, and invite them to visit the building. With very little expense and effort, the developer could get a quick response from prospective buyers or renters.

This housing survey proved to be a useful and inexpensive way to develop valuable market research. For less than $1,000, the city of Peoria now has some hard data to show developers that the areas specified in the survey will produce cost-effective and marketable investments for future developments.

Implementing the Vision: Strategies and Alternatives

While the successful redevelopment of urban areas is often a complex, frustrating, and time-consuming endeavor, the rewards for public and private stakeholders alike can be significant. The city of Peoria has assessed and quantified its opportunities and is laying the necessary groundwork to achieve its goal to revitalize the Warehouse District. However, success of future development will require the following initiatives.

DIRECT SALES OF LOFT SPACES FOR RESIDENTIAL PROPERTIES

Mature and more affluent clients will expect certain amenities and upgrades that lower income residents are willing to live without. In residential units, these may include natural stone countertops and high-end appliances in kitchens, more luxurious bathrooms with double sinks, walk-in showers and whirlpool baths, walk-in closets in bedrooms, and large, energy-efficient windows in living and dining rooms for light and views. Sustainable materials, such as low-VOC paints and carpets, bamboo flooring, and recycled materials will also be a marketing advantage for older, well-educated clients. Buildings with Leadership in Ecology and Environment Design (LEED) ratings also are more attractive to educated buyers who are willing to pay premium prices for sustainable environments.

RENTAL RESIDENTIAL UNITS FOR STUDENTS AND ARTISTS

For younger clients who are seeking minimal living requirements with the potential for work-related activities, warehouses that have been converted into lofts at a low cost per square foot will meet their expectations and pocketbooks. Minimal improvements would include new plumbing, electrical, and HVAC systems; new, energy-efficient windows; large, open live/work spaces with high ceilings; standard-grade cabinetry and appliances;

ample storage; and green materials. Finishes can be kept to a minimum, however, which allows for the possibility of exposed pipes, HVAC ducts, and electrical conduit as aesthetic features of the building.

RETIREMENT HOUSING IN SOME BUILDINGS

This is potentially a large and expanding market. Retirement housing for alumni who are affiliated with Bradley University is likely to be attractive to retirees who want to return to Peoria and live in quality housing overlooking the Illinois River. Bradley University could even hold continuing education classes in one of the buildings. Retirees from other businesses and institutions, such as the hospitals and Caterpillar, may also consider living close to the downtown, where they can walk or take public transportation to shopping, entertainment, and cultural activities.

A BED AND BREAKFAST OR BOUTIQUE HOTEL IN ONE OF THE CONVERTED LOFTS

The future residents of this neighborhood might not currently live in Peoria. A quality bed and breakfast or boutique hotel could attract visitors and entice them to spend time in the area.

EMPHASIZE THE AREA AS THE "RIVERFRONT ARTS DISTRICT"

The city and developers can work together to attract the "creative class" to locate in the district. Artists, photographers, architects, designers, and other creative professionals seek interesting areas

Figure 12.4. Waterfront Place in Peoria has antique and specialty shops that bring visitors to the district. (Courtesy of Paul J. Armstrong)

FIGURE 12.5. Redevelopment of the Kelleher's Block in the Warehouse District of Peoria has inspired other building owners and demonstrates the potential of the district. (Courtesy of Paul J. Armstrong)

of cities in which to live and work. In turn, they create and support various "microeconomies" that include retail, offices, and service businesses (Fig 12.4). Bradley University and Illinois Central College could also be recruited to hold art classes and develop studios in the district.

WORK WITH THE CITY TO CREATE AN ENHANCED STREETSCAPE

Improve Washington Street from Main Street south through the Arts District with additional landscaping, signage, parking, and sculpture.

CONSTRUCT PEDESTRIAN-FRIENDLY STREETSCAPES IN THE ALLEYS

The alleys on both sides of Washington Street are exceptionally wide and invite significant pedestrian-friendly development. Whereas alleys are desirable for bringing food and services to and from buildings, they can have a dual purpose in the Warehouse District: (1) to bring goods and services to businesses and residences and to remove trash during nonpeak hours, and (2) to act as interior block walking streets for pedestrians lined with shops, galleries, and offices. In the SynergiCity mas-

terplans (see chapter 2), the alleys were also an opportunity to introduce parking and pervious paving materials and filter strips to manage storm water ecologically. New streetlighting, ballards, plantings, and seating were also proposed to give the district historical character as well as enhance the livability of the alleys themselves (plate 4).

CONSTRUCT DIAGONAL PARKING TO OPTIMIZE PARKING POTENTIAL ON EXISTING AND NEW STREETS

The district streets are exceptionally wide and can easily accommodate parking. Diagonal parking has several benefits in this case, especially since it creates more compact parking areas adjacent to key businesses and residences.

BUILD NEW SINGLE-FAMILY AND TOWNHOUSE DEVELOPMENTS ON DEPOT STREET

There are people who would like to live in the area but will not want to own a converted loft space in an existing period building. Density can still be achieved by developing townhouses and midrise condominiums and apartments. The SynergiCity masterplan proposed designating the blocks along Persimmon Street as a Mixed-Use/Office/Residential district, which would enable mixed-use multifamily development for living and working.

CREATE INDOOR PARKING IN ONE OF THE SINGLE-STORY INDUSTRIAL BUILDINGS

Convert the first 30 feet of the street face of these buildings to retail. In planning, allow the conversion of these single-story parking garages into multistory parking decks if and when demand is sufficient. We also noted that many of the existing warehouses are built robustly enough to accommodate the weight of automobiles.

Will It Play in Peoria?

Since the days of vaudeville, Peoria's Midwest sensibilities and values have provided stage acts, products, and services "tested" in our community with a measure of market viability and success before introduction to the national marketplace. If something successfully "played in Peoria," chances were very good it would succeed anywhere in the United States.

Obviously, a targeted comprehensive urban redevelopment effort initiated during one of the most challenging economic environments experienced in a generation is no "stage act." Only time will tell us if our community can weather the current downturn and successfully build on the substantial foundation already put in place by the city, planners, developers and others in this River City (fig. 12.5).

Note

1. Durable goods manufacturing saw a significant decline between 1996 and 2003 but has returned sharply between 2003 and 2005, though it remains below 1996 levels.

References

Duany, A., and E. Plater-Zyberk. 2003. *Heart of Peoria.* Peoria, IL: City of Peoria Economic Development Department.

Hullinger, C. H. 2006. *Peoria, Illinois Economic Development Plan.* Peoria, IL: City of Peoria Economic Development Department.

Hullinger, C. H., and L. McClellan. 2001, January. "Do You Have a Smart Growth Plan?" *Illinois Municipal Review Magazine.*

Hullinger, C. H., L. Schendl, and C. Setti. 2006, January 10–February 10. Survey Tells Developers "If You Build It They Will Come." Med/tech market survey commissioned by the City of Peoria and administered jointly by the Economic Development Department and iceCentric, Inc. Available at the website of the City of Peoria, http://www.ci.peoria .il.us/index.php?module=resourcesmodule&action =view&id=779. Accessed January 6, 2012.

Tracy Cross & Associates. 2008, February 26. *Residential Market Analysis: Downtown Peoria and the Warehouse District.* Report presented to the City of Peoria.

CHAPTER THIRTEEN

Developing SynergiCity

THE REAL ESTATE DEVELOPMENT PERSPECTIVE

EMIL MALIZIA

MANY INDUSTRIAL CITIES IN AMERICA'S HEART-land and others elsewhere in the United States have endured long-term economic decline. Their manufacturing base has been undermined, and their central areas have lost many traditional economic functions, as well as population and employment, to peripheral locations. In an era of limited financial assistance from state or federal government, many cities are struggling to shore up their economic base and to strengthen central areas. Local civic and political leaders, economic developers, and downtown advocates have worked hard to attract private investment against long odds. In recent years, many can point to increases in private and public investment that indicate improvement. Although the recession that began in 2008 has derailed or delayed planned investments, redevelopment projects that leverage public infrastructure investments have become the favored vehicles for urban revitalization.

Even when markets improve, private investors are usually too risk-averse to pursue redevelopment projects without significant public assistance. That is why almost all urban redevelopment ef-forts involve public-private partnerships (Frieden and Sagalyn 1989; Kotin and Peiser 1997; Sawicki 1989). Local governments, community-based organizations, foundations, neighborhood groups, and other community advocates typically represent the public sector. Real estate developers and investors, commercial bankers, and tenants or their brokers represent the private sector. These participants seek ways to increase private returns in order to attract investment capital to redevelopment projects at reasonable public cost. In some cases, however, scarce public resources have not been utilized effectively, which slows the pace and reduces the impact of redevelopment (Meyer and Lyons 2000).

Since the mid-1980s, income tax rates, capital gains treatment, depreciation schedules, and loss provisions have significantly reduced the tax-shelter benefits of real estate ownership. The federal tax credit programs that exist are for low-income housing, historic preservation, or low-income areas (New Markets). Even when these programs are fully utilized, socially beneficial urban redevelopment projects must be both economically viable and fi-nancially feasible if private equity and debt are to be secured on reasonable terms (Adair et al. 1999; Gyourko and Rybczynski 2000).

Local leaders and concerned citizens often have a physical vision of revitalized central areas that is far ahead of market realities, as it should be. The difficult task involves attracting sufficient local and/or external demand to expand the local market in order to make the vision feasible. We must merge civic vision with economic and financial realities to achieve urban redevelopment.

This chapter focuses on real estate redevelopment in postindustrial cities. Rather than survey success stories, the emphasis is on the economic and financial dimensions of redevelopment at both the project and strategic levels. These dimensions must be addressed to achieve greater investment and improve property values. Ideas and guidelines are presented about ways to increase private investment through public-private partnerships. When local demand increases, private investment can be stimulated by increasing revenues, reducing costs, or—most important—lowering the perceived risk associated with redevelopment. Numerical examples are provided to help the reader understand the economic and financial realities of urban redevelopment more fully. (For an excellent review of this general topic, see Sagalyn 2007.)

Project-Level Approaches

Private developers use "back-of-the-envelope" techniques of financial analysis to compare value to cost in order to gauge the attractiveness of competing development opportunities at the outset of the development process. Project value is found by dividing estimated net operating income (NOI) by the appropriate market-determined capitalization (cap) rate. Net operating income is simply gross revenue (current market rent multiplied by the number of units or square footage of the project) reduced by vacancy allowance and operating expenses. The cap rate comes from transactions involving comparable properties. The cap rate can be considered the overall return investors expect per dollar invested. In other words, a 9% cap rate reflects the expectation that investors will earn 9 cents for every dollar used to purchase a property. Project cost is estimated by adding to the cost of the site construction costs per unit or square foot. Developers consider many projects, but few are sufficiently attractive to pursue.

The urban redevelopment context is quite different. The city administration, local economic development organization, or downtown advocacy group identifies potential redevelopment sites in central areas. The lead entity usually calls for public input on redevelopment options. Through *charrettes* or other means, it fashions a plan or vision for the physical redevelopment of small areas or specific sites. This plan or vision should be consistent with legal and institutional requirements as well as the site's physical constraints. At this point, the decision to redevelop depends on whether the numbers will work. In other words, feasibility depends on economic and financial considerations.

One difference in approach is that private developers almost always begin with a use (property type) and then try to find the most appropriate site. Local developers limit their search to available sites in the local market. Regional and national developers survey larger geographic areas and then narrow down to neighborhoods and finally specific sites. On the other hand, redevelopment projects promoted by the public sector almost always begin with specific sites within redevelopment areas. The question becomes: what is the most fitting and appropriate use for the site?[1] Private developers begin with a use and then determine whether an appropriate site exists for the project. Publicly inspired projects do not have this flexibility and must do sufficient feasibility research to review many potential uses as well as a combination of uses (mixed use).

Another rather obvious difference is that private developers usually build new products on "greenfield" sites. Urban redevelopment projects begin with infill sites that have been used previously or buildings that should be preserved through adaptive reuse (fig. 13.1). Both differences reflect the fact that private developers and their equity investors are footloose, whereas public redevelopers are committed to specific places.

Figure 13.1. The lobby of Harvester Lofts in Minneapolis combines historic elements and contemporary furnishings and finishes to attract young buyers. (Courtesy of Paul J. Armstrong)

Given an infill site or existing building, the first step is to estimate the cost of the redevelopment project. Although an array of public incentives and subsidies is usually available, cost estimates should be made without the inclusion of subsidies. These cost estimates are organized in the capital budget for the project. The budget should include best estimates of land and site development costs, construction costs including the structure and all systems (hard costs), and associated cost of services (soft costs).[2] Appendix A shows a hypothetical capital budget for an urban redevelopment project.

Once the capital budget is estimated, financial and market realities can be introduced. James Graaskamp developed a straightforward static method to conduct this analysis (Appraisal Institute 2008; Ciochetti and Malizia 2000; Graaskamp 1981). The cost-driven approach begins with the project capital budget and estimates the rent levels required to support this cost. The market-driven approach begins with existing market conditions and finds the project cost afforded by the market.

With the cost-driven approach, project cost as presented in the capital budget needs financing. Most real estate projects are leveraged, which means that the project is financed with permanent debt as well as equity. By introducing debt and equity, the financial dimension essentially links the cost estimates to existing market conditions.

Lenders apply two basic criteria to evaluate any loan request—the loan-to-cost (or loan-to-value) ratio and the debt service coverage ratio. In this case, the loan-to-cost ratio would be used to determine how much private debt could be provided. This ratio would usually vary in the 60–80% range. Private equity would be sourced to provide the rest of the financing.

The annual cost of private debt is not difficult to ascertain. Commercial lenders can quote the expected terms of the permanent loan—interest rate, amortization period, term of loan, and other provisions. These parameters can be used to find the monthly amount of debt service needed to repay the loan. The mortgage constant is amount of monthly debt service paid per dollar of principal. This constant is multiplied by 12 to find the annualized monthly mortgage constant.

The cost of equity is less accessible since real estate developers often rely on informal sources of equity (friends, family, business associates, etc.). In this static model, what is needed is an estimate of the cash-on-cash return on equity. In other words, how much cash would the project have to generate for equity investors to contribute one dollar of equity?

The annual return on equity and cost of debt add to NOI. The logic here is that the project's NOI will be split between the lenders and owners of the project. Project revenue is estimated by adding operating expenses, including real estate taxes and the vacancy allowance to NOI. The project size, either in square feet (SF) or units, is divided into project revenue to find the rent level required to develop the project. For most urban redevelopment projects, market rents will be below the rent required to support project cost. The question is, how large is the difference between market rents and the rent level needed to make the project feasible? Cost-driven analysis is shown in appendix B. With the costs reflected in the capital budget (appendix A) the cost-driven analysis indicates that the hypothetical redevelopment project is not feasible. The spreadsheet showing the market-driven analysis is included in appendix B.

Cost-driven/market-driven analysis is a powerful tool to evaluate redevelopment alternatives. The analysis is especially valuable because the information needed is not extensive or difficult to gather. Given the existing preference for mixed-use redevelopment projects, the analysis involves finding the combination of uses that offers the least infeasible projects. These projects are financially infeasible because project cost is greater than project value. Still, they represent the ones that require lowest amount of public subsidy, given market realities. The analysis can be refined by figuring out how much of each use should be included in the project and by evaluating this mix of uses on several potential redevelopment sites. The best options that come out of this analysis can be described in a Request for Qualifications (RfQ) or Request for Proposals (RfP) (described below) in order to attract the most qualified private developers.

PUBLIC SUBSIDIES

The lead public entity must decide whether subsidizing the project at the required level is financially and politically feasible. If the entity wants to pursue the project, the dynamic (discounted cash flow; DCF) analysis or static analysis (cost-driven/market-driven analysis) can be used to examine the impact of different forms of public participation in the project (sensitivity analysis). The underlying question to be answered is: does the redevelopment project provide sufficient public benefits to justify the public subsidy (Malizia 1999; Sagalyn 1997)?

Infeasible projects show cost (as reflected in the capital budget) greater than value (NOI/cap rate). For the redevelopment project, this difference is an initial estimate of the amount of subsidy required.

However, DCF analysis should be used to get more accurate results. The DCF methodology for estimating public subsidies is described and illustrated in appendix C.

It should be noted that entities promoting redevelopment often do not conduct this type of analysis. Instead, they employ what might be called the "buffet" approach. They usually have many types of subsidies available, everything from facade improvement programs to concessionary financing. They invite the private developer to select all the items from the buffet that appeal to his or her taste. With this approach, the developer can figure out whether to proceed with the project, but the public will learn nothing about the economics of the deal or whether too much subsidy has been provided. The public needs to know the economic and financial details of the project, given the objective of fashioning cost-effective public-private partnerships.

In general, urban redevelopment projects can be subsidized by increasing revenue, reducing cost, or lowering risk (Hodge 2004). The public entity can increase project *revenues* by boosting rent or decreasing vacancy. It is not prudent for the public to overpay for space. However, every project expects some level of vacancy loss, and the public can boost revenues by occupying space at market rents for the long term that otherwise might have remained empty.

By far, the most common subsidies involve lowering project *cost*. The capital budget in appendix A provides many subsidy opportunities. Lowering or eliminating site acquisition cost is one of the most popular.[3] Public entities can also provide or pay for site development, including demolition costs.[4] Although less common, the public can also contribute to the long list of professional fees and studies needed to plan and review the project. For example, public entities could conduct surveying, appraisals, or land planning. Or the public entity could encourage private consultants to provide some of these services pro bono. The public may also waive fees or pay for impact studies.

With respect to operating expenses, many jurisdictions have the authority to reduce, rebate, or eliminate ad valorem property taxes (fig. 13.2). Although the impact can be significant, the reduction of tax revenues and potential increases in public borrowing should be explicitly addressed as opportunity costs. The best approach is to conduct a fiscal impact analysis.[5] For projects with positive fiscal impacts, the tax abatements could be limited to equal the excess revenues. For fiscally neutral or negative projects, the public entity would have to gauge how much burden to place on the public sector to offer tax abatements. For these projects, the abatement could be limited to the early years of the project and reduced over time as NOI increases.[6]

Finally, many public entities participate in redevelopment through concessionary financing. Typically, some portion of the permanent financing is provided by a community development financial institution (CDFI). In comparison to private financing available in the market, the CDFI's financing is offered at lower cost (interest rate), longer term, longer amortization period (or interest only), and in some instances flexible repayment schedules. The financing is subordinated to private debt. Although the public entity may take an equity position in the project, this is not typical. Most public objectives can be achieved with flexible debt financing without assuming the complications and risk of project ownership (Malizia 1997; Meeker 1996).

The importance of *risk reduction* at the project

FIGURE 13.2. Urban projects are often made possible through incentives provided to developers by the city, for example the 730 Lofts, designed by Urban Works Architecture, on 4th Street in the Warehouse District of Minneapolis. (Courtesy of Paul J. Armstrong)

level is not widely recognized, in part because it is indirect. Yet its impact can be profound and cost effective. All participants in the redevelopment project price their services in relation to risk; the higher the risk, the higher the necessary return. Equity investors, permanent and construction lenders, and general contractors are the most important participants in this regard.

For the contractor, site development and building restoration are the most difficult costs to assess. The public entity could assist in site assessments, including soil borings, and in building inspections and testing. The public entity should ascertain the estimated cost reductions forthcoming from the contractor before pursuing these activities. In general, the contractor should work for a lower margin and/or require less contingency when the public entity reduces development risk.

The construction lender can reduce project cost when the public entity participates to lower risk, increase revenues, or reduce costs. The construction lender should respond by requiring a smaller project contingency and/or lower adjustable interest rate. Construction interest is also lessened when the project takes less time to complete. Although few options exist to reduce construction time, the public sector can offer timely building inspections and the certificate of occupancy (CO) issuance on completion.

In addition to lowering project cost, concessionary permanent financing lowers financial risk and should therefore impact the permanent private loan. When the public provides a subordinated second mortgage loan, the private lender's exposure is greatly reduced. The impact is similar to increasing equity, which reduces the loan-to-cost ratio. Concessionary financing often boosts the debt

service coverage ratio, which also reduces risk. Moreover, the public entity can directly reduce private lending risk by guaranteeing the private loan.

In response, private lending terms should be improved, lowering project cost further. When concessionary financing is in play, the private loan should be negotiated at better terms—lower interest, longer term, and/or longer amortization period. The amount of the loan may also be increased, lowering project cost further by replacing some of the equity required for the project. This outcome reflects the fact that debt is cheaper to secure than equity because creditors assume less risk and earn less than equity investors.

Equity investors form expectations by comparing risk and return for different opportunities.[7] They view urban redevelopment projects as carrying more risk than projects in locations where the market is more established or robust. Therefore, their return requirements are higher.

Public entities can work with developers to help educate their equity sources about the many ways that project risk is expected to be lowered through public participation. All of the methods that reduce costs or raise revenues could reduce equity return requirements to some extent. The problem is that most equity investors have experience only with new development in peripheral locations. These projects appear to be lower risk than urban redevelopment projects. Even with information about how the public-private partnership is lowering risk for project owners, many equity investors may still require higher returns. The fact that typical equity investors lack experience with redevelopment would elevate return requirements even if the redevelopment project were objectively no more risky than a suburban alternative.[8] Return requirements are

ultimately subjective. Still, any reduction achieved in equity return requirements would increase project value at no additional public cost.[9]

In addition, public entities could try to recruit potential investors directly and educate them about urban redevelopment. As a result, these investors may seek more modest returns on projects they come to understand well. With effective communication about the details of redevelopment projects, the cost of equity could be reduced with minimal additional public outlay.[10]

When the redevelopment project has achieved stabilized occupancy, it is an operating enterprise that should have positive cash flow with public subsidies included. Effective property management is essential to maintaining and improving this enterprise over time. Public entities promoting urban redevelopment should network to find good property management firms, since many real estate developers do not have property management capacity within their firms (fig. 13.3). The public sector can use the RfQ/RfP process to identify and select the most attractive property managers.

Generally, public entities initiate the redevelopment process by issuing RfQs. The responses enable the public to consider how different developers would approach the prospective redevelopment in relation to their development experience. Once the qualified firms are selected, the public entities issue RfPs. Only the qualified firms can respond to the RfP. Once the firm is selected, the public entity formalizes the partnership agreement that lays out the expectations and responsibilities of all participants.[11]

This discussion of redevelopment at the project level assumes that the objective is to increase private investment in urban areas for economic

Figure 13.3. Interior of Franco's Restaurant, a prime tenant in the Soulard Square Lofts in St. Louis. Successful businesses bring people to urban districts and encourage further development. (Courtesy of Paul J. Armstrong)

revitalization and physical renewal. The important related objective is to redevelop in a sustainable manner. Sustainable development has many meanings. In this context, sustainable redevelopment or green redevelopment pertains both to construction and ongoing building operations.[12] The evidence suggests that construction costs are increased marginally as a result and that operating costs can be lowered substantially. Although the research is limited, sustainable/green projects also achieve higher than average market value (Dermisi 2009). Evidence also exists that worker productivity and turnover are lower in healthier work environments (Miller et al. 2009). Sustainable practices in construction are promoted by Leadership in Energy and Environmental Design (LEED) whereas ENERGY STAR is the best known vehicle promoting sustainable/green building operations.

Strategic Approaches

Public strategies that promote urban redevelopment can be designed to influence the expectations and behaviors of private actors. The sources of debt and equity capital are addressed here to cover the financial dimension. The next section considers ways to increase local demand, which covers the economic dimension. (This section draws from Malizia and Accordino 2001 and Malizia 2003; see also Leinberger 2005.)

In general, lenders and other sources of debt capital underwrite urban redevelopment projects more conservatively than more robust projects and commit less debt capital to them.[13] Another disincentive is that commercial lenders do not have access to secondary markets, given the uniqueness of urban redevelopment projects. Therefore, the capital devoted to these projects remains committed and is not replenished by another financial source that purchases the loan. For a related discussion of development lending, see Gordon (1997) and Jackson (2001).

Commercial lending behavior deserves further attention, especially during periods when credit is difficult to access. Unlike investors who can seek higher returns by accepting greater risk, prudent lenders have to take a different approach to the deployment of debt capital. Lenders determine a comfortable, presumably modest, range of risk in identifying "creditworthy" projects. They charge similar interest rates to these projects when they allocate funds to them. If the project exceeds its expected rate of return, the owners benefit; lenders earn the same amount of interest. Therefore, lenders worry about downside risk much more than the upside earnings potential. They ration credit to the projects they prefer.

On the other hand, if lenders pursued projects with the highest expected returns and charged higher interest rates afforded by these high return expectations, they would end up holding a portfolio of loans that would be high risk. The conventional wisdom is that greater potential earnings from high-risk loans would not compensate for the additional risk assumed (Wood and Wood 1985).

With respect to equity capital, investors consider both amount and timing of equity infusions, as well as holding period, in determining return require-

Figure 13.4. In many places in the United States, low financing rates for housing help both developers and buyers, for example Cotton Mills Condos in New Orleans, the first complex in the Warehouse District to be approved for FHA financing. (Courtesy of Paul J. Armstrong)

ments. They expect to earn more than tax-credit investors who infuse equity late in the development process, after construction and substantial leasing have been completed. When equity investors are asked to infuse equity during early stages of the project or provide the balance sheet that is used to guarantee the construction loan, their equity return requirements increase.[14]

Given these expectations and behaviors, public sector entities should formulate strategies to lower risk in order to promote urban redevelopment. Four strategies to reduce financial risk are presented below: (1) develop and steadfastly imple-ment small-area revitalization plans, (2) concen-trate infrastructure improvements, (3) use triage when necessary, and (4) promote competition.

All of these strategies are designed to reduce the uncertainty and risk involved in urban redevelop-ment. The most significant source of uncertainty is the wide range of informed and uninformed opinions that exist concerning the redevelopment potential of central areas. Appraisers have difficulty valuing inner-city projects accurately, due to thin markets (few transactions). The absence of good comparables increases the influence of opinions and other subjective factors. Existing property owners who derive income from current land uses have a vested interest in having an optimistic outlook on the long term. Developers may envision viable uses for central-area sites, but only if the properties can be secured in the near term at reasonable prices (fig. 13.4).[15] Investors usually have a wider range of as-sessments about risk and uncertainty than develop-ers or property owners. Some investors are attracted to urban redevelopment projects; others have little interest in them. Because transactions are infre-quent and projects are complex, markedly different investment outlooks may be justified for central areas. However, such differences of opinion form a major barrier to attracting the resources needed for urban redevelopment because they ultimately lower the value of potential projects.[16]

SMALL-AREA PLANS

Physical plans have always served as a framework to guide development over the long term. As a risk reduction technique, small-area planning is critical because it significantly reduces the number of alternative futures that could pertain to specific central areas or neighborhoods. Good graphics and visual representations of what the neighborhood could become are important ingredients in changing attitudes about places. However, risks will not be decreased with visioning or general land-use proposals alone. The best plans identify which public improvements will be made, where they will be located, and when they will become operational. In other words, planning and zoning should be linked to capital improvements programming to carry small-area plans forward.

Considerable political will is needed to implement such specific small-area plans, but jurisdictions that reduce risk and uncertainty in this way should be rewarded with increased private investment. At the same time, local governments should pursue strategic land banking to help ensure that asking prices for land in locations earmarked for redevelopment that may well increase do not become a disincentive to further redevelopment.[17]

CONCENTRATED INFRASTRUCTURE INVESTMENTS

Local politics as usual calls for resource allocations that spread funds among neighborhoods. Small-scale public investments that are dispersed widely rarely change perceptions that can reduce risk. It is much more effective, but politically difficult, to concentrate resources in strategic locations. Such investment can encourage larger projects that achieve adequate scale. Projects that cluster development around strong neighborhood anchors are likely to be more successful.

Urban redevelopment resembles an invasion that must first establish a beachhead in one location before it can spread to adjacent land. Without adequate infrastructure, project scale, and concentrated development, a beachhead cannot be firmly established. With success at one location, redevelopment should gradually spread to proximate sites. As projects accumulate and deals become self-sustaining, market information improves. As a result, confidence intervals around forecasts should narrow, and the associated risk should go down. Over time, property values in targeted central areas or neighborhoods should increase.

TRIAGE

Certain areas may be too expensive to help, at least in the near term, given limited resources and the need to concentrate public investments spatially to achieve adequate scale. In these areas, most residents and businesses will want to stay, but some may want to be relocated. The public entity should help them find more viable locations. As harsh as this option may seem, private investors will come to understand that the public sector intends to ignore these areas for some period of time. As a result, asset values may decline. Over time, increased certainty about the future of these areas will narrow the range of investment alternatives considerably. More certainty should provide a countervailing tendency that may gradually increase investment. Eventually, asset values in these areas may begin to increase.

The triage strategy is worth considering even if eventual increases in asset values are not forthcoming. As will be discussed later, successful urban redevelopment draws on many different ideas that require different spatial locations. Relatively cheap sites and structures are often needed in central areas because many desirable businesses and residents can only afford modest rents.

More broadly, not all cities are experiencing sustained population and employment growth. In declining places, the market is implementing the triage strategy as firms close and people move out. It is extremely difficult for the public sector to invest sufficiently to overcome these market forces. It is usually prudent to accept them. On the other hand, the political challenges of implementing the triage strategy decline significantly in shrinking cities.

COMPETITION

The public sector can promote competition among developers and investors if central areas, in fact, provide viable investment opportunities. Strategic public investments and specific small-area plans should increase the attractiveness of specific sites and the value of property at locations where the market becomes strong. Currently, most redevelopment opportunities exist in "buyers' markets," where private developers are scarce and are able to exact major concessions from the public in return for buying sites and investing in redevelopment projects.

Local jurisdictions should try to make certain areas sufficiently attractive to create "sellers' markets," where private developers are lining up to buy or option sites in order to participate in urban redevelopment. The competition among private developers should drive up asset values, make redevelopment projects in these locations more feasible, attract even more private investment, and create opportunities to recapture appreciating property values for the benefit of the community (plate 8). As more private capital flows to urban redevelopment projects, community residents should realize more local services, jobs, business opportunities, and wealth creation.

The shift from buyers' to sellers' markets can only occur when local governments have targeted attention and resources to a few strategic sites in key locations, rather than dispersing scarce resources throughout the entire city. In addition to basic infrastructure, the public entity should identify public investments that create anchors on strategic sites. Such investments can conserve public resources in the long term by lowering the public subsidies required to promote public-private redevelopment projects. Potential anchor investments include city or county government facilities, educational institutions, sports facilities, civic centers, performing arts centers, museums, and public or civic open space.

Market Expansion

Urban redevelopment is limited by the extent of the market. In this context, the economic dimension of real estate development is most usefully addressed by focusing on market expansion. Real estate developers rely on real estate market research to gauge the depth and breadth of the market. They conduct in-house research and also rely on market analysts and appraisers to conduct formal market and marketability studies (Ciochetti and Malizia

2000; Fanning 2005). This work generally involves forecasting demand and competing supply to determine whether sufficient excess demand exists to warrant the project. Market risk is mitigated when development projects can provide the supply response to identified market opportunities.[18]

The challenge is to increase space demand in order to solicit supply response in the form of urban redevelopment. Economic developers work hard to increase the competitive advantage of their location to investment. Place-based strategies attract, expand, retain, or create businesses that provide jobs.

Recruiting businesses is by far the most common local economic development strategy and the core practice of economic developers (plate 15). Investment from external sources provides local jobs and increases the tax base. Economic developers also work with existing businesses to assist with expansions or restructurings that retain employment. Since most employment is provided by these businesses, attention to their needs is important. Strategies to promote local entrepreneurship (creation strategies) have become increasingly popular, especially during economic downturns. They range from providing basic support for small businesses to creating the milieu for new businesses to mobilizing the resources needed to identify and foster emerging growth companies. (A detailed discussion of economic development planning, strategies, and practice is presented in Blakely and Green Leigh 2010 and Malizia and Feser 1999. For more specific applications, see chapter 12.)

People-focused strategies have recently become popular, partly inspired by the work of Richard Florida (Florida 2004, 2005). Many jurisdictions have developed strategies designed to attract people under the assumption that jobs will fol-

low. However, it is not clear that this strategy is more effective than traditional approaches to job creation. (See, for example, Donegan et al. 2008.) These strategies include downtown redevelopment, tourism development, adaptive reuse of industrial properties, historic preservation in residential areas, increases in parks, trails, and open space, improvements in education at all levels, public health initiatives related to physical activity and nutritional local food, and so on (plate 13). But these strategies can only succeed if in-migrants are in fact able to find jobs. These people-focused approaches are clearly easier to implement in large or growing metropolitan areas. However, they can succeed in declining areas when linked to effective place-focused strategies.

Thus, it makes sense to combine these approaches since the local market will expand either way. Successful local economic development expands the local market as aggregate disposable income increases due to job growth. Employment opportunities in the regional economy are just as important, because they can provide jobs for local residents who become out-commuters. Jobs are also created when the existing population and tourists/visitors are better served. Moreover, the ability of the local workforce to bargain for higher wages and salaries is another effective way to increase aggregate demand.

In summary, place-based strategies attempt to expand or improve the local economic base in order to increase the demand for labor (job creation). People-based strategies attempt to increase or improve labor supply, either by providing education or training or with more attractive living opportunities. A third approach is to consider ways to expand nonbasic sectors, which are the ones that serve only the local market.

It may seem unnecessary to be concerned with nonbasic sectors when success from either place-focused or people-focused strategies will automatically generate demand in these sectors. However, in the context of the global economy, the linkage between increased local demand and growth in local businesses is far from automatic. First, "leakage"—the difference between local disposable income and local purchases—may increase. In addition to mail-order purchases, internet purchasing is increasing. More mobility leads to more purchases during trips outside the local area. Second, "inflow"—purchases from outside the primary market area—may decline. Neither residents nor nonresidents (tourists) will purchase from local businesses that do not meet their quality or price standards; as noted, convenient alternatives exist. Thus, it is vitally important to attend to strategies designed to assist local businesses. Chambers of commerce should want to assume leadership in this area.

One strategy with considerable potential would focus on local entrepreneurs. To the extent that entrepreneurs are exporting goods or services (part of basic sectors), they are already in the scope of local economic developers pursing "creation" strategies. Ones that are in nonbasic sectors are more likely to be overlooked. Two groups exist. One group of local entrepreneurs is running unique local businesses. The other group own or manage franchises, usually more than one.

Some owners in the first group may be in a position to seek locations in urban redevelopment projects. Forging the connection between these entrepreneurs and local developers should contribute to their mutual success.

One barrier stems from the fact that these young local businesses often have weak credit ratings.

Some form of credit enhancement would increase their attractiveness to redevelopment project owners. It may be possible to find locally based corporations, hospitals, universities, or public entities willing to guarantee the rent payments of these businesses. The established entity would cosign the lease.

Other local businesses may have outgrown the home office but are not seeking upscale office space. These young businesses need cheap space. Areas not targeted for redevelopment that are physically safe could offer "funky" space for these prospective tenants. As noted, areas not targeted for redevelopment are very important, because they represent affordable locations for young local businesses or even somewhat marginal ones. Business incubators and business accelerators could be located in these areas (plate 7).

The franchisees may not need additional business support, but local chambers of commerce or business associations should solicit their ideas. Simply convening them to facilitate the development of peer groups and networks can be beneficial.

In most areas, franchise businesses are not in central locations. Since most are creditworthy, they would be attractive tenants in urban redevelopment projects. As housing expands in central areas, it may become feasible to attract these businesses to redevelopment projects in these areas.

Taken together, strategies to foster both types of businesses in nonbasic sectors hold considerable promise. Certainly, latitude exists for creative thinking. More local jobs, more out-commuting, more successful local businesses, and higher wages and salaries will increase disposable income and aggregate local demand. These outcomes would expand the local market and foster urban redevelopment as a result.

Conclusion

Effective public interventions at the project and strategic levels can promote urban redevelopment. At the project level, techniques of financial analysis can be used to gauge project feasibility, estimate appropriate subsidies, and conduct sensitivity analysis. Financial feasibility can be increased by increasing project revenue, reducing project cost, and, most important, mitigating financial risk. At the strategic level, small-area planning, public infrastructure investments, and consistently applied priorities can make selected locations more attractive to private investment. Economic development strategies can enhance the local market, which will increase demand for redevelopment. They may focus on place, people, or entrepreneurs operating in nonbasic sectors.

Appendix A

CAPITAL BUDGET EXAMPLE

The hypothetical redevelopment project is located on an infill site where demolition is required. The proposal is to develop retail and office space at an estimated total cost of about $20 million. The summary budget provides estimates of land acquisition and development costs, hard costs, soft costs, and costs associated with construction financing (table 13A.1). General contractors estimate hard costs in much greater detail. The unit price categories typically used are shown in table 13A.2.

TABLE 13A.1 *Capital Budget*

ASSUMPTION			
Gross buildable area (SF)			115,000
Net leasable area (SF)			103,500
Project contingency			10.0%
Operating expenses (per SF)			$4.50
Taxes (% of total development cost)			1.5%
Cost of equity (%)			10.0%
Cost of debt (%)			6.5%
Loan term (years)			10
Loan amortization (years)			20
Loan to cost (%)			75%
Debt service coverage Ratio			1.15
Vacancy rate			7%

LAND DEVELOPMENT COSTS	SQUARE FEET	$ / SF	BUDGET
Acquisition of site	35,000	$65.00	$2,275,000
Demolition	45,000	$2.50	$112,500
On-site improvements	21,000	$15.00	$315,000
Total land development			*$2,702,500*

HARD COSTS (shell & interior construction)	SQUARE FEET	$ / SF	BUDGET
Office	90,000	$120.00	$10,800,000
Retail	25,000	$155.00	$3,875,000
Total hard costs			*$14,675,000*

TOTAL ACQUISITION & HARD COSTS (before financing)			$17,377,500

SOFT COSTS	
Architecture & engineering	
Survey	$12,000
Phase 1 environment report	$5,000
Building design	$115,000
Geotechnical engineering	$14,000
Total architecture & engineering	*$146,000*
Legal	
Partnership organization	$15,000
Loan documents	$45,000
Entitlement	$55,000
Total legal	*$115,000*
Marketing	
Marketing studies	$14,000
Advertising & public relations	$7,500
Commissions	$69,000
Total marketing	*$90,500*
Taxes, title, appraisal	
Construction period taxes	$48,000
Title/closing/escrow	$32,000
Property appraisal	$12,000
Total financial	*$92,000*
Government relations	
Application fees	$25,000
Total government relations	*$25,000*
General & administration	
Insurance	$12,500
Project contingency	$1,785,850
Total general & administration	*$1,798,350*
TOTAL SOFT COSTS	$2,266,850

TOTAL DEVELOPMENT COSTS (before financing)	$19,644,350

FINANCING COSTS	
Construction loan	
Origination/commitment fee (1%)	$137,510
Interest	$446,909
Permanent loan	
Origination/commitment fee (1%)	$137,510
Tenant improvements & maintenance reserve	$287,500
Total financing costs	*$1,009,430*

TOTAL DEVELOPMENT COSTS (after financing)	$20,653,780

TABLE 13A.2 *Site Work and Hard Construction Cost Elements (based on Construction Specification Institute Format)*

Division 1	General requirements	*Division 3*	Concrete work	*Division 8*	Openings	*Division 11*	Equipment
	Payment and	*Division 4*	Masonry		Doors and frames	*Division 12*	Furnishings
	performance bond	*Division 5*	Metals		Finish hardware	*Division 13*	Special Construction
	Design/estimating		Structural steel		Glass and glazing	*Division 14*	Conveying Systems
	contingency		Miscellaneous metalwork	*Division 9*	Finishes		and Equipment
	General liability insurance	*Division 6*	Wood, Plastics,		Drywall	*Division 21*	Fire Suppression
	Builder's profit		and Composites		Hard tile		Fire protection systems
Division 2	Demolition		Rough carpentry		Ceilings	*Division 22*	Plumbing systems
	Site preparation/		Rough hardware		Resilient flooring	*Division 23*	Heating, ventilating, and
	excavation		Millwork		Carpeting		air conditioning systems
	Site utilities (water, storm,	*Division 7*	Thermal and		Painting	*Division 26*	Electrical systems
	and sanitary systems)		Moisture Protection	*Division 10*	Specialties		
	Site improvements		Waterproofing		Toilet partitions		
	Landscaping		Caulking and sealants		and accessories		
	Earth retention systems		Insulation				
			Roofing				

Appendix B

COST-DRIVEN/MARKET-DRIVEN ANALYSIS

The static cost-driven analysis begins with the project costs that are given in the capital budget and ends with an estimate of the required rent needed to make the project feasible. Since retail and office are the projected uses, current market rent is the weighted average of current rent for each use. The proposed redevelopment project requires rent that is 9% over market, which means that the project is infeasible (see table 13A.3). The market-driven approach is shown in table 13A.4. Given market rents, the project can attract only 85% of the capital needed to redevelop the site.

As noted, one can conduct sensitivity analysis with these static models to examine the impact of various subsidies. However, it is more accurate to use the dynamic DCF model to analyze the project's performance over time, as shown in appendix C. This model should be used to conduct sensitivity analysis.

TABLE 13A.3 *Cost-Driven Analysis Using Loan-to-Cost Ratio*

COSTS

Acquisition	$2,702,500
Construction	$14,675,000
Soft costs	$2,266,850
Other (Financing)	$1,009,430
Total development cost	*$20,653,780*

EQUITY

Loan-to-cost ratio	0.25
*Cost	$20,653,780
= Equity needed	*$5,163,445*
*Cash-on-cash return rate	10%
= Required "cash throw off"	*$516,344*

DEBT

Total development cost	$20,653,780
*Loan-to-cost ratio	0.75
= Allowable mortgage amount	*$15,490,335*
*Annual mortgage constant	0.08946878
= Annual debt service	*$1,385,901*

Net operating income	$1,902,246
+ Operating expenses	$517,500
+ Real estate taxes	$309,807
= Effective gross income	*$2,729,553*
+ Vacancy	$205,450
= Gross revenue required	*$2,935.003*
/ Net leasable area	103,500
= Required rental income/SF	*$28.36*

Debt coverage ratio	*1.37*
	OK
Monthly	*$0.0074557*
Annually	*$0.0894688*

Market rent per SF—office	$26.00
Market rent per SF—retail	$22.00
Market rent—weighted value	$25.13
Your rent/market rent	*109%*

Infeasible

TABLE 13A.4 *Market-Driven Analysis Using Debt Coverage Ratio*

COSTS

Market rent per SF—office	$26.00
Market rent per SF—retail	$22.00
Market rent—weighted value	$25.13
* Net leasable area	103,500
= *Gross rental revenue*	*$2,601,000*
– Vacancy	$182,070
= *Effective gross income*	*$2,418,930*
– Operating expenses	$517,500
– Real estate taxes	$309,807
Net operating income	*$1,591,623*

EQUITY

NOI	$1,591,623
– Debt service	$1,384,020
= *Available "cash throw off"*	*$207,603*
/ Cash-on-cash return rate	10%
= *Justified equity investment*	*$2,076,030*

DEBT

NOI	$1,591,623
/ Debt coverage ratio	1.15
= *Cash available for debt service*	*$1,384,020*
/ Annualized mortgage constant	0.0894688
= *Justified mortgage amount*	*$15,469,310*

Justified project investment	$17,545,341
– Anticipated capital improvement costs	$22.00
= *Justified land development costs*	*($405,939)*
Total development costs	$20,653,780

Your justified investment / total development costs 84%

Infeasible

TABLE 13A.5 *Discounted Cash Flow*

ASSUMPTIONS

Vacancy: 7.0%
Rent growth: 2.0%
Expense growth: 2.0%
Operating expenses per SF: $4.50
Going-out cap rate: 10.5%
Selling expense: 6.0%

YEAR	1	2	3	4	5	6	7	8	9	10	11
Gross rent receipts (GRR)	$ 2,601,000	$ 2,653,020	$ 2,706,080	$ 2,760,202	$ 2,815,406	$ 2,871,714	$ 2,929,148	$ 2,987,731	$ 3,047,486	$ 3,108,436	$ 3,170,604
– Vacancies (VAC)	$ 182,070	$ 185,711	$ 189,426	$ 193,214	$ 197,078	$ 201,020	$ 205,040	$ 209,141	$ 213,324	$ 217,591	$ 221,942
Total income	$ 2,418,930	$ 2,467,309	$ 2,516,655	$ 2,566,988	$ 2,618,328	$ 2,670,694	$ 2,724,108	$ 2,778,590	$ 2,834,162	$ 2,890,845	$ 2,948,662
– Operating expenses (OE)	$ 517,500	$ 527,850	$ 538,407	$ 549,175	$ 560,159	$ 571,362	$ 582,789	$ 594,445	$ 606,334	$ 618,460	$ 630,830
– Real estate taxes	$ 309,807	$ 316,003	$ 322,323	$ 328,769	$ 335,345	$ 342,052	$ 348,893	$ 355,871	$ 362,988	$ 370,248	$ 377,653
Net operating income (NOI)	*$ 1,591,623*	*$ 1,623,456*	*$ 1,655,925*	*$ 1,689,043*	*$ 1,722,824*	*$ 1,757,281*	*$ 1,792,426*	*$ 1,828,275*	*$ 1,864,840*	*$ 1,902,137*	*$ 1,940,180*
– Debt service (DS)	$ 1,384,020	$ 1,384,020	$ 1,384,020	$ 1,384,020	$ 1,384,020	$ 1,384,020	$ 1,384,020	$ 1,384,020	$ 1,384,020	$ 1,384,020	$ 1,384,020
Before tax cash flow (BTCF)	*$ 207,603*	*$ 239,436*	*$ 271,905*	*$ 305,023*	*$ 338,804*	*$ 373,260*	*$ 408,406*	*$ 444,255*	*$ 480,820*	*$ 518,117*	*$ 556,160*
Debt service coverage ratio	*1.15*	*1.17*	*1.20*	*1.22*	*1.24*	*1.27*	*1.30*	*1.32*	*1.35*	*1.37*	*1.40*
Return on cost											
(NOI / total development cost)	*7.7%*										
Cash-on-cash return	*4.0%*										
BTIRR	9.0%										

CASH FLOWS FROM DISPOSITION

Property cash flows

Gross selling proceeds	$ 18,477,904
Selling expenses	$ 1,108,674
Net selling proceeds	$ 17,369,230

Financing cash flows

Net selling proceeds	$ 17,369,230
Unpaid mortgage	$ 10,157,382

Before tax equity reversion (BTER)	*$ 7,211,847*

Weighted-average cost of capital	7.4%
Required BTIRR	12.0%
BTIRR	9.0%
NPV (discounted at required BTIRR)	$ (1,013,098)

INVESTMENT PERFORMANCE

YEAR	0	1	2	3	4	5	6	7	8	9	10
Equity contributed	$ (5,184,470)										
BTCF		$ 207,603	$ 239,436	$ 271,905	$ 305,023	$ 338,804	$ 373,260	$ 408,406	$ 444,255	$ 480,820	$ 518,117
BTER											$ 7,211,847
Total cash flows	*$ (5,184,470)*	*$ 207,603*	*$ 239,436*	*$ 271,905*	*$ 305,023*	*$ 338,804*	*$ 373,260*	*$ 408,406*	*$ 444,255*	*$ 480,820*	*$ 7,729,964*

PARTITIONING NPV AT BTIRR

YEAR	CASH FLOW	PV CF	PV DISPOSITION	
0				
1	$ 207,603	$190,420		
2	$ 239,436	$201,440		
3	$ 271,905	$ 209,822		
4	$ 305,023	$215,897		
5	$ 338,804	$219,958		
6	$373,260	$ 222,271		
7	$ 408,406	$ 223,070		
8	$ 444,255	$222,566		
9	$ 480,820	$ 220,947		
10	$ 7,729,964	$ 218,379	$ 3,039,699	
Total		*$ 2,144,771*	*$ 3,039,699*	*$ 5,184,470*
% of total NPV		41%	58.6%	
		Outflow	$ (5,184,470)	
		NPV (at BTIRR)	$_____	

Appendix C

DISCOUNTED CASH FLOW ANALYSIS

This type of analysis is used to examine the financial dimension of the redevelopment project and, most important, to estimate the subsidy needed to make it feasible. The simplified analysis assumes that equity is invested in year 0, the project achieves stabilized occupancy in year 1, cash flows for the 10-year holding period are driven by the assumed rents and expenses, the project is sold at the beginning of year 11, and expected NOI in year 11 is divided by the going-out cap rate of 10.5% to estimate sales value.

The accuracy of this analysis can be improved by using months as the time period instead of years. In this way, cash solvency over the development period and the important development risk areas, such as entitlement risk and lease-up risk, can be examined. In addition, returns can be estimated more accurately with monthly figures. Although the developer should conduct monthly analysis, public participants will find the inputs for annual analysis easier to estimate than monthly figures. They should prefer annual analysis because it is sufficiently accurate and would tend to estimate lower required subsidies, given the time value of money.

From the analysis presented in table 13A.5, return on cost is 7.7%, cash-on-cash return at stabilized occupancy (year 1) is 4.0%, and before-tax internal rate of return (BTIRR) for the holding period is 9.0%. An analysis is also shown that calculates the share of returns from cash flow compared to the share from the residual, which represents the net proceeds from the sale of the project after the mortgage balance is paid. Almost 59% of total returns come from the residual.

Discounted cash flow analysis can be conducted using the 12.0% BTIRR that equity investors expect as their hurdle rate (discount rate). At this hurdle rate, net present value (NPV) is in the red by more than $1.0 million. Thus, equity investors would not invest in this project because it fails to meet their return requirements. The project would become feasible if the public sector generated $1.013 million in subsidies. With these subsidies, NPV would be approximately zero at the 12% discount rate.

As noted, public subsidies could either increase project revenues or, more likely, reduce project costs. Project feasibility is also affected by risk perceptions. Three typical ways to lower project costs and their impact on returns are presented. First, if the public sector donates the redevelopment site, it will generate $1.4 million more subsidy than needed and 16.3% BTIRR, well above the required 12.0%. Second, reducing site cost to $38 per SF should enable the developer to do the deal. Third, if the public sector abates taxes from 1.5% to 1.0% of total development cost, which is used as the estimate of assessed value, the project becomes feasible. Similarly, concessionary financing at 5.0% interest provides slightly more subsidy than needed.

Changes in risk perceptions can significantly impact returns. Since risk perceptions can change without incurring the costs of direct subsidies, public participants should try to influence private perceptions in positive ways. If the going-out cap rate were reduced by 160 basis points to 8.9% to reflect growing investor optimism about the redevelopment area, the project becomes feasible without direct subsidies. At this cap rate, the residual value (sales price) of the project increases significantly from $7.7 million to $10.9 million.

Although the numbers in these spreadsheets are all based on assumptions and represent forecasts, DCF analysis is a powerful tool to use in negotiating public-private partnerships. First, the public entity can calculate the impact of various tactics for lowering project cost or project risk. Then, the analysis can be presented to the private entity, used to estimate the subsidy, and fleshed out when negotiating the final agreement.

Notes

1. The reader may wonder why reference is not made to the highest and best use of the site. Highest and best use in property appraisal calls for the identification of the most economically profitable use given legal and physical constraints (Appraisal Institute 2008). Most fitting and appropriate use is a broader concept that requires attention to collective users and even future users as well as current private users who are willing to pay market rents to occupy the property (Malizia 2009; Vandell and Carter 2000).

2. Soft costs include architectural and engineering fees and fees resulting from legal work, accounting, surveying, land planning, appraisal, market research, and marketing. Costs associated with the construction loan are included; construction-period interest is an important line item. All costs incurred to take the project through the development review process (entitlement process) are added, such as fees, cost of impact studies, community relations efforts, etc. Contractor fees, overhead, and contingency can

be listed under soft costs but are often built into the hard cost estimates. Soft costs also include the developer fee (profit) and project contingency. The size of the latter reflects the perceived risk of the redevelopment. In private suburban projects, soft costs may be less than 25% of hard costs, but in complex urban redevelopment projects they can exceed that benchmark.

3. The ill-fated urban renewal program of the 1950–60s relied on eminent domain to condemn private property, assembled parcels into development sites, and sold these sites for nominal consideration. Public entities can contribute the land for redevelopment projects following this tradition. If the site is improved, the structure can also be contributed, but this may be both expensive and unnecessary. The developer may prefer to incur the cost of the building if historic preservation tax credits are envisioned. (When the developer purchases the building, it becomes part of the qualified basis used to calculate the tax credit.)

4. Of course, providing infrastructure within public rights-of-way is not a project subsidy but rather one way the public supports private development (see chapter 7). The subsidy begins when infrastructure is extended onto the site.

5. FIA compares the net increase in revenues to the net increase in costs. Although the redevelopment site often generates some tax revenues and requires expenditures for public services, the absolute amounts are probably not large. In the FIA, the present value of public expenditures is compared to the present value of the taxes paid to determine whether the fiscal impact of the redevelopment project is positive, negative, or neutral.

For infill sites in central areas, the redevelopment project will require public services. All uses will require police and fire protection, general

governmental services, roads, utilities, etc. Projects with residential components additionally require social services, public schools, and parks and open space. Large-scale projects may well generate the need for new facilities and require additional capital outlays.

The people and businesses occupying the redevelopment project would pay municipal and county taxes downstream. In almost all states, they would pay ad valorem property taxes and sales taxes. In some areas, personal income taxes are also assessed at the local level.

6. Tax Increment Financing (TIF) is a popular way to afford subsidies to urban redevelopment projects. The property taxes forthcoming from redevelopment are dedicated to the project. Formal TIFs often float debt to finance infrastructure and then use the tax revenue stream to repay the debt. But TIFs can be used to subsidize the project directly with public support in lieu of property taxes. Informal TIFs (synthetic TIFs) can be established by mutual agreement as part of a public-private partnership and used as a source of public subsidy.

7. For example, government securities pay a return that is usually considered the risk-free rate. Other investments yield higher returns because the investor assumes more risk. General obligation bonds that are backed by jurisdictions offer lower yields than the revenue bonds because risk is less.

8. This situation is similar to differences in risk assessment among commercial lenders based on their prior experience. For example, lenders in Texas and Oklahoma are comfortable making loans for oil and natural gas exploration because they have become very familiar with that industry. Lenders without this experience would certainly shy away from these lending opportunities.

9. Project value increases when estimated NOI is

divided by a lower cap rate that reflects lower return requirements.

10. The most risky stage of the development process is after the CO is issued but before the project has reached the occupancy level required by the permanent lender (stabilized occupancy). The developer seeks to increase occupancy as rapidly as possible, since the project is paying interest on the entire construction loan during this period. The public entity may be able to help market the project, but this risk is borne by the developer partly to justify his or her fee.

11. Once the private developer is selected, it is important to ensure that it will be able to carry out the redevelopment project. If the partnership is not properly structured with the appropriate lead public agency, another developer may be able to take over the project by making a nominally more attractive financial offer after all of the feasibility work and technical studies are completed (called an upset bid).

12. General contractors are learning how to reduce energy consumption during the construction process and from the materials and equipment employed. Techniques range from using locally sourced or recycled materials to worker training that reduces waste. Energy-efficient fixtures and materials are being used with greater frequency. Some projects using solar power or other non-petroleum-based sources of power are aiming to add energy to the grid on a net basis. Site development is another way to conserve resources and mitigate environmental impacts. Innovative techniques are being used for storm water management. Projects are increasingly collecting rainwater and using this gray water in place of potable water. Furthermore, urban redevelopment itself is more sustainable than new greenfield development, due to the embodied energy in existing buildings that

are reused rather than replaced with new construction. (For an introduction to the topic and guide to the literature, see Federal Reserve Bank of Atlanta 2009).

13. In addition to lowering financial risk through more conservative underwriting, commercial lenders often try to lower their financial exposure further by including their Community Development Corporation (CDC) subsidiary, since bank CDCs often have the contacts needed to bring public and private financing sources together for redevelopment projects.

14. Developers often reduce the holding period and financial exposure of equity investors through refinancing. If the redevelopment project is successful, it should generate more NOI and before-tax cash flow over time, which should increase project value. As debt service reduces the principal balance of the loan, equity builds in the project. Project owners can usually refinance the higher-valued project at a higher loan-to-value ratio than the ratio used for the original loan, often loan-to-cost. As a result, the owners receive the portion of the refinancing left after the principal balance of the original loan is paid, which is used to reduce investors' financial exposure or even buy one or two out of the project.

15. It should be noted that private developers who are attracted to public-private urban redevelopment projects tend to be less experienced, because more seasoned developers are able to pursue projects that are less complex, less time consuming, and potentially more profitable. Moreover, newer developers want to build their reputations; carrying out a highly visible redevelopment project often leads to recognition at the local and regional levels. However, major, well-established real estate developers do participate in urban redevelopment. Their participation is correlated with downturns in the building cycle when private development opportunities become limited.

16. In essence, more variation in expected returns translates into higher risk premiums. For elaboration, see Luscht, 1997, chs. 14-15.

17. This proposal is not meant to deemphasize the importance of long-range master plans. In some jurisdictions, the master plan may be sufficiently detailed to lessen the need for small-area plans. In these cases, it would certainly be more cost effective to forego small-area planning. However, in many places, small-area planning is essential to flesh out the preferred uses of land within districts and corridors. The cost is usually justified because portrayal of small-area plans in three dimensions adds valuable information that is rarely presented in master plans.

18. Projects have been justified not through market research but on the belief that supply will create its own demand (build it and they will come). Usually, this belief is dashed by market realities.

References

Adair, A., S. McGreal, B. Deddis, and S. Hirst. 1999. "Evaluation of Investor Behaviour in Urban Regeneration." *Urban Studies* 36(12): 2031-45.

Appraisal Institute. 2008. *The Appraisal of Real Estate*. 13th ed. Chicago.

Blakely, E. J., and N. Green Leigh. 2010. *Planning Local Economic Development: Theory and Practice*. 4th ed. Los Angeles: Sage.

Ciochetti, B. A., and E. E. Malizia. 2000. "Ch. 8: The Application of Financial Analysis and Market Research to the Real Estate Development Process." In *Essays in Honor of James A. Graaskamp*, ed. J. DeLisle and E. Worzala. Dordrecht: Kluwer Academic, 135-65.

Dermisi, S. V. 2009. "Effect of LEED Ratings and Levels on Office Property Assessed and Market Values." *Journal of Sustainable Real Estate* 1(1): 23-47.

Donegan, M., J. Drucker, H. A. Goldstein, N. J. Lowe, and E. E. Malizia. 2008. "Which Indicators Explain Metropolitan Economic Performance Best?" *Journal of the American Planning Association* 74(2): 180-95.

Fanning, S. F. 2005. *Market Analysis for Real Estate*. Chicago: Appraisal Institute.

Federal Reserve Bank of Atlanta. 2009. "Green Development Primer." Special Issue. *Green Partners in Community and Economic Development* 19(2).

Feser, E. J., and E. E. Malizia. 1999. *Understanding Local Economic Development*. New Brunswick, NJ: Center for Urban Policy Research.

Florida, R. 2004. *Cities and the Creative Class*. New York: Routledge.

———. 2005. *The Flight of the Creative Class*. New York: HarperCollins.

Frieden, B. J., and L. B. Sagalyn. 1989. *Downtown Inc: How America Rebuilds Cities*. Cambridge, MA: MIT Press.

Gordon, D. L. 1997. "Financing Urban Waterfront Redevelopment." *Journal of the American Planning Association* 63(2): 244-65.

Graaskamp, J. A. 1981. *Fundamentals of Real Estate Development*. Development Component Series. Washington, DC: Urban Land Institute.

Gyourko, J., and W. Rybczynski. 2000. "Financing New Urbanism Projects: Obstacles and Solutions." *Housing Policy Debate* 11(3): 733-50.

Hodge, G. 2004. "The Risky Business of Public-Private Partnerships." *Australian Journal of Public Administration* 63(4): 37-49.

Jackson, T. O. 2001. "Environmental Risk Perceptions of Commercial and Industrial Real Estate Lenders." *Journal of Real Estate Research* 22(3): 271-88.

Kotin, A., and R. Peiser. 1997. "Public-Private Joint

Ventures for High Volume Retailers: Who Benefits?" *Urban Studies* 34(12): 1871-1997.

Leinberger, C. B. 2005. *Turning Around Downtown: Twelve Steps to Revitalization.* Washington, DC: Brookings Institution.

Luscht, K. M. 1997. *Real Estate Valuation.* Chicago: Richard D. Irwin.

Malizia, E. E. 1997. *Economic Development Finance.* 2nd ed. Rosemont, Illinois: American Economic Development Council.

———. 1999. "The Garvey Retail Center Case: Redeveloping an Inner-City Site." *Journal of Real Estate Practice and Education* 2(1): 63-120 and teaching notes.

———. 2003. "Structuring Urban Redevelopment Projects: Moving Participants Up the Learning Curve." *Journal of Real Estate Research* 25(1): 463-78.

———. 2009. "Site Use in a Redeveloping Area." *Journal of Real Estate Practice and Education* 12(1): 81-104.

Malizia, E. E., and J. Accordino. 2001. *Financing Urban Redevelopment Projects.* Community Affairs Office, Federal Reserve Bank of Richmond Research Report.

Meeker, L. 1996. *Doing the Undoable Deal.* Federal Reserve Bank of Kansas City Monograph.

Meyer, P., and T. T. Lyons. 2000. "Lessons from Private Sector Brownfield Redevelopers: Planning Public Support for Urban Regeneration." *Journal of the American Planning Association* 66(1): 46-57.

Miller, N. G., D. Pogue, Q. D. Gough, and S. M. Davis. 2009. "Green Buildings and Productivity." *Journal of Sustainable Real Estate* 1(1): 65-89.

Sagalyn, L. B. 1997. "Negotiating for Public Benefits: The Bargaining Calculus of Public-Private Development." *Urban Studies* 34(12): 1955-70.

———. 2007. "Public/Private Development: Lessons from History, Research, and Practice." *Journal of the American Planning Association* 73(1): 7-22.

Sawicki, D. S. 1989. "The Festival Marketplace as Public Policy." *Journal of the American Planning Association* 55(3): 347-61.

Vandell, K. D., and C. C. Carter. 2000. "Ch. 15: Graaskamp's Concept of Highest and Best Use." In *Essays in Honor of James A. Graaskamp,* ed. J. DeLisle and E. Worzala. Dordrecht: Kluwer Academic, 307-19.

Wood, J., and N. Wood. 1985. *Financial Markets.* New York: Harcourt Brace Jovanovich.

Conclusion

PAUL HARDIN KAPP

THE CREATORS AND CONTRIBUTORS OF SynergiCity share the following points of general consensus:

We are pro-development.

We are pro-density.

We are pro-community.

We are pro-environment.

We are pro-sustainability.

We believe in the heritage of the built place.

We believe in large-scale visioning.

We believe in small-area revitalization.

We are against development centered on the automobile.

SynergiCity is, in fact, the product of synergy. More than just an area of architecturally rehabilitated buildings, it is the transformation of dormant factories and warehouses into inviting attractors of small businesses, incubators, offices, retail shops, green public places, and residences. It is the result of five distinct environmental design professions (architecture, planning, historic preservation, landscape design, and urban design) and cities working together to produce a singular vision addressing postindustrial urban redevelopment that is far greater than the individual visions of each entity. It is the culmination of the meeting of industrial heritage with nature, architecture with social eco-

nomics, and urban revitalization with environmentally sustainable design. It is a city-within-a-city, a neighborhood for residents, a destination for shoppers, and a community for creative entrepreneurship. It is the ideal postindustrial community of the twenty-first century comprised of the creative capital of economy, marketable talent, and industrious people.

Manufacturing began in the Midwest in the late nineteenth century with significant industrialization occurring between 1860 and 1920 (Meyer 1989). This industrial maturation resulted in large factories built to produce more goods, mostly built between 1890 and 1940. Manufacturing in the United States began to decline in the 1970s. During the 1980s corporate takeovers precipitated this decline; in the 1990s and the first decade of the twenty-first century, manufacturing began its current steep decline as globalization took hold in the world economy. Nearly every city in the Midwest has been affected by this change. Cities such as Cleveland and Youngstown, Ohio; Detroit and Flynt, Michigan; and Elkhart, Indiana, have lost significant portions of their populations as more and more people have left former manufacturing cities for work elsewhere (McCormack 2010). Today, warehouses sit empty, factories are shuttered, and smokestacks, once towering symbols of industrial might, are reduced to either nostalgic relics or rubble. This book not only presents the

case for their preservation, but provides direction for their redevelopment as a base for the twenty-first century and green economy, the theoretical core of SynergiCity.

Postindustrial redevelopment is hardly new; it is even older than the term "postindustrial," as Daniel Bell dubbed it in 1973. Originally, such redevelopment was considered part of the fringe element of American culture; artists, low-level retail, and ethnic groups, such as first-generation immigrants, engaged in this kind of development, since "normal" development (central business districts in cities) and use of urban space was cost prohibitive to them (Jacobs 1961). Today, transformed districts such as Milwaukee's Third Ward, the Minneapolis Warehouse District, and Lowertown in Saint Paul are, after 30 years of intensive work, once again serving the economic needs of the city. These successes, combined with today's sustainable culture of reduce, reuse, and recycle, make the case for rehabilitating postindustrial districts an easy one. The utilization of these historic existing buildings and the reuse of their materials for living and working keeps viable materials out of the landfill and keeps the production of new raw materials at a minimum. The vastness and size of these districts will accommodate the need for space required in small-batch manufacturing. All of these factors will help keep the new industry ideas alive in the Midwest despite the effects of the Great Recession.

Manufacturing continues to be a vital component of the economy of midwestern cities. Within one year after the mass layoffs of employees of Caterpillar in 2009, Peoria was still ranked by *Money* as one of the best cities in the United States to start a small business (Tarter 2010). Sometimes unemployment of skilled workers can give rise to new industries, such as the production of wind turbines for green energy, medical devices for the expanding biotech market, and agricultural equipment for agribusiness, an industry started in Peoria by Caterpillar's former middle management. Small, innovation-based companies such as these are emerging in the postindustrial Midwest—precisely the shift to creative and innovation-based jobs that Richard Florida calls the "Great Reset" (Florida 2009). With its flexible infrastructure, vast amounts of space, visual and historic character, and location near central business districts, the postindustrial district can be redeveloped to become environmentally sustainable, pedestrian friendly, and the ideal location for these twenty-first-century businesses (plates 2 and 3). It is precisely this type of major transformation the district must undergo if it is to survive the shift from manufacturing sector jobs to service sector jobs, which the American economy is currently undergoing, as described by Mark Gillem in chapter 7. Today, very few postindustrial districts are being used as centers for innovation businesses. Cities such as Rockford, Illinois (fig. 14.1), and Elkhart, Indiana, need to "reset" their postindustrial districts (McCormack 2010).

However, before midwestern cities "reset," they should reconsider, analyze, and plan their postindustrial districts for a new and productive future that will generate highly valued technologies, experiences, products, and services. Rather than being based on simply mechanical production, the new, innovative economy of the twenty-first century will be powered by imagination, creativity, and teamwork. In order for it to thrive, it requires a highly educated and motivated workforce, institutions of higher education (for training and business collaboration), and buildings and places that are conducive to human interaction and collaboration. Postindustrial districts revitalized in accordance with the concept of SynergiCity have the attributes to attract the highly educated and creative minds needed for the innovation economy to emerge. The challenge is the transformation of the postindustrial district for the new economy.

This book answers this challenge by presenting one viable option for economic renewal through the rebuilding of the industrial districts of midwestern cities. Each of our contributors has proposed ideas to help facilitate the redevelopment of buildings, underground infrastructure, and streets with the creation of public parks and plaza spaces. Their ideas also address immediate and broader challenges facing America today, including unemployment, poor air quality, declining real estate values, addiction to fossil fuels, suburban sprawl, and an impending lack of potable water.

The SynergiCity idea of postindustrial urban redevelopment is a three-part approach, ecological, interactive, and adaptive. This approach strives to renew the urban ecology as it redevelops the postindustrial district (fig. 14.2). An interactive approach, it proposes active environments that emphasize walking and active living, pedestrian movement instead of automotive movement—all of which stimulates social interaction and provides environments that aspire to do more than be engaging and instead to become "environments that educate." Finally, the SynergiCity approach embraces the industrial heritage of the postindustrial district. Through adaptive use, it seeks to transform large buildings that have a vast amount of adaptable, useable space and robust structures for new uses that complement the original character of the buildings.

SynergiCity begins with ecological design. In the Midwest, potable water must be a major criterion in urban redevelopment, especially in attracting new innovation-based "green" industries and a creative, well-educated workforce. Water certainly attracted industrialists well over a century ago, who used it to provide transportation systems for people and manufactured goods in Rockford and St. Louis, to manufacture whiskey in Peoria and beer in Milwaukee, and to generate power for mills such as the St. Anthony Falls in Minneapolis — and water continues to attract industry today. The Midwest is blessed with the largest bodies of freshwater (the Great Lakes) in the world, the great Mississippi and Ohio rivers, and aquifers full of high-quality fresh water. Mercer, a global human resource and financial consulting firm that provides rankings produced exclusively to inform top companies and their top talent which cities are the most livable, has taken note. In Mercer's first "Eco-City" ranking of the most environmentally friendly cities in the world, Minneapolis ranked sixth and St. Louis ranked forty-third. The criteria for this ranking included water availability, water portability, waste removal, sewage, air pollution, and traffic congestion. Water is now not only a public health issue but also an economic development and marketing issue: mayors, city administrators, and public officials should make the availability of potable water a priority as they plan for future development, since companies today consider a city's commitment to environmental stewardship a criterion for location.

For the past 15 years, water experts throughout the Great Lakes region have been concerned about the future of potable water (Illinois-Indiana Sea Grant 2010). The value of this precious resource increases even more as sources from aquifers around the United States are now being used at a faster rate than they can be replenished, especially in areas that lack large bodies of fresh water such as the Southeast and Southwest (Illinois-Indiana Sea Grant 2010). In chapter 1, Don Carter correctly sets the ecological tone when he recodifies these regional disparities in America by redefining former "rust belts" as "water belts" and so-called sun belts as arid "drought belts." Thus, he maintains, in the twenty-first century a potable water source will no longer be continual. If water becomes a finite resource and as precious as oil in the twenty-first century, then the states that border the upper Great Lakes are likely to be the new "OPEC of water." Therefore, planners and government officials all throughout the Midwest where fresh water is abundant should take note of the future economic and ecological potential of potable water.

Potable water, the environment, and their relationships to the SynergiCity approach have been discussed in a variety of ways by contributors Christine Scott Thomson, James Wasley, and Mark Gillem. Together they present a common overarching urban, landscape, and design vision that can best be called Ecological Urbanism. At the heart of this design theory is a fundamental belief that the Earth is indeed a closed system. As we design with the SynergiCity approach, a new balance between natural systems and urban systems must be established. Thomson proposes an urban-scale ecological

FIGURE 14.1. The Barber Colman Factory sits idle along the Rock River in Rockford, Illinois. Without public-private investments buildings like these will deteriorate further, resulting in higher land reclamation and new construction costs in the future. (Courtesy of Paul J. Armstrong)

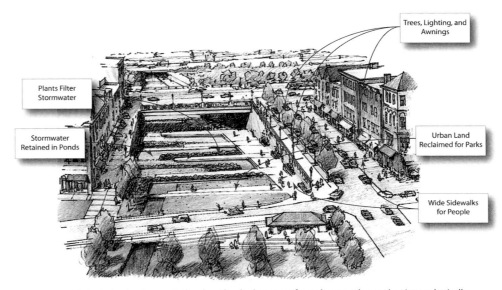

FIGURE 14.2. Ecological redevelopment of underutilized urban areas for parks can enhance the city aesthetically. (Courtesy of U.S. Pipe/Wheland Foundry and LA Quatra Bonci Associates/Edward Dumont)

solution that protects natural estuaries and tributaries of waterways that provide the filtration of storm water before it enters rivers or lakes. By relating the natural role of an urban greenway (which is based on estuaries and tributaries) to its recreational use in the city, she proposes the greenway as a primary urban feature for the city. Redeveloping natural spaces in and adjacent to postindustrial districts can benefit the city in three ways: (1) improve the water quality, (2) improve the natural habitat of the city, and (3) provide recreational venues for all citizens. Using the proposed nearly 900-acre Milwaukee River Greenway Master Plan as a case study, Thomson presents an idea for midwestern cities that celebrates the heritage of the postindustrial city and its historical relationship to the waterways and estuaries that provide havens for wildlife and fauna. These parks can also become a recreational venue in the city with nature walks, playing fields, and rowboat opportunities. There are numerous benefits of the large-scale park and nature sanctuary in the SynergiCity approach. As Thomson states in chapter 9, the greenway can "connect people with places, both natural and human-made, connect past to present, and bring the boater into contact with the rivers and surrounding lands."

Brownfield remediation should occur regardless of use. Pollution resulting in contaminated soil and water has and will continue to be a significant challenge in the redevelopment of postindustrial sites. As we reconsider what is left on these sites after industry has discarded them for cheap labor and fewer restrictions overseas, we must plan now not only for their remediation but also for their redevelopment and reintegration into the city. In chapter 7, Mark Gillem asserts that environmental remediation of brownfield sites, which is nec-

essary for clean groundwater and public health, can also serve as the catalyst for the betterment of the public realm. For example, Gillem showcases the remediation of contaminated sites in the Pearl District in Portland, Oregon, which allowed recyclable infrastructure to be reutilized and existing industrial buildings to be adapted for new uses. This can have two significant benefits: sites that should never have originally been developed can become parkland and nature sanctuaries, and the district's buildings and infrastructure (streets, alleys, and rail lines) can be redeveloped.

Development in the postindustrial district should be done in a "closed-loop" manner. Storm water removal should equal a site's predevelopment rate of stormwater runoff. Simply diverting storm water into large pipes and sending it to natural waterways is no longer a responsible or feasible option. In chapter 8, James Wasley proposes developing a "Zero-Discharge Zone" (ZDZ) for the University of Wisconsin–Milwaukee as a sensible ecological design strategy for storm water management. All urban districts, especially midwestern postindustrial ones with their proximity to large waterways, should not only retain but also recycle their storm water, using design strategies ensuring that the water discharged from the district be as clean as possible. By implementing best management practices for storm water management, thoroughly remediating postindustrial sites, and achieving a regional vision of greenways, the industrial heritage of the city and nature can coexist in "SynergiCity" (plate 2).

Unfortunately, incentives for new site development in cities today often discourage this type of sustainable redevelopment and the emergence of a "SynergiCity." As Gillem states in chapter 7, cheap

land, access to interstate highways, and cheap financing encourage developers to build on greenfields and abandon brownfields. The magnitude of effort and expense coupled with the liability of remediating brownfield sites is enough to discourage any developer to engage in such a daunting project. In chapter 6, John Norquist, CEO of the Congress of New Urbanism, proposes a clear line of demarcation between the responsibilities of the public and private sectors in the redevelopment of postindustrial districts. The public sector should take on the task of remediation, which includes upgrading the infrastructure of utility and sewerage services, while the private sector should redevelop the buildings and sidewalks. In his opinion, tax incremental financing (TIF), a current governmental program that communities use to promote private development through capturing the projected property tax revenue stream created by the development and investing those funds into the district that is being redeveloped, should be discouraged and used as a last resort. This way, public financing directly serves the public realm and private financing directly benefits the investor (Norquist 2010). This is not to say that federal and state programs such as the federal and state historic preservation tax credits or low-income tax credits and enterprise zone tax incentives should not be used; these are proven effective tools for urban redevelopment. But by clearly defining the role of the municipal government in development, the perception that some property owners are paying more taxes than their neighbors could be avoided. This perception has and will most likely continue to be a stumbling block for postindustrial district redevelopment. Until recently, environmental remediation did little to attract private investment in postindustrial re-

FIGURE 14.3. The interior of the Deere & Company building in Minneapolis combines existing materials with new, upscale elements. (Courtesy of Paul J. Armstrong)

Amble, Density, Sustainability, Epicenters, and Synergy (developed by the Peoria design studios at the University of Illinois and described in greater detail in chapter 2) did not seem so difficult to determine (plates 2 and 3). In fact, they were almost self-evident, since warehouse districts such as the one in Peoria were built with these ideas in mind. As Norquist observes: "There is nothing wrong with the warehouse district. It does everything we want a city to do" (Norquist 2010). Norquist is right. The pedestrian scale is intact, with streets and alleys originally built to accommodate large amounts of traffic. Existing warehouse buildings can be economically adapted to a wide variety of new uses. And the district's inherent "grittiness" attracts a new "creative class" of artists and entrepreneurs.

In the past, accommodating large numbers of automobiles in postindustrial districts has been perceived as an obstacle. Instead of designing transportation systems to move automobile traffic as quickly as possible in and out of a district, a new approach to transportation design should be used that enhances the district's sense of place and takes advantage of all of the attributes the existing transportation system offers, including wide streets, alleys, and on-street parking. In chapter 10, Norman Garrick proposes a "city-friendly" transportation planning approach that sets "maximum," not "minimum," parking requirements for developments and advocates that once the maximum amount of parking spaces has been reached in the district, postindustrial districts should then implement "nonauto" forms of transportation (mass transit, bicycle lanes, and parking racks). Garrick's "city-friendly" approach promotes healthier lifestyles for people who live in the urban district as well as enhancing its historic character (fig. 14.4).

development, but this is also beginning to change. As always, the market influences development. In today's green-based economic environment, investors are attracted to what an environmentally sensitive postindustrial redevelopment can offer. People who are interested in building a business or relocating their residences are taking note of this new kind of development, its synergy between nature and industrial character, and its sense of "totality" through its diverse social, economic, and environmental opportunities in harmony with the natural and urban environments.

Midwestern postindustrial cities are, for the most part, entire and intact. From Milwaukee to St. Paul and Peoria to St. Louis, these districts convey a sense of "wholeness," making them compelling places to restore and develop (fig. 14.3). The existing architectural and urban conditions found in postindustrial districts present exciting design opportunities. High-end architectural design, sustainable and ecological design, and historic preservation are but a few areas that can be explored in these districts. The pedestrian nature of the midwestern postindustrial district and the immense size of the warehouse districts are two significant attributes that can make "SynergiCity" a reality. While reinventing blocks of warehouse buildings, streets, alleys, and waterfronts, the design principles of

FIGURE 14.4. New infill development resides with old in the Warehouse District of New Orleans. The character of the district is maintained through the creative use of modern industrial materials. (Courtesy of Paul J. Armstrong)

Interestingly, the postindustrial district is the place where diverse and disparate design theories and philosophies converge—a synergy of architecture, preservation, landscape design, planning, and urban design. The variety of inventive design and well-planned historic preservation occurring in successfully redeveloped districts is impressive. In these successful redevelopments, New Urbanism can work hand in hand with Ecological Urbanism. Historic preservation can work with new design. Traditional or contextural architecture can co-exist with the historic landmarks of the district. "Edgy" modern design fits within the old blocks of masonry warehouses. Although districts such as Milwaukee's Third Ward have begun to enforce stricter design guidelines, essentially the use of New Urbanist "SmartCodes" and a respect for the context of street wall and building massing is sufficient for architectural expression to flourish in these districts (plate 1). Part of this reasoning is that historic warehouses in the Midwest were built with both utility and tradition in mind. Most embody traditional and classical proportion (a clearly delineated base, middle, and top composition), but they were also built using modern and industrial materials and elements including large steel framed windows, steel fire doors, and concrete structural systems—component assemblies that inspired European modernists of the early twentieth century. This architectural link between traditional and utilitarian design found in older historic warehouses allows for a visual compatibility between old and new buildings to occur. Whether it is the detailing of new against old found at the architecture offices of PSA-Dewberry in Peoria or the rooftop expansion of the old port building in the Milwaukee Third Ward, it is clearly apparent that the opportunities for interesting and innovative architecture can happen in SynergiCity.

It is also interesting to note that design expression in these districts is not necessarily prescribed by design guidelines, as one would typically encounter in a typical historic district, but is inferred by the preservation and architectural ethic of a particular city. A good example of this dichotomy of ethics can be found when comparing St. Paul to Minneapolis. In St. Paul, preservation and rehabilitation of the historic warehouses strictly followed the Secretary of the Interior's Standards for Rehabilitation. The building of new townhomes and commercial spaces in St. Paul tended to be contextual, with new buildings designed to match the existing historic buildings. Redevelopment in Minneapolis's warehouse district took a different approach. New buildings, comparable to any new modernism found anywhere in the world, are juxtaposed with historic warehouse buildings. The warehouses were transformed at the roof level with the addition of new units and roof terraces. Both approaches accomplish the same objective: the transformation of an unused industrial district into an enriching place to experience, at the same time respecting its historic character. This spatial arrangement and density of buildings found in the postindustrial district allows the dynamic urban phenomenon of "Urban Metabolism" to occur in the city. Urban metabolism is best defined as the ability to facilitate productive technical product-based economic enterprises and socioeconomic processes, resulting in urban growth, the production of social energy, and the elimination of organic and inorganic waste (Kennedy et al. 2007). Urban metabolism is essential for SynergiCity to become a reality. European cities such as Vienna, Helsinki,

and Copenhagen are well known for their improved Urban Metabolism, which is the result of improved efficiency of mass transit, active lifestyles, and social interaction, all of which enables cities to be more productive, produce less waste, and consume less energy.

The redevelopment of postindustrial districts is a long and arduous process. This is clearly evident in the Lowertown district in St. Paul, where Weiming Lu, executive director of the Lowertown Redevelopment Corporation, spent 30 years of his long and illustrious career rebuilding and preserving that district. He planned the Lowertown redevelopment one block at a time, allowing successful projects to build off each other. Each of these small-area development projects was based on a broader vision: to transform Lowertown into a vibrant urban village within St. Paul (Lu 2010). In chapter 13, Emil Malizia presents a practical approach to implementing development through small-area revitalization, improving the infrastructure in the same small areas, doing emergency structural stabilization projects when it is necessary, and finally promoting competition within the development community. This approach has been proven successful throughout the Midwest in developments such as Midtown Alley in St. Louis. In 2003, local developer Renaissance Development Associates began a redevelopment project in a concentrated small area of abandoned historic automobile factories and sales buildings that once supported St. Louis's short-lived automobile industry of the early twentieth century. By concentrating on an eight-block area near St. Louis University, the developers have been able to build their success one city block at a time, resulting in over $70 million of redevelopment in a seven-year span (Johnson 2010). Aside

from the financial attributes of this approach, there are a number of architectural and urban facets to it as well. By implementing small-area planning, primarily through preservation development, the critical first phase of a long-term, large-scale urban redevelopment can be achieved. Malizia's implementation approach, combined with initial broad visioning planning as suggested by both Carter and Thomson, is the key to making SynergiCity a reality. It can be developed block by block, with each small success story leading to a larger project, all of which is carefully coordinated to fulfill a common vision for redevelopment.

The timing of this book is also worth noting, because postindustrial districts throughout the Midwest are in various stages of redevelopment. Postindustrial districts in Milwaukee, Minneapolis, and St. Paul can now be considered redeveloped after 30 years of planning and construction. These districts are now considered successful, with new and rehabilitated buildings that have been recognized for their innovation and have received architecture, historic preservation, and sustainability awards. However, it is worth noting that once redeveloped, postindustrial districts can become victims of their own success. They can become too expensive for starting businesses or creative individuals such as artists to afford. The rise in property values and taxes that gentrification brings can stifle the innovative spirit in a district. Innovation needs to be served by both a diversity of productivity yields and a diversity of people from all income brackets and ethnic and cultural backgrounds. Simply assuming that the market or the private sector will provide affordable residential and commercial space is naive; moreover, local government mandating a percentage of affordable housing units

Figure 14.5. CommonBond, a nonprofit developer, rehabilitated the 11-story Teweles Seed Warehouse building in Milwaukee's Fifth Ward into a new mixed-income apartment building. (Courtesy of Paul J. Armstrong)

or commercial suites in a development project does not always ensure that a balance of income levels can be achieved within a district. However, another type of developer can serve this need to ensure that the economic diversity of a district is preserved: the nonprofit corporation and the charitable foundation. Throughout the United States, nonprofits have played a positive role in postindustrial redevelopment. In Milwaukee's Fifth Ward, CommonBond, a Minneapolis-based nonprofit affordable housing developer, rehabilitated the 11-story Teweles Seed Warehouse building into a new mixed-income apartment building (fig. 14.5) (Jones 2010). Rents varied in the building from small efficiencies starting at $300 per month to the penthouse at $2,500 per month. Nonprofit developers can pool together private and public funding sources; they can solicit investors, leverage equity, qualify for Department of Housing and Urban Development funding, and even use preservation tax credits.

For the past 60 years, philanthropy from charitable foundations has made an immense impact in urban redevelopment. For instance, the Heinze Foundation helped to finance the redevelopment of the warehouse districts of Pittsburgh. Lowertown in St. Paul would have never been redeveloped without the initial $10 million contribution from the McKnight Foundation, and it was the generous support of the Lyndhurst Foundation that enabled the Chattanooga, Tennessee, riverfront to undergo a green rehabilitation. By bringing corporate foundations and nonprofits into the earliest stages of postindustrial redevelopment, their missions become integrated with the overall goals of redevelopment. Whether the mission is to provide affordable housing, space for startup businesses, or sustainable development, everyone benefits when the missions of nonprofit entities and foundations become a physical reality.

While a vision of sustainable community development, the use of less fossil fuel, and the promotion of healthier lifestyles are all compelling reasons to redevelop postindustrial districts, clearly the most important one is the need to increase economic production in cities. Despite predictions that the internet would decentralize industry, the opposite is, in fact, occurring. A 2007 World Bank report on productivity determined that productivity and performance is higher in urban areas (World Bank 2009). Creativity and innovation rarely occur in isolation; urban areas have always brought together and multiplied human productive efforts. Noted urban theorist Jane Jacobs asserted 50 years ago that the agglomeration of human capital is essential for innovation to occur. Placing creative enterprises in structured research parks, the prevailing development model in the postwar era, is both inefficient and inconvenient. As I wrote in chapter 3, the mixing of businesses and live-and-work experiences with aged buildings allows for a development to become dynamic. It provides businesses room to expand while at the same time minimizing expense by reusing existing buildings.

The Marine Terminal Lofts in the Third Ward District of Milwaukee, for example, integrate new high-end penthouses into the existing shell of a former port terminal building (fig. 14.6). Designed by architect James Shields of Ellerbee Becket, the Marine Terminal Lofts bring urban living directly to the shore of the Milwaukee River. Adaptive reuse projects like the ones described allow a new cycle of innovation to begin in stagnant urban districts.

In *The Death and Life of Great American Cities*, Jacobs gives an example of how businesses typically start and grow in New York. Two mechanics in Brooklyn quit their jobs working in a factory and open a business in one of their garages. The business grows, and they move into a larger building. Finally, they build a large plant in New Jersey. Whereas Jacobs's example of free enterprise occurs in New York and New Jersey, it is essentially the story of how businesses grow throughout the United States. While it is true that a business will sometimes outgrow its building, it is the hope that it will not outgrow its community of innovation. "SynergiCity" can be the host for this innovative community as a granary of old and new buildings capable of accommodating enterprises at all stages of growth and development. By adapting old buildings for new uses and adding compatible new ones within the existing urban fabric, a city can make a warehouse district once again serve the city's economic needs. Unlike the research park that caters only to manufacturing, such a district is the place where residential living, manufacturing, and

Figure 14.6. Designed by architect James Shields of Ellerbee Becket, Marine Terminal Lofts in the Third Ward District, Milwaukee, integrates new high-end penthouses into the exterior shell of a former port terminal building. (Courtesy of Paul J. Armstrong)

research and development occur simultaneously (plates 4 and 6).

Current market trends should also be considered within the context of sustainable urban development. "Green" developments are being built and successfully marketed. Developments such as Dockside Green, a 15-acre luxury development located in a brownfield in Victoria, British Columbia, employs a number of the ideas presented in this book. It mixes Victoria's industrial character with green living, combining both living and work areas, and preserves the waterways, which are also used for recreation. These features helped sell units in the development at prices ranging from $400,000 for a one-bedroom condominium to over $1 million for penthouses. Dockside Green, a product of brownfield mitigation and sustainable design, is proof that individual investors are interested in the postindustrial district development: SynergiCity is not just a theoretical idea; it's marketable and it sells (Baker 2010).

We do not believe that the SynergiCity approach can solve all of the problems facing midwestern cities today. We also do not believe that everyone will want to move to a redeveloped warehouse district in Peoria and completely change their lifestyle. There will always be suburbs, and there will always be people who prefer to live in a detached residence, enjoy a large residential lot, commute by automobile to work, and shop in retail shopping centers. However, before we use limited resources to develop rural land for suburban development, we should fully maximize the underutilized resources that postindustrial districts and historic city centers offer.

Redeveloping postindustrial districts is a challenge that requires a true synergy of diverse de-

sign professions and ideas if it is to be successful. Developers will be successful in these ventures if they take a holistic approach that incorporates urban design, planning, architecture landscape design, and historic preservation. In cities throughout the Midwest, this is already happening. From Minneapolis to St. Louis, the redevelopment of both industrial heritage and naturally wooded greenspaces has produced exceptional results. We are optimistic that the Midwest will reset itself for a brighter future in a new economy. Rumors of the demise of its manufacturing capabilities have been greatly exaggerated, but innovation of new products and new ideas will henceforth be what is typically done in midwestern cities. Ideas and entrepreneurship have always happened in the Midwest and will continue in the foreseeable future throughout the region. The Midwest is blessed with a plentiful amount of potable water. Compared to regions such as the West Coast or the East Coast, housing and commercial real estate are still reasonably affordable, along with the overall cost of living. As my coeditor often asks: "Why should a breakthrough invention or idea that happens in Champaign, Illinois, be developed in Silicon Valley?" Cities like Peoria and Rockford should provide the buildings, parks, and recreational amenities that will lead this innovative talent to remain in the Midwest. These buildings and spaces already exist and were often built out of high-quality materials with exquisite design and craftsmanship. Rather than allow them to remain stagnant and decay further, we should reinvent them in ways that embrace their industrial roots for an environmentally sustainable future. Let's create places where enterprise is welcomed—not places that the next Fortune 50 company necessarily relocates to but

places from which it emerges. We are confident that the "innovation economy" will happen in the Midwest, and when it does, it will happen first in a place called SynergiCity.

References

Baker, L. 2010, July 7. "A Housing Project That Embraces a City and Nature." *New York Times.*

Beatley, T. 1999. *Green Urbanism: Learning from European Cities.* Washington, DC: Island Press.

Florida, R. 2009, March. "How the Crash Will Reshape America." *Atlantic.* Available at www.theatlantic.com/magazine/archive/2009/03/how-the-crash-will-reshape-america/7293/.

Illinois-Indiana Sea Grant. 2010. Water Supply. Available at the website of Illinois-Indiana Sea Grant, www.iisgcp.org/topic_watersupply.html.

Jacobs, J. 1961. *The Death and Life of Great American Cities.* New York: Random House.

Johnson, J. (Renaissance Development Associates). 2010, July 14. Interview with the author at Renaissance Development, Midtown Alley District, St. Louis, Missouri.

Jones, P. (CommonBond Development Company). 2010, May 12. Interview with the author.

Kennedy, C. A., J. Cuddihy, and J. Engel Yan. 2007, May. "The Changing Metabolism of Cities." *Journal of Industrial Ecology* 11(2): 43-59.

Marsh, M., G. C. Kroll, and O. Wyman. 2010. Mercer's 2010 Quality of Living Survey Highlights—Global. Available at www.mercer.com/qualityofliving.

McCormack, R. A. 2010, March 31. "Dozens of U.S. Cities Lose Half Their Population in a Generation: A Record Last Set during the European Plague." *Manufacturing and Technology News* 17(5). Available at www.manufacturingnews.com/news/10/0331/ plague.html. Accessed September 29, 2010.

Meyer, D. 1989. "Midwestern Industrialization and the American Manufacturing Belt in the 19th Century." *Journal of Economic History* 49(4): 921-37.

Norquist, J. 2010, May 17. Interview with the author at Congress for New Urbanism, Chicago.

Tarter, S. 2010, October 16. "Peoria a Great Place for Small Business: CNN/Money Names City 5th Best on Mid-sized List, 15th Overall." *Peoria Journal-Star*. Available at http://www.pjstar.com/business/ x988292039/Peoria-a-great-place-for-small -business. Accessed January 15, 2012.

Weiming Lu. 2010, June 25. Interview with the author.

World Bank. 2009. World Development Report 2009. Available at siteresources.worldbank.org/ INTWDR2009/Resources/Outline.pdf. Accessed January 15, 2012.

Ali, Mir M., and Paul J. Armstrong, eds. *Architectural Design of Tall Buildings: Tall Building Council on Tall Buildings and Urban Habitat.* New York: McGraw-Hill, 1995.

Adair, A., S. McGreal, B. Deddis, and S. Hirst. Evaluation of Investor Behaviour in Urban Regeneration. *Urban Studies*, 1999.

Alexander, C., H. Beis, A. Anninou, and I. King. *A New Theory of Urban Design.* New York: Oxford University Press, 1987.

Appraisal Institute. *The Appraisal of Real Estate.* 13th ed. 2008.

Beatley, Timothy. *Green Urbanism: Learning from European Cities.* Washington, D.C.: Island Press, 1999.

Bell, Daniel. *The Coming of Post-industrial Society: A Venture in Social Forecasting.* New York: Basic Books, 1973.

Blakely, E. J., and N. Green Leigh. *Planning Local Economic Development: Theory and Practice.* 4th ed. Los Angeles: Sage, 2010.

Calthorpe, Peter, and William Fulton. *The Regional City.* Washington, D.C.: Island Press, 2001.

Duany, A., and E. Plater-Zyberk. *Heart of Peoria.* Peoria, Ill.: City of Peoria Economic Development Department, 2003.

Easterling, Keller. "Public Enterprise." In *Seaside: Making a Town in America*, ed. David Mahoney and Keller Easterling. New York: Princeton Architectural Press, 1991.

Fanning, S. F. *Market Analysis for Real Estate.* Chicago: Appraisal Institute, 2005.

Fine, S. *Violence in the Model City.* Ann Arbor: University of Michigan Press, 1989.

Florida, Richard. *The Great Reset: How New Ways of Living and Working Drive Post-crash Prosperity.* New York: HarperCollins, 2010.

———. *The Rise of the Creative Class: And How It's Transforming Work, Leisure, Community and Everyday Life.* New York: Basic Books, 2002.

Frieden, B. J., and L. B. Sagalyn. *Downtown Inc: How America Rebuilds Cities.* Cambridge, Mass.: MIT Press, 1989.

Fuller, R. B. *Synergetics: Explorations in the Geometry of Thinking.* With E. J. Applewhite. Introduction and contribution by Arthur L. Loeb. New York: Macmillan, 1975.

Fullilove, Mindy Thompson. *Root Shock: How Tearing Up City Neighborhoods Hurts America, and What We Can Do about It.* New York. Ballantine, 2005.

Funding Universe. "Caterpillar, Inc." In *International Directory of Company Histories.* Vol. 63. St. James Press, 2004.

Gillette, Howard, Jr. *Camden after the Fall: Decline and Renewal in a Post-industrial City.* Philadelphia: University of Pennsylvania Press, 2005.

Green, Melvin, and Anne Watson. *Building Codes and Historic Buildings.* Washington, D.C.: National Trust for Historic Preservation Press, 2005.

Grogan, Paul, and Tony Proscio. *Comeback Cities: A Blueprint for Urban Neighborhood Revival.* Boulder, Colo.: Westview Press, 2000.

Howard, J. Myrick. *Buying Time for Heritage: How to Save an Endangered Historic Property.* Raleigh: Preservation North Carolina, 2007.

Hudnut, William H., III. *Cities on the Rebound: A Vision for Urban America.* Washington, D.C.: Urban Land Institute, 1998.

Jacobs, Jane. *The Death and Life of Great American Cities.* New York: Random House, 1961.

Kelbaugh, D. *Common Place: Toward Neighborhood and Regional Design.* Seattle: University of Washington Press, 1997.

Kromer, John. *Fixing Broken Cities: The Implementation of Urban Development Strategies.* New York: Routledge, 2010.

Kunstler, J. Howard. *The Long Emergency: Surviving the Converging Catastrophes of the Twenty-First Century.* New York: Atlantic Monthly Press, 2006.

Leopold, Aldo. *A Sand County Almanac with Essays on Conservation from Round River.* New York: Ballantine Books, 1996.

Lorant, Stefan. *Pittsburgh: The Story of an American City.* 5th ed. Pittsburgh: Esselmont Books, 1999.

Lubove, Roy. *Twentieth-Century Pittsburgh.* Vol. 1. *Government, Business, and Environmental Change.* Pittsburgh: University of Pittsburgh Press, 1969.

———. Vol. 2. *The Post-steel Era.* Pittsburgh: University of Pittsburgh Press, 1996.

Malizia, E. E. *Economic Development Finance.* 2nd ed. American Economic Development Council, 1997.

Malthus, T. R. *An Essay on the Principle of Population.* 1st ed. (1798) with excerpts from 2nd ed. (1803).

Edited with an introduction by Philip Appleman. Norton Critical Editions. New York: Norton.

Marshall, Alex. *How Cities Work: Suburb, Sprawl and the Road Not Taken*. Austin: University of Texas Press, 2001.

Meadows, D. H., D. L. Meadows, and J. Randers. *Beyond the Limits: Global Collapse or a Sustainable Future*. London: Earthscan, 1992.

Nasaw, David. *Andrew Carnegie*. New York: Penguin, 2006.

Norton, Peter D. *Fighting Traffic*. Cambridge, Mass.: MIT Press, 2008.

O'Neill, Brian. *The Paris of Appalachia: Pittsburgh in the Twenty-First Century*. Pittsburgh: Carnegie Mellon University Press, 2009.

Oswalt, Philipp, ed. *Shrinking Cities*. Vol. 1. *International Research*. Ostfildern: Hatje Cantz, 2006.

———. Vol. 2. *Interventions*. Ostfildern: Hatje Cantz, 2006.

Rypkema, Donovan D. *The Economics of Historic Preservation: A Community Leader's Guide*. Washington, D.C.: National Trust for Historic Preservation Press, 1998.

Silvetti, J. "The Beauty of Shadows." Reprinted in *Architecture Theory since 1968*, ed. K. M. Hays. Cambridge, Mass.: MIT Press, 1998.

Stivers, R. *The Sustainable Society: Ethics and Economic Growth*. Philadelphia: Westminster Press, 1976.

Vale, Lawrence J., and Thomas J. Campanella. *The Resilient City: How Modern Cities Recover from Disaster*. Oxford: Oxford University Press, 2005.

Willis, Daniel. "Architecture as Medicine." In *The Emerald City and Other Essays on the Architectural Imagination*. New York: Princeton Architectural Press, 1999.

Wood, J., and N. Wood. *Financial Markets*. New York: Harcourt Brace Jovanovich, 1985.

Paul J. Armstrong, RA, is Associate Professor and Chair of the Design Faculty in the School of Architecture at the University of Illinois at Urbana-Champaign. He received a Bachelor in Fine Arts degree from the University of Wisconsin–Superior and a Master of Architecture degree from the University of Wisconsin–Milwaukee. He is a licensed architect, and prior to joining the faculty at the University of Illinois, he was a senior designer for Harding and Associates in Chicago. Professor Armstrong has written extensively on urban design and, most notably, on the architecture of tall buildings.

Donald K. Carter, FAIA, FAICP, LEED-AP, is David Lewis Director of Urban Design and Regional Engagement of the Remaking Cities Institute, Carnegie Mellon University. He also teaches in the Master of Urban Design program in the School of Architecture. Prior to joining Carnegie Mellon University in July 2009, Professor Carter was President of Urban Design Associates, where he led many of the firm's most complex projects, drawing on his broad international experience as an architect, urban designer, and developer. He continues to serve as consulting principal to the firm. He is a Fellow of the American Institute of Architects (AIA), a Fellow of the American Institute of Certified Planners, a member of the Congress for the New Urbanism, and a member of the Urban Land Institute (ULI), where he was national Chair of the Inner City Council. Previously, at ULI he served on the Affordable Housing Forum, Infill Development Forum, Residential Development Council, and Entertainment Development Council. Professor Carter is past Chair of the ULI Pittsburgh District Council, and past President of the Pittsburgh Chapter, AIA. He has lectured and published internationally on urban design and architecture. He currently serves on the board of the Andy Warhol Museum, and previously served on the boards of the Pittsburgh Downtown Partnership, Pittsburgh Zoo, Leadership Pittsburgh, Pittsburgh Chamber of Commerce, Pittsburgh Public Theater, and LaRoche College Board of Regents. Don earned a Bachelor of Architecture from Carnegie Mellon University and did postgraduate work in urban design and regional planning at the University of Edinburgh, Scotland.

Lynne M. Dearborn, Ph.D., is Associate Professor in the School of Architecture at the University of Illinois at Urbana-Champaign. Professor Dearborn's research explores residential choices and residential qualities for marginalized populations, architectural responses to social injustice, and the role of the environment in the lives of immigrant and minority populations in the United States. Professor Dearborn currently serves as Co-director of the East St. Louis Action Research Project. She is a licensed architect and received her Ph.D. from the University of Wisconsin–Milwaukee in 2004.

Richard Florida has spent his life studying, living in, and helping to revitalize great industrial cities. Shaped by his childhood in working-class enclaves in and around Newark, New Jersey, he has lived and taught in Columbus, Ohio; Pittsburgh, Pennsylvania; and most recently Toronto, Ontario. He directs the Martin Prosperity Institute at the University of Toronto's Rotman School of Management, and is Senior Editor of the *Atlantic*. His books include the *Rise of the Creative Class*, *Who's Your City?* and, most recently, *The Great Reset*.

Norman W. Garrick, Ph.D., PE, is Associate Professor in the Department of Civil and Environmental Engineering and Director of Transportation and Urban Planning at the University of Connecticut. Professor Garrick serves as a board member for the Congress of New Urbanism and has written extensively on transportation issues in city centers. He has served as a transportation consultant for numerous cities including North Charleston, South Carolina, and Hartford, Connecticut, and for the Mississippi Gulf Coast, post-Katrina. He holds a Master's degree and a Ph.D. in civil engineering from Purdue University.

Mark L. Gillem, Ph.D., is Associate Professor in the Department of Architecture at the University of Oregon School of Architecture and Allied Arts. Professor Gillem's teaching and research centers on the balance between theory and practice and is interested in developing new ways community participation can play a more important role in urban design. His book *America Town: Building the Outposts of Empire* (University of Minnesota Press,

2007) explored the impact of U.S. armed forces on the landscape of foreign countries. Professor Gillem is a licensed architect and received his Ph.D. in architecture from the University of California at Berkeley in 2004.

Robert Greenstreet, Ph.D., is an architect and Dean of the School of Architecture and Urban Planning. Dr. Greenstreet specializes in the legal aspects of construction. He is the author or coauthor of seven books, has contributed to twenty other texts and handbooks, and has published over 150 working papers and articles. He is a Fellow of the Royal Society of Arts and is listed in fifteen international Who's Who publications. In addition to being a registered architect in the United Kingdom, he is a practicing arbitrator, mediator, and expert witness recognized in both the United States and Europe.

Craig Harlan Hullinger, AICP, is Partner in the City Planning and Economic Development consulting firm of Ruyle Hullinger and Associates. He has over 35 years of experience in city planning and economic development. Hullinger holds a Master's degree in Environmental Planning from Governor's State University. He is member of the American Institute of Certified Planners, is a Vietnam veteran, and is a retired Colonel in the Marine Corps Reserve.

Paul Hardin Kapp, AIA, LEED-AP, is Associate Professor and Chair of the History and Preservation Faculty in the School of Architecture at the University of Illinois at Urbana-Champaign. Prior to teaching, he was a practicing architect in historic preservation. He received his Bachelor of Architecture degree from Cornell University

and his Master of Science degree in Historic Preservation from the University of Pennsylvania. He was the historical architect of the University of North Carolina at Chapel Hill (UNC) and was also a lecturer in the Department of City and Regional Planning at UNC.

Ray Lees is Principal with the national architectural/ engineering firm PSA-Dewberry. During his 34 years of practice in the architectural/engineering industry, he has been responsible for project and client development throughout the United States for a wide range of commercial, health-care, education, justice, civic, and wellness/fitness facilities, with a total market value of over $3 billion. He is very active in civic affairs, developing a particular interest in and passion for effective and sustainable community planning through his two decades of service on the City of Peoria Planning Commission, for which he has served as chair the past 15 years. Ray is a graduate of the University of Illinois at Urbana-Champaign.

Emil Malizia, Ph.D., is Professor and Chair, Department of City and Regional Planning, University of North Carolina at Chapel Hill. His areas of expertise include real estate and economic development, with emphasis on urban redevelopment, market research, development finance, and fiscal and economic impact analysis. His recent work focuses on impact fee methodologies and the relationships between the built environment and public health. For over four decades, he has conducted research, taught graduate-level and in-service courses, and engaged in consulting for private, foundation, public, and community-based clients. Dr. Malizia is the author

or coauthor of four books and over 140 scholarly articles, monographs, and other publications. During leaves, he has worked as a senior adviser at MONY Real Estate Investment Management in New York City, as a visiting professor at School of City and Regional Planning, Georgia Institute of Technology, and in federal service at the U.S. Department of Labor. His planning and development work abroad has taken him to Austria, Colombia, Jamaica, and Nova Scotia. He is a member of the American Planning Association, American Real Estate Society, International Economic Development Council, and Urban Land Institute. He received his master's and doctoral degrees from Cornell University in city and regional planning and his baccalaureate from Rutgers University.

John O. Norquist is President and CEO of the Congress of the New Urbanism. Mr. Norquist works to promote New Urbanism as an alternative to sprawl and antidote to sprawl's social and environmental problems. He was the Mayor of Milwaukee from 1988 to 2004. Under his leadership, Milwaukee experienced a decline in poverty, saw a boom in new downtown housing, and became a leading center of education and welfare reform. He has overseen a revision of the city's zoning code and reoriented development around walkable streets and public amenities such as the city's 3.1-mile Riverwalk. He has drawn widespread recognition for championing the removal of a 0.8-mile stretch of elevated freeway, clearing the way for an anticipated $250 million in development in the heart of Milwaukee. A leader in national discussions of urban design and educational issues, Mr. Norquist is the author of *The Wealth of Cities* and has taught courses in urban policy and urban planning at the University of Chicago, University of Wisconsin–Milwaukee School of Architecture and Urban Planning, and Marquette University. Mr. Norquist received both his undergraduate and master's degrees from the University of Wisconsin.

Christine Scott Thomson, Adjunct Professor and Researcher in the Department of Architecture, received a master's in Architecture and a master's in Urban and Environmental Planning from the University of Virginia and an undergraduate degree in Geology and Urban Studies from Brown University. Her research interests include undergraduate and graduate design, urban planning, and site and community ecology. She is currently teaching an undergraduate course in architectural design and pursuing grant opportunities in green building and sustainable community design. Professor Thomson recently copresented with collaborators from the Technical University in Graz, Austria, at the Fabos International Conference on Landscape and Greenway Planning in Budapest, Hungary, on the topic of ecological urbanism as a framework for renewing small communities.

James H. Wasley, AIA, LEED-AP, is an associate professor in the Department of Architecture at the University of Wisconsin–Milwaukee (UWM). He is a past president of both the Society of Building Science Educators and the Wisconsin Green Building Alliance: An Affiliate of the United States Green Building Council, which he helped to found in 1997. In relation to this essay, Professor Wasley's current research and teaching involves the creation of a "zero-discharge" stormwater masterplan for the UWM campus and the design and implementation of demonstration projects within that ecologically progressive framework. In 2005 he was recognized by the American Institute of Architects Committee on the Environment for promoting "Ecological Literacy in Architectural Education" for courses and activities featuring a similar blend of academic research, teaching, and environmental activism promoting the adoption of green building standards throughout the University of Wisconsin System.

The University of Illinois Press is a founding member of the Association of American University Presses.

Designed by Mindy Basinger Hill
Composed in 10/15 pt Warnock Pro
with Meran Light display
Manufactured by Bang Printing

University of Illinois Press
1325 South Oak Street
Champaign, IL 61820-6903
www.press.uillinois.edu